CONDUCTOR

ESSENTIAL TECHNIQUE

Intermediate To Advanced Studies
Essential Elements Band Method

I0794416

Tom C. Rhodes • Donald Bierschenk • Tim Lautzenheiser
John Higgins • Linda Petersen

WHY BAND?

Everyone loves music. From the awakening musical notes of the radio alarm to the final chord of your favorite television show's theme song, music is an important part of every day. Through melody and rhythm, music offers a level of communication that makes life itself more exciting and fulfilling.

Being in band gives you the opportunity to explore your own musical talents and skills while developing a life-long family of friends who share this artistic journey with you. You will discover a higher level of success in many parts of your life because of your experiences in band.

BAND IS MUSIC.
BAND IS FRIENDS.
BAND IS SELF-DISCIPLINE.
BAND IS PERFORMANCE.
BAND IS EXCITING.
BAND IS WORKING TOGETHER FOR A COMMON GOAL.
BAND IS A CHANCE TO EXPRESS YOUR TALENT.
BAND IS ENJOYMENT.
BAND IS HIGH ENERGY.
BAND IS YOU!

STRIKE UP THE BAND!

- Tim Lautzenheiser

ISBN 0-7935-1817-2

HAL•LEONARD®
CORPORATION
7777 W. BLUEMOUND RD. P.O. BOX 13819 MILWAUKEE, WI 53213

00863562

SEQUENCE OF

Director Page / Student Page / CONCERT KEY	4-35 **2-5** **B♭ Major**	36-60 **6-10** **E♭ Major**	61-99 **11-17** **F Major***	100-109 **18-19** **D Minor**	110-131 **20-22** **A♭ Major**	132-143 **23-24** **C Major***
Ear Training	Balance Builder	Balance Builder Ear Training Technique	Balance Builder	Ear Training Technique	Balance Builder	Balance Builder
Chorale Full Band Arr.	Ex. 2 - Prelude from *Hansel and Gretel*	Ex. 15 - Based on a Theme by Palestrina	Ex. 34 - Based on a Theme by J.S. Bach	Ex. 65 - Based on a Theme by Tchaikovsky	Ex. 72 - *Erhalt Uns In Der Wahreit* (J.S. Bach)	Ex. 80 - *Navy Hymn*
Scale Technique and Chromatic Studies	Ex. 3, 12	Ex. 16, 28	Ex. 35, 38, 42, 45, 52	Ex. 62, 63, 64, 66, 69	Ex. 73, 76	Ex. 81
Rhythms and Meters			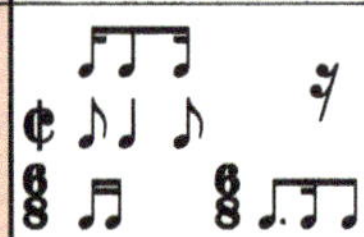			
History	J.S. Bach	Johann Strauss Jr. Amy Marcy Beach Native American Indian Music	Claude Debussy Jazz (Dixieland) Korean Folk Song Cajun Music Renaissance Music		*Star Spangled Banner* Antonio Vivaldi	Black American Spirituals
Theory	Interval	Chords Key Signature Names		Natural, Harmonic, Melodic Minor Scales Minor Chords		
Terms	Articulation Style Mark Dolce	***pp ff*** Lento Lento mysterioso	Giocoso Divisi Marcato accent ∧ Allegro marziale Andante grazioso Animato			
Special Features	Director Communication Kit (score pages 4-13) Conducting 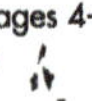 Duet Sightreading Stars System	Conducting  Conducting 	Conducting 		Woodwind Trills Brass Double Tonguing Drum Set Intro.	
Quiz Purpose or Sight - reading	Sightreading Challenge #1 Review Rhythms Quiz	Sightreading Challenge #2 Key Signature Names Quiz	Rhythm Challenge Quiz	Sightreading Challenge #3		Meter Mania #1 Quiz

* Includes exercises which reinforce previous keys.

NEW NOTE SEQUENCE:

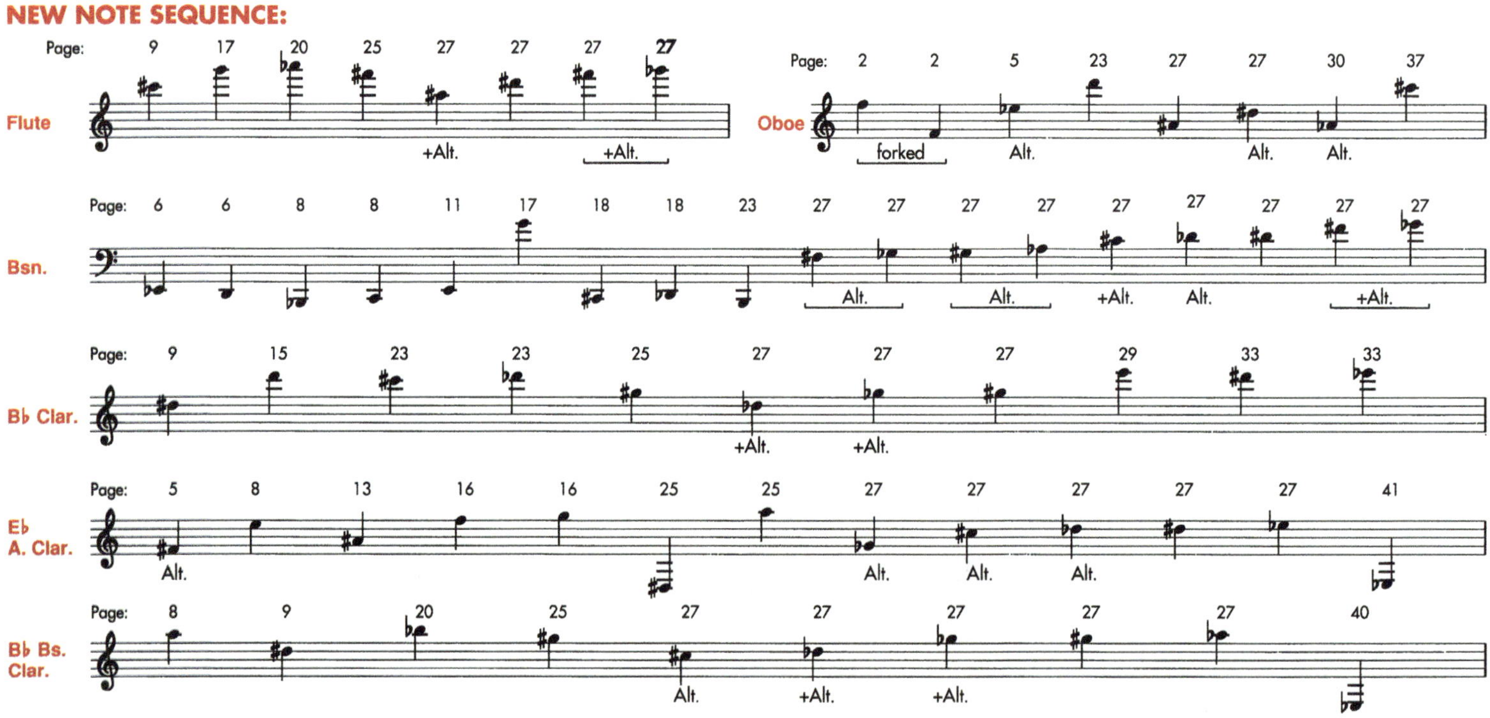

ESSENTIAL TECHNIQUE

Director Page / Student Page / CONCERT KEY	144-155 **25-26** **G Minor**	156-199 **27-35** **REVIEW KEYS**	200-212 **36-37** **G Major**	213-223 **38-39** **D Major**	224-229 **40** **D♭ Major**	230-233 **41** **G♭ Major**	234-294 **42-48** **ALL KEYS**
Ear Training	Balance Builder		Balance Builder	Balance Builder Ear Training Technique	Balance Builder	Balance Builder	
Chorale Full Band Arr.	Ex. 87 - *Prelude* (Chopin)		Ex. 126 - *All Beautiful The March Of Days* (Vaughan Williams)	Ex. 133 - *With One Voice* (Higgins)			
Scale Technique and Chromatic Studies	Ex. 88, 91	Ex. 93, 118, 121, 123	Ex. 127	Ex. 134, 138	Ex. 141	Ex. 144	2-Octave Major Scales, Arpeggios Minor Scales, Arpeggios
Rhythms and Meters		3/8 9/8 12/8 3/2 5/4 3 (triplet) 3/2					
History	Native Japanese Instruments Late 19th Century French Composers	Russian Composers African Folk Music W.C. Handy/Blues George F. Handel	Edvard Grieg 20th Century Composers	Latin American Music			
Theory		Transposing Instruments					
Terms		Allegro agitato Grace Note Tempo di Valse Andante espressivo Leggiero Alla marcia Swing	Andante grazioso				
Special Features		Enharmonics Conducting	Duet				Woodwind Trill Chart Brass Lip Slurs Percussion Rudiments Fingering Chart Glossary
Quiz Purpose or Sight-reading		Key Signature Quiz Meter Mania #2 Quiz Mixed Meter Quiz					

FOREWORD

The success of any organization is dependent on the effectiveness of its communication network. It is important that we adapt this universal law to our band programs to ensure the continued growth and development of the various patron elements, i.e., parents, administration, business sponsors, community patrons, and all other supportive individuals and groups.

Most teacher schedules allow for a preparation period, but for band directors that time is often consumed with private or class lessons, administrative details, necessary phone calling, or a host of other tasks which fill an already overflowing agenda. The luxury of sitting down and creating a letter, let alone a file of appropriate communiqués, is usually next to impossible. Unfortunately, this is one of the first director responsibilities that falls to the low end of the priority list. Avoiding this crucial obligation will predictably bring about unfavorable conditions for the band program in the future.

The following *Essential Technique Communication Kit* is designed to provide the dedicated music educator with a blueprint of ideas that will offer a constant exchange of information to those directly or indirectly involved with the band program. The communications are constructed in such a manner they can be used in their present form or individual paragraphs can be extracted and added to handbooks, newsletters, booster speeches, administrative memorandums, etc. The key is making certain the data reaches the appropriate people and nurtures the underlying support of the band program.

The worst possible communication is no communication. With this truth in mind, the following library of suggested mailings will offer a vitally important commentary to inform everyone, reminding them that music is one of the *essential elements* in the growth of every child.

The *Essential Technique Communication Kit* is certain to become a welcomed companion of every successful band program. We invite you to explore the many possibilities of its positive potential.

— Dr. Tim Lautzenheiser

Research has shown that it is not the *amount* of information we send to our constituents that has the most impact, but rather the *frequency* of the message. In other words, repetition of data at measured timely intervals is more effective than any other plan of action. We also know the ideal length for reader comprehension and retention. Therefore, the following sample documents have been written using test-proven guidelines as the basis for length and style of the suggested texts.

Although it is possible to simply use the chosen letter or memo almost verbatim, it is advisable to embellish the communication with select self-generated paragraphs that will personalize the exchange and create a friendlier atmosphere for the reader. Experiment with various forms of mailings until you find the best avenue of communication for your particular situation.

With the advent of computers and the popularity of direct mail, you are competing for the time of the reader. Here are some hints to assure a higher level of response to your communication program;

- **A letter should not be over one page in length.** Make the paragraphs easily accessible by writing in a friendly style involving the reader at all times.

- **Each communication should not have more than two important themes.** It is often tempting to share every bit of applicable data in one epistle, but is not an effective form of writing, and will probably not be read or retained.

- ***Personalizing* is the key.** A hand-written note on the envelope as well as a penned-message at the end of the page is certain to catch the reader's eye. It *is* worth the extra time it takes to remind then they are deserving of your personal attention. Avoid using artificial forms of signatures (rubber stamps, etc.) Make and take the time to sign each document.

- **Mail at two-to-three week intervals.** Frequency develops a solid bridge of communication between reader and the program. These constant reminders establish a healthy pattern for you and for your band supporters.

- **Always write in the style that you would enjoy reading.** Do not try to impress others with your extensive vocabulary. Be professional and courteous in your written creation and write in a language they can understand and appreciate.

- **Focus each communication on the benefits of band to the students, NOT your position.** Always put the band members in the spotlight.

Communication is a skill. It is something every person can learn to do, and do with an artistic-personal style. The more you communicate with people, the more proficient you will become. With each mailing, you will begin to see the growing support for the program and the continued interest from everyone as you promote the development of a quality musical organization.

Good luck in the exciting journey ahead!

BAND: A PREPARATION FOR LIFE

In today's society there is much conversation about school curriculum, use of academic time, and the applicable value of the knowledge that is brought to the classroom. With an emphasis on "back to the basics," it becomes increasingly more significant to bring the *importance of band* to the forefront in this ongoing educational discussion.

WHY SHOULD A YOUNG PERSON CONSIDER JOINING THE BAND?

HOW LONG SHOULD THEY STAY IN BAND?

WHAT WILL IT MEAN TO THEIR LIFE?

CREATIVITY: Since *creativity* is the source of all possibilities, we are constantly challenged to explore this area of the mind. To avoid being confined to a repetition of patterns, the human can take information from various sources, combine it and arrive at a new level of understanding. Music appeals to the part of the mind which opens new horizons. The study of music supports wonderment, imagination, appreciation, and sensitivity. Experiencing *creativity* can become a personal choice and music offers a pathway to this inventive thinking style.

COMMUNICATION: Music is a language unto itself. It is beyond words or visual images. Music can only be explained by music. The various styles and textures elicit a human emotion which cannot be generated by any other art form. If we do not expose the human to music, we are depriving the individual of an array of personal understandings that cannot be found in any other part of life. MUSIC IS FUNDAMENTAL TO THE HUMAN SOUL.

CRITICAL ASSESSMENT: Intelligence is the ability to conceptualize and respond according to the given situation. Emotional stability stems from the capacity to deal with the various consistencies and inconsistencies of life, which involves opening the mind and analyzing the available data. To accomplish either or both of these ends, the individual must be able to access both the cognitive (factual) and affective (emotional) sides of the mind. MUSIC is one of the key disciplines which demands this ability and reinforces the learning patterns to allow for greater *critical assessment.*

COMMITMENT: The key to success in any endeavor is *going the distance.* In many areas of the academic world, it is quite easy to give up, simply quit. One is not obligated to complete a test, turn in a paper, or finish reading the assigned material. In band every student at the concert performance will be required to play from the beginning of the composition to the end. Although there may be errors in the performance, it is most unusual to see an individual simply stop and put the instrument away. The importance of tenacity and personal persistence are given top billing in the establishment of habits for positive, productive living.

Most certainly all of these attributes can be brought to any subject area, however the study of MUSIC does not make it an option, but it is a fundamental necessity from the first note ever played. Participation at the level of excellence is not a personal preference, it is an expected requisite. Success breeds success in every avenue of life, therefore a successful and well-trained musician does tackle life with a knowledge of "what it takes to get there," and the wisdom of "what it brings to life."

LET THE MUSIC BEGIN!

DATELINE: Send whenever appropriate to Board of Education members.

Dear Board of Education Members:

Educational reform has become a way of life. We are constantly remodeling our present curriculums to expose our students to a more effective preparation for their adult lives. Only recently have we come to understand the importance of the arts in this basic agenda. Extensive research reveals that students who have an educational background in the arts achieve at a higher level than their counterparts who have not been exposed to any form of arts education.

The Center for Arts in the Basic Curriculum (CABC) in Washington, D.C. has based its work on the following three principles developed by the Harvard Project Zero that has been engaged in research in the arts since 1970.

- *The arts are cognitive domains that trigger multiple forms of learning. They engage students in long-term, open ended projects that integrate production of original works with perception of the work of others.*

- *Effective arts education, using such open-ended projects, is an important model for all educators. It involves a process of critique and reflection of one's own work, and it naturally produces exhibitions, portfolios, and performances that are more meaningful than other traditional forms of assessment.*

- *Arts education holds promise for community development by enhancing cultural and civic pride, fostering inter-cultural understanding, and giving professionals in the community opportunities to mentor our students.*

Unfortunately we have, over the years, ignored the importance of the arts as a fundamental building block of the development of the mind. Those beliefs are now being overturned based on the work of neurologists, cognitive psychologists and quantum physicists. We realize the intellect and the senses represent a combined system of reasoning interacting with the other, and each dependent on the other for maximum understanding and problem-solving skills. We simply cannot ignore the expressive-creative side of the mind developed via the study of the arts.

The arts are cognitive domains, representing our multiple intelligences as well as forms of organized perceptions. Perception when combined with intellect leads to high yield education. This explains why students of music are scoring 60+ points higher on SAT scores. While the national average of SAT scores from 1969 to 1991 fell, the scores of music students actually went up. These young people are more prepared to use their minds at a more productive level, and are capable of more demanding agendas in life.

Our music program is doing far more than teaching notes, rhythms, tone quality, etc. We are preparing students for the assignment of life. History tells us, the young ladies and gentlemen sitting in our music classrooms are destined to be the leadership of tomorrow. Your support in seeing they have the chance to experience this dramatic learning process is much appreciated.

Please join us for the next concert (date) and see why it is so important we continue to *Strike Up The Band.*

Respectfully,

Name of Director
Director of Bands

The Center for Arts in the Basic Curriculum quote is used with permission.
Please call the CABC office at 202-638-5196 for additional information.

DATELINE: Send whenever appropriate.

Dear (Correct title/name),

This letter comes to you as a personal *thank-you* for your continued support of our band program. So much of our success is directly tied to the administrative encouragement and help we receive in our continued efforts to create a quality band experience for our students. Although busy agendas often seem to get in the way of expressing our appreciation, we do not take for granted your genuine efforts on the organization's behalf.

Every committed educator sees his/her discipline as vital to the growth and development of the child. Likewise, I feel the same about MUSIC and how it relates to the fundamental value system we should be bringing to every young boy and girl who walks through our school doors. Recently I came upon a quote by Illinois U.S. Senator Paul Simon. It is not a political statement, but rather a viewpoint of education expressing a unique logic and a different position concerning the benefit of music in our schools. I hope you will enjoy it.

"Very few days go by that the media does not compare our economy, educational system, business endeavors and productivity to those of the Japanese. Ironically, the Japanese consider Western music as a basic part of their children's education. Beginning in the first grade, music is taught as an academic subject in a step-by-step program in which a combination of music history, theory, conducting, instrumental and choral performance, plus the reading and writing of music has resulted in a populace that has received lessons on two instruments and can read music.

We cannot forget that music is an integral part of a student's educational element. We must insure that the present 'back to basics' mentality includes access to arts and music education. As we push to increase high school graduation and college entrance requirements, we must not ignore the cultural and artistic development of our students."

— *U.S. Senator*
Paul Simon

Knowing your sensitivity concerning the welfare of our students, I thought you would profit from this man's perspective. Obviously it agrees with all that we do in our band program, but demonstrates the positive implications of music education from a more global vantage point.

We look forward to having you with us at our next concert scheduled for (date and time) at (location.) If you would like to say a few words to our audience of band supporters, the invitation is extended. It would mean much to the band members and to their parents.

Thank-you for your time and continued interest in our band program.

Sincerely,

Name
Director of Bands

DATELINE: Send whenever appropriate.

Dear (Correct title/name.):

Each day in band rehearsal we are working to develop the musical skills and talents of the students. Musicians enjoy a common, but unattainable goal of perfection. There are always wrong notes to correct, phrases to be shaped, greater dynamics to achieve, and an ongoing list of improvements to develop a better language of personal expression. In the midst of all these busy activities, we must find time to inform students and parents about the reason we have band in the first place. It is more than just an entertainment group which shows up at various athletic events, marches in the local parade and plays select concerts during the year on appropriate holidays. It is clear that as a music educator, I must make it my responsibility to inform others that band is an *art form*. By doing so there will be a clearer understanding of *why* we have band in our school curriculum.

The following condensed outline has serves helped me in this important communication and I offer a copy for your perusal.

WHY BAND?

Band is intrinsic. As with all art, it is about *expressing* oneself via a different and unique language. Much of academia is *impressionistic* which requires a definitive skill of following instructions. Band adds to that requirement the option of self-expression.

Band is a group effort. Members are required to shift from an *I/Me* reasoning to a *We/Us* concept. This means extending oneself beyond the normal considerations of much of our day-to-day living. Instead of the logic being, *what's in it for me,* it becomes, *what's in it for us?* The values of cooperation, communication, concentration, correlation, and completion come into play each rehearsal and performance.

Band builds positive self-worth. Although we share many similarities with our athletic counterparts, BAND is a place for everyone. Rarely is a person serving as an alternate or a substitute. Everyone in the band plays a varsity role.

Band is a preparation for life. Through the discipline of MUSIC, we are developing a consistent understanding between the intellectual (cognitive) and the emotional (affective) thought processes. It allows the person to create formulas and not just solutions that are directly transferable to other facets of life.

Although these four points may seem lofty in character, they make up the fundamental framework of our band program. As an administrator, I know you are faced with many questions concerning the various aspects of our school curriculum. Hopefully this brief overview will give you a first-hand look at the foundation that supports our musical education program

The band room door is always open to you. Join us at any time, and thank you for helping us as we continue our journey towards musical excellence.

Sincerely,

Name
Director of Bands

DATELINE: Send one week after starting *Essential Technique.*

To the Parents of (name of student),

It is my pleasure to inform you that (name of child) has mastered many of the fundamental skills in the development of (his/her) instrumental talent and is now ready to advance to the next step in the journey of musical competence. Our new text, *Essential Technique,* offers us a perfect roadmap for our continued exploration of artistry. The students who have achieved this level of proficiency are to be commended for their exemplary commitment and dedicated practice. Much has been covered since the first day of band, and the joy of musical expression is now the benefit that awaits all those who have attained this important level of expertise. As supporting parent/s, you also are to be *congratulated,* for your continued encouragement has played a vital role in this exciting personal success of your child.

We are all invested in the goals ahead. As parents, you have sacrificed time, revenue, and an immeasurable amount of patience in the initial stages of your child's instrumental education. Along with other members of our band, (name of child) has devoted (his/her) practice to reaching a prescribed proficiency which has brought him/her to this upper echelon of technique development. As the director, I have enjoyed the experience of sharing MUSIC with all the students who chose to participate in the band and am delighted to inform you that (name of child) is one of the key players we see as having a very rewarding future in band.

Reaching *excellence* in any endeavor requires self-discipline, personal sacrifice, and a support group of caring individuals who will continue to serve as a base of inspiration when the road to success becomes a bit bumpy. You can quickly see what a vital role you play in this upcoming agenda. Because we are limited in the amount of time we can rehearse the band, it is crucial each student continues a positive practice schedule at home. Your inclusion in this common goal is essential. Knowing the exciting progress which (name of child) has made in the first part of (his/her) band career, I know we can continue to count on you for your important contribution as a band supporter as well as proud parent/s. Thank-you.

In future weeks you shall be receiving several communications about the importance of MUSIC as it relates to the growth and development of the individual. There is very exciting news about the advantage that young musicians have when entering society and taking on the responsibilities of adult life, and it is going to be a thrill to share all of this information with you. There is no question, musical understanding is an *essential technique* in the quest for success.

Thank you for your time and continued interest as we band together.

Musically yours,

Name
Director of Bands

DATELINE: Send one month after starting *Essential Technique.*

To the Parents of (name of student),

As promised, I shall continue to update you on the progress of (name of child) and our entire band program as well as communicate many of the *benefits of band* which are often overlooked in our haste to develop a higher level of technical proficiency. We are moving along at a fast pace and much of our ongoing success is directly due to the admirable parent support and involvement we traditionally enjoy. We are fortunate to have people in our community who appreciate and realize the importance of the ARTS in the educational development of every child. Our own band program reflects this understanding and a vote of thanks is extended to you and all the members of our organization.

WHY BAND? Perhaps this question is not a new one to your ears. There must be times when other options seem like a higher priority than taking the instrument out of the case and investing that needed hour of personal practice. Every young person deals with this same frustration and anxiety, so do not let it be a sign of discouragement. It is a part of the total learning experience. Some persuasive suggestions concerning time-on-task would be most helpful at this point. We're counting on your help in this area.

The answer to the question has some life-long implications. MUSIC offers every individual the chance to experience the pleasure of self-expression at a new level. It is *intrinsic*; the process itself provides the reward. Music is music for its own sake. It is beauty within itself and offers the performer new realms of self-satisfaction. The mental stimulation of wonder and imagination is a highly intellectual activity and brings about a unique personal joy that can only be felt through personal accomplishment. It stretches one's understanding and this growth can be transferred to every facet of learning. Many feel this expansion of comprehension and awareness mixed with the development of positive self-discipline habits, is the reason those who study MUSIC perform at a higher level in academic classes. Exhaustive research confirms this theory.

Band, in many respects, is a microcosm of our society demanding high levels of responsibility, social skills, ongoing communication, analytical talents, and the important ability to work with others. Simply put, learning a musical instrument and continuing to explore the limitless possibilities of music provide an excellent preparation for life.

It is from this position I encourage your continued emphasis of the importance of band to the (name of child)'s educational agenda. Realizing band is an elective, it is necessary we constantly emphasize the essential role it plays in the overall development of the individual. Do not let a moment of anxiety become the deciding factor of future participation. Giving up the study of music cannot be an option. The value of your parental encouragement is of utmost value at this point. Thank-you.

Should you have any questions or comments about (name of child) or any facet of our band program, please feel free to contact my office at your convenience. As always, your inclusion in our band family is acknowledged and appreciated.

Musically yours,

Name
Director of Bands

DATELINE: Send two months after starting *Essential Technique.*

To the Parents of (name of student),

I bring good news with this letter; *the band is playing beautifully* and (name of child) is a solid contributor to our success. A well-deserved commendation is extended to all the young musicians and to the secret key to our success; YOU and the model parental support we receive in our common mission.

As with any skill development, the more advanced the material, the higher the demand for a focused effort on the part of the learner. The temptation to avoid the responsibility of practice or ignore the need for a more intense application of effort will be apparent. The required fuel to catapult one to the next level of proficiency comes from reassuring parents creating an increased level of motivation.

Through all of this, you are certain to hear the now familiar question, WHY BAND? Your answer will be of untold value in continuing the important forward progress of learning. Band is more than just playing notes, memorizing a few rhythms, attending extra rehearsals, or opting for personal practice instead of an hour in front of the television. The study of MUSIC helps develop an appetite or all forms of learning. It teaches us: *concentration, alertness, memory skills, and self-control.* It allows us to use acquired knowledge to develop all aspects of life including: *values, ethics, and creative decision-making.* It reinforces all the essential elements of our development as caring-sharing human beings and brings us to a higher level of emotional maturity. Ultimately, it allows us to have a greater understanding and appreciation for life itself.

To a teenager, these concepts may seem well-beyond their grasp, however a constant reinforcement of the ideals will stimulate that often forgotten side of the mind and begin to generate important introspective questions which are the basis of personality development. MUSIC can serve as an important bridge to the building positive self-esteem for every individual. It is a personal journey and we (parents and teachers) can only point the way and lend our unconditional encouragement, and to that end we must pledge ourselves.

I once again extend my personal thanks for your genuine support of our band program. You are not only making a positive difference to (child's name), but also to every young musician who is a part of our program. Everyone involved can feel a sense of PRIDE in our band. It is apparent the students are mastering the *essential technique* of music while we are also learning the *essential technique* of developing a program of excellence for them. You count and I count on you.

As always, I look forward to our continued communication and am excited to share this important *good news.* The upcoming concert on (date of performance) will evidence the thrilling progress the band has made since its last performance. It is going to be the best concert of their careers. I'll see you there!

Musically yours,

Name
Director of Bands

DATELINE: Send one month prior to upcoming concert.

To the Parents of (name of student,)

Although it seems like only yesterday, several weeks have passed since we initiated the study of the advanced band series, *Essential Technique.* I am pleased to report the progress of the group is incredibly satisfying. *Musicality* is now a part of every rehearsal and the thrill of seeing the young musicians enjoying the chance to express themselves through music is beyond words. The band is setting new standards of excellence which will become a signature of our program from this point forth. There is something quite special about this committed and dedicated group of fine performers. As parents, you should share in the joy of their achievements and do know you have played an integral part in their success.

Arnold Schopenhauer, one of our modern day philosophers, said, *"Victory once attained should lead only to further victory. Happiness lies rather in the act of attempting rather than in the completion."* With that bit of wisdom in hand, we cannot rest on our laurels, but must relish the moment and then begin the journey to greater musical heights. You can rest assured, that *is* the upcoming agenda for the band.

By now you are well aware of the growth process BAND brings to every student. While much of education is *impressionistic,* MUSIC is *expressionistic.* It is not a mere repetition of suggested data, but rather a chance to create, express, and contribute to the overall final performance. It allows the musician to bring something to the art form. In doing this the child's positive self-worth rises and the desire to explore the potential of personal talents becomes dominant. In short, it is a chance to bring one's uniqueness to the game of life. Logically, the performer begins to understand; *I matter. I am not just another person. I have value and am a source of unlimited potential. I count.*

Every parent wants the best opportunities for (his/her) child. We all want to see them succeed by living a healthy and happy existence. The positive attitude of the individual is crucial in this quest, and it is absolutely necessary for the child to feel a sense of self-worth as (s/he) takes on the responsibilities of life. What better way to sense this importance than through the constructive habits learned in band? It is no accident that the "band community" continues to score higher on college entrance exams, maintain significantly superior grade point averages in academic classes, and be the first people sought by employers in our working world.

As you can see, the curriculum offers a second benefit package that assures success in every aspect of life. If it were "just the music," we would be able to gain all of this by listening to recordings, but it is the *process* of learning the music and the self-confidence which is instilled as a result of this effort. Reaching the top of the mountain is NOT the thrill, rather it is the knowledge one gains during the climb.

The education that goes on each day in band provides the *essential technique* for all of life. With that, I shall bid you good-bye, walk out to the podium and *STRIKE UP THE BAND.*

Musically yours,

Name
Director of Bands

Director

Concert keys in **Essential Technique** are introduced in the following format:

Balance Builder
- A, B and C parts for all students

Chorale - Full Band Arrangement
- Rehearse woodwinds alone, brass alone and full band

Scale
- Marked articulations
- Scale in Thirds
- Arpeggio

Articulation Work-Out
- Focus on accuracy

If you wish to warm-up in specific key(s), ask students to turn to the indicated pages:

Concert Key	Score Pg.	Student Pg.
B♭ Major	14	2
E♭ Major	36	6
F Major	61	11
D Minor	100	18
A♭ Major	110	20
C Major	132	23
G Minor	144	25
G Major	200	36
D Major	212	38
D♭ Major	224	40
G♭ Major	230	41

Tune and shape each note on *Balance Builder* exercises, and experiment with different instrument combinations. Rehearse brass alone, woodwinds alone and the full band on each *Chorale* to improve balance and intonation. Include various dynamic levels on each *Scale* and *Articulation Work-Out*, including ***mf***, ***f***, ***p*** and crescendo/decrescendo.

Additional scale studies are found on score pages 234 - 240 (student book pages 42 - 44). All scale studies are transposed for group or individual practice. *Chromatic Technique* studies are found throughout the book, in addition to multicultural songs, rhythm reinforcement and theory exercises.

NEW NOTES INTRODUCED ON 1. BALANCE BUILDER

Oboe **F**

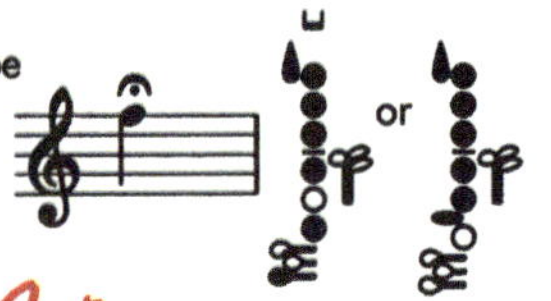

Oboe **F**

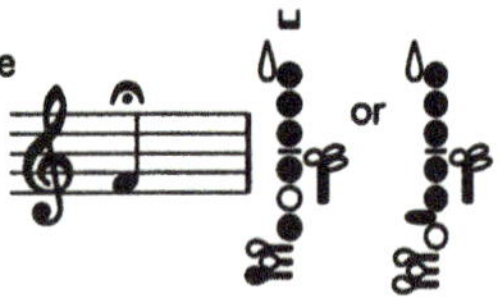

Director All oboe F forked fingerings are marked with a ⊔ in the student books.

Ear Training

Concert B♭ Major Ear training helps you blend in with the rest of the ensemble by teaching you to listen carefully. Tune each note on *Balance Builders,* starting with the lowest pitch.

1. BALANCE BUILDER

Woodwinds & Upper Brass

Low Brass, Woodwinds & Timpani

Director All chorales in this book are written with a divided trumpet part. Be sure to explain *divisi* to the trumpet section. *Divisi* is introduced to the full band on page 14 (score page 80).

2. CHORALE - Full Band Arrangement (Prelude from Hansel and Gretel)

Englebert Humperdinck
Arr. by John Higgins

5
Flute
Oboe
Bassoon
B♭ Clarinet
E♭ Alto Clar.
B♭ Bass Clar.
E♭ Alto Sax.
B♭ Ten. Sax.
E♭ Bari. Sax.
5
B♭ Trumpet
F Horn
Trombone
Baritone
Tuba
Keyboard Percussion
Tri.
Percussion
mp
F to E♭
Timpani

9
Flute
Oboe
Bassoon
B♭ Clarinet
E♭ Alto Clar.
B♭ Bass Clar.
E♭ Alto Sax.
B♭ Ten. Sax.
E♭ Bari. Sax.
B♭ Trumpet
F Horn
Trombone
Baritone
Tuba
Keyboard Percussion
Percussion
S.D.
B.D.
Timpani
cresc.
mp
mf

13
Flute
Oboe
Bassoon
B♭ Clarinet
E♭ Alto Clar.
B♭ Bass Clar.
E♭ Alto Sax.
B♭ Ten. Sax.
E♭ Bari. Sax.
13
B♭ Trumpet
F Horn
Trombone
Baritone
Tuba
Keyboard Percussion
Cr. Cym.
Percussion
E♭ to F
Timpani

17
Flute
Oboe
Bassoon
B♭ Clarinet
E♭ Alto Clar.
B♭ Bass Clar.
E♭ Alto Sax.
B♭ Ten. Sax.
E♭ Bari. Sax.
17
B♭ Trumpet
F Horn
Trombone
Baritone
Tuba
Keyboard Percussion
Percussion
Timpani
rit.
mp

Articulation

Articulation is the way we tongue or slur notes. Staccato dots, tenuto marks and slurs tell us how to articulate each note. Notes without articulation marks should be tongued and played for full value. Articulations often occur in patterns, such as:

A.

B.

C.

Percussion and Keyboard Percussion: Articulation is the way wind and brass players tonque or slur notes. Staccato dots, tenuto marks and accents are common articulation marks. Percussionists should follow the written articulations, and try to imitate wind and brass articulation sounds. Play staccato notes lightly and with separation. To play staccato, snap your wrist a little faster.

NEW NOTES INTRODUCED ON 3. CONCERT B♭ MAJOR SCALE TECHNIQUE

B♭ Tenor Sax

B

F Horn

G

3. CONCERT B♭ MAJOR SCALE TECHNIQUE

Practicing scales is the best way to improve your playing ability. Try them in various tempos, always keeping a steady pulse.

Scale

Scale In Thirds

Arpeggio

4. ARTICULATION WORK - OUT

Play even rhythms at all tempos.

► Practice this exercise as a wrist builder with RRRR and LLLL sticking.

NEW NOTES INTRODUCED ON 5. CHILDREN'S SHOES

B♭ Tenor Sax

E

5. CHILDREN'S SHOES

Black American Spiritual

Flute
Oboe
B♭ Clarinet
B♭ Bass Clar.
E♭ Alto Sax
E♭ Bari Sax
B♭ Tenor Sax
B♭ Trumpet
F Horn
Trombone
Baritone
Bassoon
Tuba
Keyboard
Percussion
Flam Taps
Percussion

Flute
Oboe
B♭ Clarinet
B♭ Bass Clar.
E♭ Alto Sax
E♭ Bari Sax
B♭ Tenor Sax
B♭ Trumpet
F Horn
Trombone
Baritone
Bassoon
Tuba
Keyboard
Percussion
Percussion

Conducting

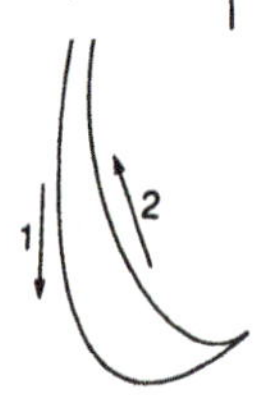

The two-beat conducting pattern is used for pieces written in 2/4, C, or 2/2, and fast 6/8 meters. Practice conducting this two-beat pattern.

6. COME DOWN TO HILO

English Sea Song

Flute
Oboe
B♭ Clarinet
B♭ Bass Clar.
E♭ Alto Sax
E♭ Bari Sax
B♭ Tenor Sax
B♭ Trumpet
F Horn
Trombone
Baritone
Bassoon
Tuba
Keyboard
Percussion
Percussion

ALL BOOKS:
Where is the "&" of beat 2?
Flute
Oboe
B♭ Clarinet
B♭ Bass Clar.
E♭ Alto Sax
E♭ Bari Sax
B♭ Tenor Sax
B♭ Trumpet
F Horn
Trombone
Baritone
Bassoon
Tuba
(6)
Keyboard
Percussion
Percussion

7. RESTS ALWAYS COUNT

8. THE MOUNTAIN DEER CHASE

North American Folk Song

Flute
Oboe
B♭ Clarinet
B♭ Bass Clar.
E♭ Alto Sax
E♭ Bari Sax
B♭ Tenor Sax
B♭ Trumpet
F Horn
Trombone
Baritone
Bassoon
Tuba
(6)
Keyboard
Percussion
Percussion

Flute
Oboe
B♭ Clarinet
B♭ Bass Clar.
E♭ Alto Sax
E♭ Bari Sax
B♭ Tenor Sax
B♭ Trumpet
F Horn
Trombone
Baritone
Bassoon
Tuba
Keyboard
Percussion
Percussion

Theory **Interval** The distance between two notes. Start with "1" on the lower note, and count each line and space between the notes. The number of the higher note tells us the name of the interval.

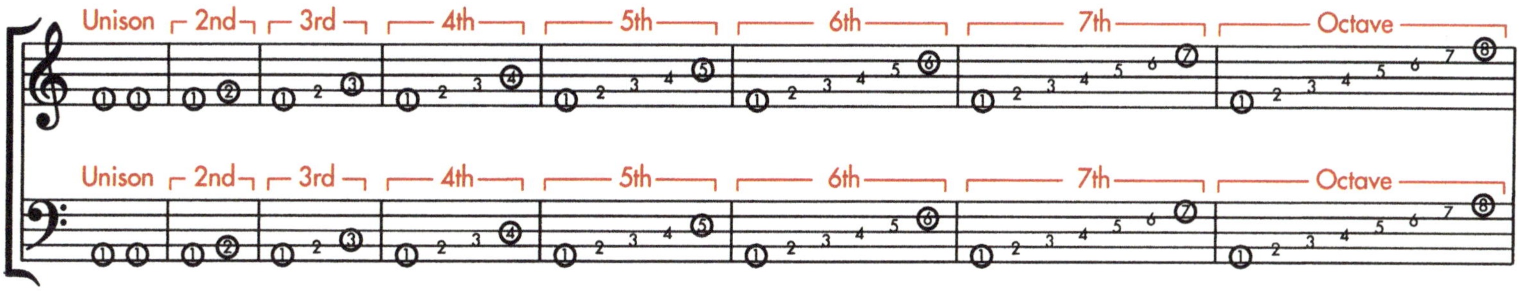

9. INTERVAL TECHNIQUE

Write in the numbers of the intervals. Remember to count **up** from the lowest note.

Sightreading Playing a musical selection for the first time. The key to sightreading success is knowing what to look for before playing the piece. Follow the guidelines below, and your band will be sightreading STARS! Use the word **STARS** to remind yourself what to look for before reading a selection the first time.

S — **Sharps or flats** in the **key signature** Identify the key signature first. Silently practice notes from the key signature. Look for key signature changes in the piece.

T — **Time signature** and **tempo markings** Identify and look for changes in the piece.

A — **Accidentals** Check for any accidentals not found in the key signature.

R — **Rhythm** Slowly count and clap all difficult rhythms. Pay special attention to rests.

S — **Signs** Look for all signs that indicate dynamics, articulations, tempo changes, repeats, 1st and 2nd endings, and any other instructions printed on your music.

10. SIGHTREADING CHALLENGE #1

Puerto Rican Folk Song

Allegro

ALL BOOKS: Where is beat 4?

History German composer **Johann Sebastian Bach** (1685-1750) is the most famous composer of the Baroque era (1600-1750). Bach wrote many cantatas, which are long works for chorus, soloists and orchestra. "Sheep May Safely Graze" is from *Cantata 208,* written in 1713. European immigrants began to settle in the American colonies during Bach's lifetime.

Style Mark Indicates the manner or style in which the piece should be played. Style marks are usually found above the time signature.

11. SHEEP MAY SAFELY GRAZE - Duet

Johann Sebastian Bach

Flute
Oboe
Bb Clarinet
Bb Bass Clar.
Eb Alto Sax
Eb Bari Sax
Bb Tenor Sax
Bb Trumpet
F Horn
Trombone
Baritone
Bassoon
Tuba
Keyboard
Percussion
Percussion
Timpani
very softly
rit.

NEW NOTES INTRODUCED ON 12. CHROMATIC TECHNIQUE

E♭ Alto Clarinet

F♯

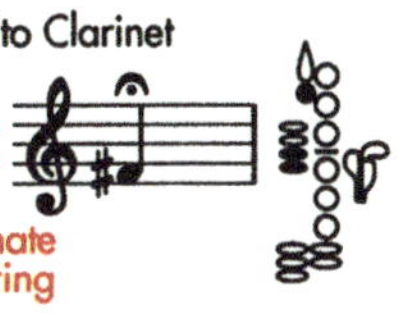

Alternate fingering

B♭ Tenor Sax

F♯

Alternate fingering

12. CHROMATIC TECHNIQUE

13. ESSENTIAL TECHNIQUE QUIZ - SPINNING SONG

Johann Ellmenreich

D.S. al Fine
Flute
Oboe
B♭ Clarinet
B♭ Bass Clar.
E♭ Alto Sax
E♭ Bari Sax
B♭ Tenor Sax
B♭ Trumpet
F Horn
Trombone
Baritone
Bassoon
Tuba
Keyboard
Percussion
Percussion
Timpani

Director

Concert keys in **Essential Technique** are introduced in the following format:

Balance Builder
- A, B and C parts for all students

Chorale - Full Band Arrangement
- Rehearse woodwinds alone, brass alone and full band

Scale
- Marked articulations
- Scale in Thirds
- Arpeggio

Articulation Work-Out
- Focus on accuracy

If you wish to warm-up in specific key(s), ask students to turn to the indicated pages:

Concert Key	Score Pg.	Student Pg.
B♭ Major	14	2
E♭ Major	36	6
F Major	61	11
D Minor	100	18
A♭ Major	110	20
C Major	132	23
G Minor	144	25
G Major	200	36
D Major	212	38
D♭ Major	224	40
G♭ Major	230	41

Tune and shape each note on *Balance Builder* exercises, and experiment with different instrument combinations. Rehearse brass alone, woodwinds alone and the full band on each *Chorale* to improve balance and intonation. Include various dynamic levels on each *Scale* and *Articulation Work-Out*, including ***mf***, ***f***, ***p*** and < >.

Additional scale studies are found on score pages 234 - 240 (student book pages 42 - 44). All scale studies are transposed for group or individual practice. *Chromatic Technique* studies are found throughout the book, in addition to multicultural songs, rhythm reinforcement and theory exercises.

NEW NOTES INTRODUCED ON 14. BALANCE BUILDER

Ear Training

Concert E♭ Major Singing is a common ear training exercise. Play each exercise below, then sing it in your natural voice range. Make sure you can hear all the notes when playing and singing.

14. BALANCE BUILDER

15. CHORALE - Full Band Arrangement (Based on a Theme by Palestrina)

Arr. by John Higgins

5
Flute
Oboe
Bassoon
B♭ Clarinet
E♭ Alto Clar.
B♭ Bass Clar.
E♭ Alto Sax.
B♭ Ten. Sax.
Alt.
E♭ Bari. Sax.
5
B♭ Trumpet
F Horn
Trombone
Baritone
Tuba
Keyboard Percussion
Percussion
Timpani
f - p

9
Flute
Oboe
Bassoon
B♭ Clarinet
E♭ Alto Clar.
B♭ Bass Clar.
E♭ Alto Sax.
B♭ Ten. Sax.
E♭ Bari. Sax.
9
B♭ Trumpet
F Horn
Trombone
Baritone
Tuba
Keyboard Percussion
Tri.
Percussion
Timpani
mf

Flute
Oboe
Bassoon
B♭ Clarinet
E♭ Alto Clar.
B♭ Bass Clar.
E♭ Alto Sax.
B♭ Ten. Sax.
E♭ Bari. Sax.
B♭ Trumpet
F Horn
Trombone
Baritone
Tuba
Keyboard Percussion
Percussion
Timpani
17
p - f
2nd time only
f

Flute
Oboe
Bassoon
B♭ Clarinet
E♭ Alto Clar.
B♭ Bass Clar.
E♭ Alto Sax.
B♭ Ten. Sax.
E♭ Bari. Sax.
B♭ Trumpet
F Horn
Trombone
Baritone
Tuba
Keyboard Percussion
Percussion
Timpani
21
pp rall.
rall.
B♭ to C, E♭ to D

NEW NOTES INTRODUCED ON 16. CONCERT E♭ MAJOR TECHNIQUE

B♭ Tenor Sax

F

16. CONCERT E♭ MAJOR TECHNIQUE

Practice scales at all dynamic levels and in various tempos. Always keep a steady pulse.

17. ARTICULATION WORK - OUT

Play even rhythms at all tempos.

► Practice this exercise as a wrist builder with RRRR and LLLL sticking.

Conducting

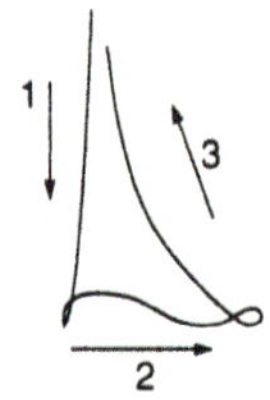

The three-beat pattern is used for pieces written in $\frac{3}{4}$, $\frac{3}{2}$ and $\frac{3}{8}$ meters. Practice conducting this three-beat pattern.

Director *The Birthday Song* uses the same melody as the folk song *Good Morning To You.* Students could conduct the band playing this popular tune on their birthday.

18. THE BIRTHDAY SONG

Dynamics

pp *(pianissimo)* Play very softly. ***ff*** *(fortissimo)* Play very loudly.
Always use full breath support to produce your best possible tone and intonation.

19. DYNAMIC CONTRASTS

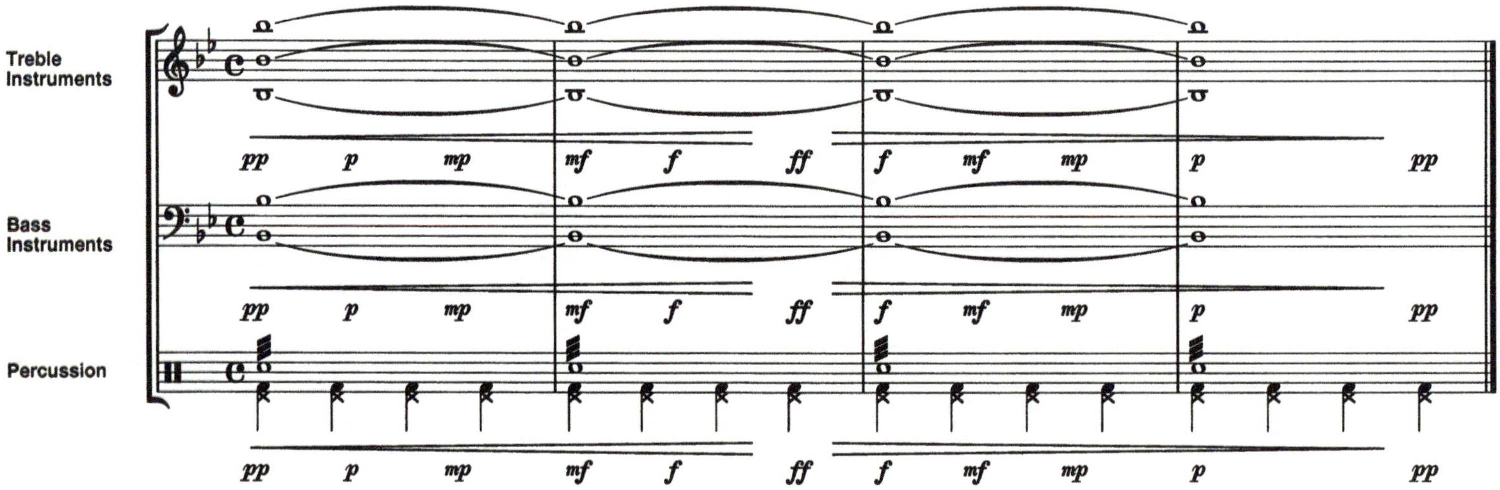

Director The first five notes of the Concert E♭ scale and complete tonic chord are transposed in each student book on this example. Ask students to select a chord tone and play the chord. Singing before playing improves aural awareness and intonation.

Theory **Chords** Two or more different notes sounding simultaneously. Chords can be formed from scale steps. The most common chord is made up of the 1st, 3rd, and 5th scale steps. Here is a chord from the E♭ Major scale:

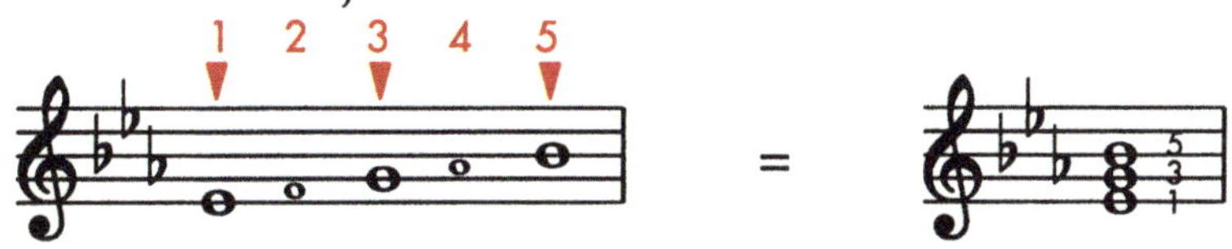

Director This exercise is transposed in each student book. A single note appears in the final measure. The chord voicings function as a teaching exercise. Play the chord, and ask students to identify their chord tone. Substitute different chord tones throughout the band, and experiment with balance and textural sounds. You may wish to have a few students play or sing the root, then add band members singing the third and fifth before playing.

20. EAR TRAINING TECHNIQUE

Play each exercise below, then sing it in your natural voice range. Make sure you can hear all the notes of the chord in the last measure.

History Austrian composer **Johann Strauss Jr.** (1825-1899) is also known as "The Waltz King." He wrote some of the world's most famous waltzes (dances in 3/4 meter). This waltz is from *Die Fledermaus* ("The Bat"), Strauss' most famous operetta. Operettas were the forerunners of today's musicals, such as *Oklahoma, The Sound Of Music* and *The Phantom Of The Opera.*

21. ADELE'S SONG

Bright waltz tempo

Johann Strauss Jr.

Flute
Oboe
B♭ Clarinet
B♭ Bass Clar.
E♭ Alto Sax
E♭ Bari Sax
B♭ Tenor Sax
Alt.
Alt.
B♭ Trumpet
F Horn
Trombone
Baritone
Bassoon
Tuba
Keyboard
Percussion
Percussion
Timpani
Flute
Oboe
B♭ Clarinet
B♭ Bass Clar.
E♭ Alto Sax
E♭ Bari Sax
B♭ Tenor Sax
Alt.
B♭ Trumpet
F Horn
Trombone
Baritone
Bassoon
Tuba
Keyboard
Percussion
Percussion
Timpani

NEW NOTES INTRODUCED ON 22. O TANNENBAUM

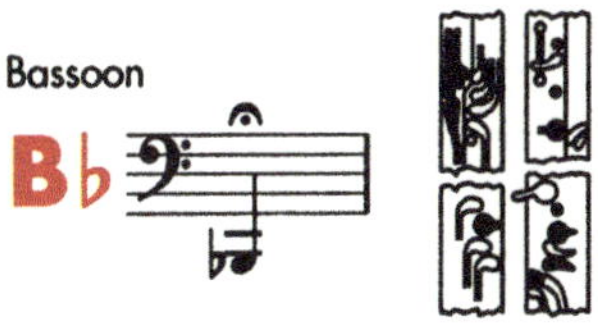

22. O TANNENBAUM

German Carol

Director *Rhythm Raps* introduce new rhythms and meters to the band. The Percussion book includes the single clapping line plus an accompaniment. Follow this four-step teaching sequence:

- Ask the full band to count, clap and tap the single line until everyone demonstrates it satisfactorily.
- Add the percussion accompaniment while the rest of the band claps and counts the single line.
- Clap the line as a round, with and without percussion accompaniment.
- Sing the *Rhythm Rap* using syllables (or simply "tah") with percussion accompaniment.

23. RHYTHM RAP

24. KEEPIN' SECRETS

Appalachian Folk Song

Moderato

► Choke Cym. on beat two of every measure to create a closed hi-hat effect.

SPECIAL PERCUSSION EXERCISE

This exercise will help you develop smooth, even rolls.
Practice at various tempos and dynamics.

American composer **Amy Marcy Beach** (1867-1944) was the first woman composer to have a major symphonic work (*Gaelic Symphony*, 1896) performed by the New York Philharmonic. She toured and performed in Europe after 1910, and was recognized as the first American woman composer to write works in the European style. Amy Marcy Beach, known at the time as Mrs. H. H. A. Beach, was a pioneer for today's women composers and performers.

NEW NOTES INTRODUCED ON 25. SCOTTISH LEGEND

25. SCOTTISH LEGEND

Amy Marcy Beach

Lento ◄ Very slow tempo

26. THE KEEL ROW

Sea Song

ALL BOOKS:
Count carefully!
Flute
Oboe
B♭ Clarinet
B♭ Bass Clar.
E♭ Alto Sax
E♭ Bari Sax
B♭ Tenor Sax
B♭ Trumpet
F Horn
Trombone
Baritone
Bassoon
Tuba
Keyboard
Percussion
Percussion
Timpani
Alt.

27. SMOOTH SAILING

Conducting

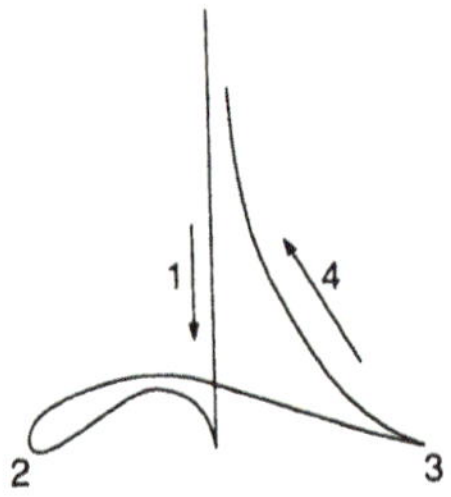

The four-beat pattern is used for pieces written in 4/4, 4/2 and 12/8 meters. Practice conducting this four-beat pattern.

NEW NOTES INTRODUCED ON 28. CHROMATIC TECHNIQUE

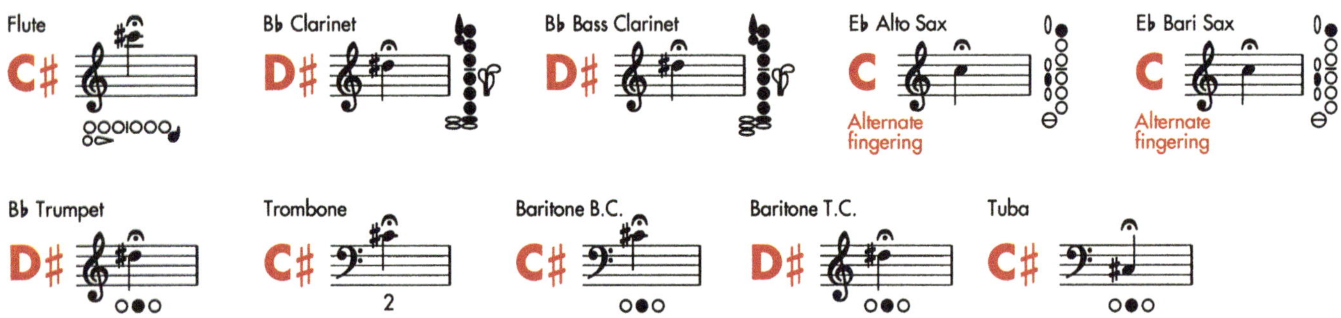

28. CHROMATIC TECHNIQUE

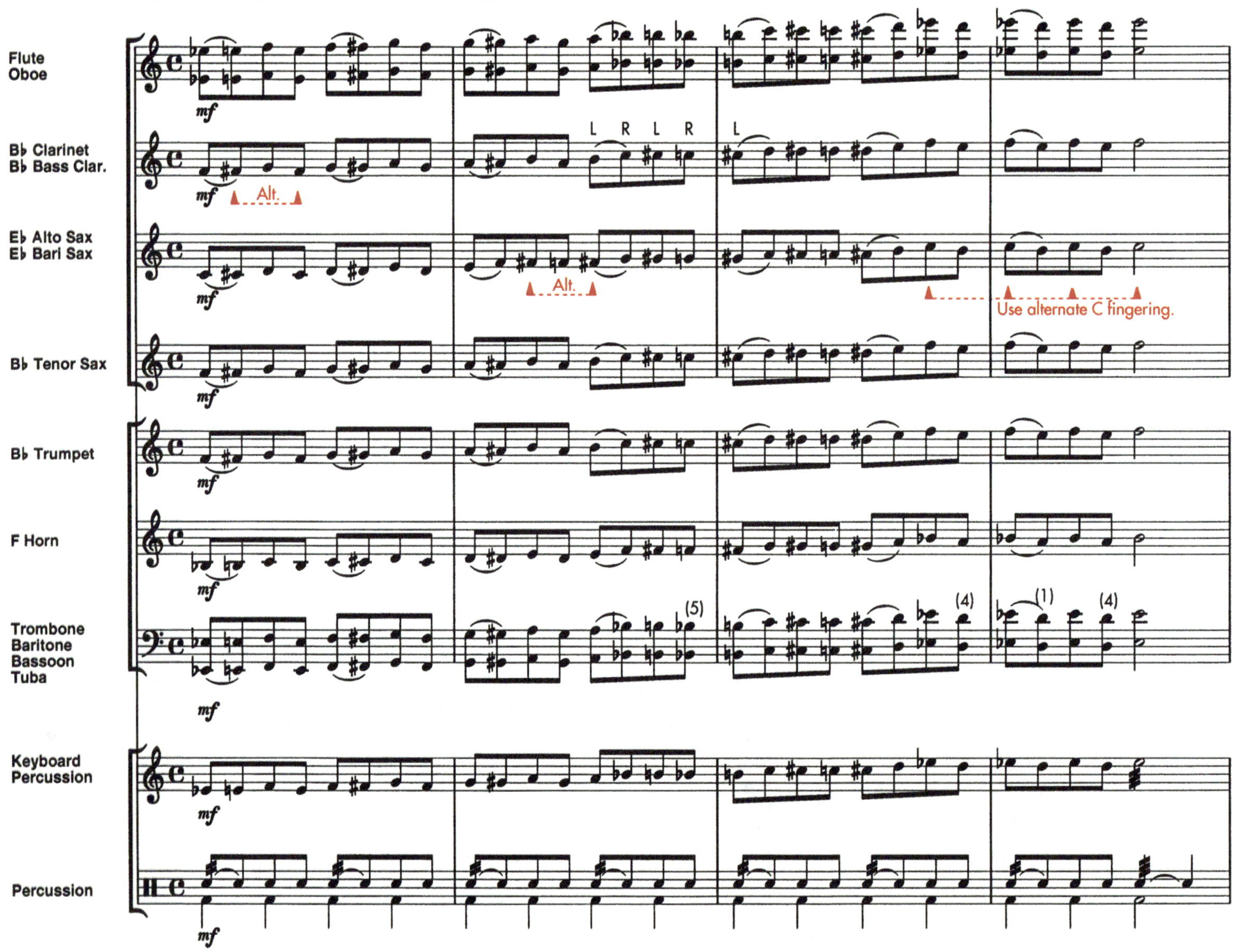

Flute
Oboe
Bb Clarinet
Bb Bass Clar.
L
L R L R
Alt.
Eb Alto Sax
Eb Bari Sax
Alt.
Bb Tenor Sax
Alt.
Bb Trumpet
F Horn
(6)
Trombone
Baritone
Bassoon
Tuba
Keyboard
Percussion
Percussion

Director Review the **STARS** guidelines before playing this exercise. Ask students to tell you how each element pertains to this exercise. Encourage your band to memorize this acronym, and apply it to all band literature.

Review the **STARS** guidelines before sightreading.

- **S** — Sharps or flats in the key signature
- **T** — Time signature and tempos
- **A** — Accidentals
- **R** — Rhythm
- **S** — Signs

29. SIGHTREADING CHALLENGE #2 - COMIN' THROUGH THE RYE

Scottish Folk Song

Flute
Oboe
B♭ Clarinet
B♭ Bass Clar.
E♭ Alto Sax
E♭ Bari Sax
B♭ Tenor Sax
B♭ Trumpet
F Horn
Trombone
Baritone
Bassoon
Tuba
Keyboard
Percussion
Percussion

History

For centuries, **Native American Indian music** has been an important part of tribal dancing ceremonies. Apache fiddles, rattles, flutes and log drums accompanied simple songs. Much of today's Indian music has been influenced by Western and Afro-American cultures due to the forced migration of Indian tribes to reservations. American composer **Charles Wakefield Cadman** (1881-1946) wrote this song in 1914 based on Indian melodies he researched throughout his lifetime.

30. SONG OF THE WEEPING SPIRIT

Native American Indian Melody
Adapted by Charles Wakefield Cadman

Lento mysterioso ◄ Slowly and mysteriously

31. CELEBRATION SONG

Malaysian Wedding Song

Theory: Key Signature Names

Key signature names tell us the "key" of the musical composition. The key is the tonal center, or "home base." A key signature without sharps or flats is usually called C Major. Identify the name of key signatures by remembering two simple rules:

1) **Flats look back.** The second-to-last flat tells us the key signature name.

For example, a key signature with 3 flats (B♭, E♭, A♭) is E♭ Major:

A key signature with one flat is F Major:

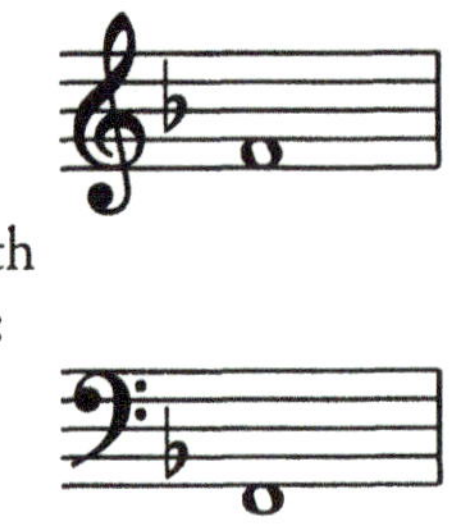

2) **Sharps look up.** The note one half-step above the last sharp tells us the key signature name.

For example, a key signature with one sharp is G Major:

Here are some common key signatures:

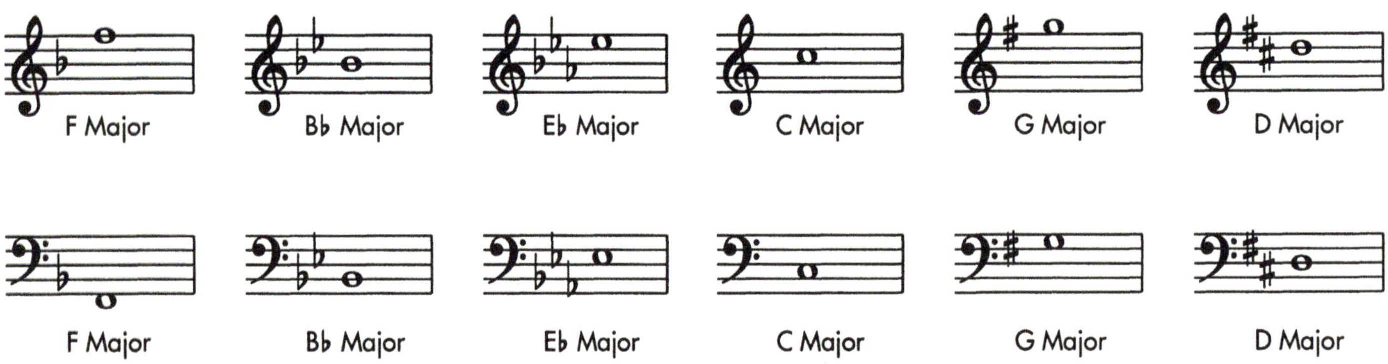

Director The treble clef key signature sequence above is found in all treble clef instrument books. The bass clef key signature sequence appears in all bass clef books, and the percussion books include both treble and bass clef key signatures. Verbal questions such as "What key signature has three flats?" "Name the two flats in the B♭ major key signature" and "Name the sharps found in G Major key signature" also help reinforce key signature recognition.

32. ESSENTIAL TECHNIQUE QUIZ

Write the names of the following key signatures. The name of the whole note is the name of the key signature.

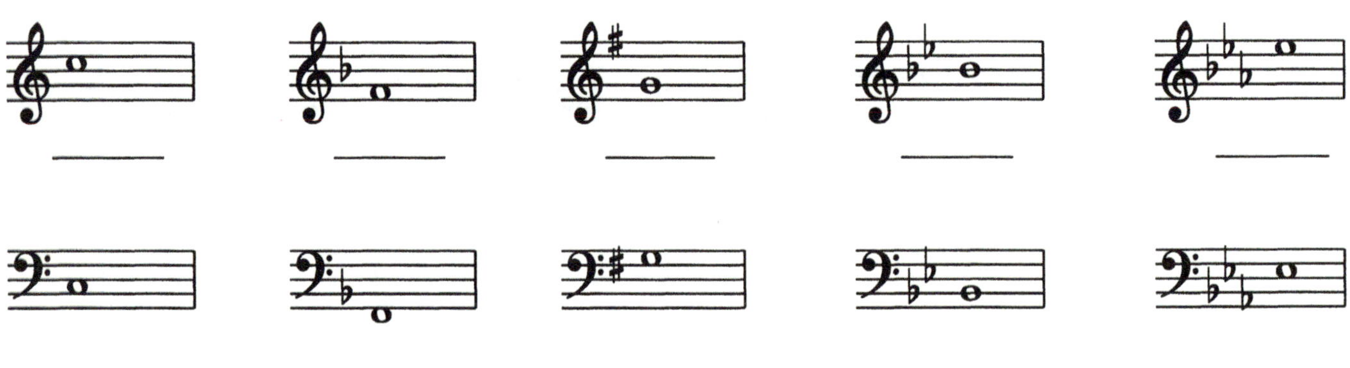

Director

Concert keys in **Essential Technique** are introduced in the following format:

Balance Builder
- A, B and C parts for all students

Chorale - Full Band Arrangement
- Rehearse woodwinds alone, brass alone and full band

Scale
- Marked articulations
- Scale in Thirds
- Arpeggio

Articulation Work-Out
- Focus on accuracy

If you wish to warm-up in specific key(s), ask students to turn to the indicated pages:

Concert Key	Score Pg.	Student Pg.
Bb Major	14	2
Eb Major	36	6
F Major	61	11
D Minor	100	18
Ab Major	110	20
C Major	132	23
G Minor	144	25
G Major	200	36
D Major	212	38
Db Major	224	40
Gb Major	230	41

Tune and shape each note on *Balance Builder* exercises, and experiment with different instrument combinations. Rehearse brass alone, woodwinds alone and the full band on each *Chorale* to improve balance and intonation. Include various dynamic levels on each *Scale* and *Articulation Work-Out,* including ***mf***, ***f***, ***p*** and < >.

Additional scale studies are found on score pages 234 - 240 (student book pages 42 - 44). All scale studies are transposed for group or individual practice. *Chromatic Technique* studies are found throughout the book, in addition to multicultural songs, rhythm reinforcement and theory exercises.

NEW NOTES INTRODUCED ON 33. BALANCE BUILDER

Bassoon

E

Ear Training

Concert F Major

Play each line below, then sing it in your natural voice range. Make sure all chord tones are heard equally well and are in "balance." Begin tuning with the lower instruments of the band.

33. BALANCE BUILDER

34. CHORALE - Full Band Arrangement (Based on a Theme by J. S. Bach)

Arr. by John Higgins

5
Flute
Oboe
Bassoon
B♭ Clarinet
E♭ Alto Clar.
B♭ Bass Clar.
E♭ Alto Sax.
B♭ Ten. Sax.
E♭ Bari. Sax.
5
B♭ Trumpet
F Horn
Trombone
Baritone
Tuba
Keyboard Percussion
Tri.
S.D.
Percussion
mf
p
Timpani

9
Flute
Oboe
Bassoon
B♭ Clarinet
E♭ Alto Clar.
B♭ Bass Clar.
E♭ Alto Sax.
B♭ Ten. Sax.
E♭ Bari. Sax.
B♭ Trumpet
F Horn
Trombone
Baritone
Tuba
Keyboard Percussion
Percussion
B.D.
Timpani
rit.

35. CONCERT F MAJOR TECHNIQUE

36. ARTICULATION WORK - OUT

Play even rhythms at all tempos.

► Practice this exercise as a wrist builder with RRRR and LLLL sticking.

Director *Rhythm Rap* teaching sequence: Entire band claps • Add percussion accompaniment • Clap as a round • Sing on "tah."

37. RHYTHM RAP

Director The rhythms of *37. Rhythm Rap* and *38. Concert F Major Scale* are identical. Be sure to count, clap and tap all exercises before playing them.

38. CONCERT F MAJOR SCALE (Your F Major)

History

French composer **Claude Debussy** (1862-1918) created moods and "impressions" with his music. While earlier composers used music to describe events (such as Tchaikovsky's *1812 Overture*), Debussy's new ideas helped shape today's music. The style of art and music created in this time is called "impressionism." The first automobile was produced during Debussy's lifetime. He died the same year that World War I ended.

39. THE LITTLE CHILD

Claude Debussy

Giocoso ◄ Lightly, happily

40. TURKEY IN THE STRAW

American Folk Song

Allegretto

Flute
Oboe
B♭ Clarinet
B♭ Bass Clar.
E♭ Alto Sax
E♭ Bari Sax
B♭ Tenor Sax
B♭ Trumpet
F Horn
Trombone
Baritone
Bassoon
Tuba
Keyboard
Percussion
Percussion
(6)
mf
2

Director The rhythms of *41. Rhythm Rap* and *42. Concert F Major Scale* are identical. These exercises are cut-time versions of *37. Rhythm Rap* and *38. Concert F Major Scale,* which appear on student book page 12 (score page 67). It may be helpful to review the 4/4 rhythms before playing the cut-time versions. Divide the band and perform the matching exercises in unison rhythms. *Rhythm Rap* teaching sequence: Entire band claps • Add percussion accompaniment • Clap as a round • Sing on "tah."

41. RHYTHM RAP

¢ or 2/2 - 2 beats per measure - ♩ or ▬ gets one beat

42. CONCERT F MAJOR SCALE

43. INDONESIAN DANCE

Indonesian Folk Song

Flute
Oboe
B♭ Clarinet
B♭ Bass Clar.
E♭ Alto Sax
E♭ Bari Sax
B♭ Tenor Sax
B♭ Trumpet
F Horn
Trombone
Baritone
Bassoon
Tuba
Keyboard
Percussion
Flam Tap
Percussion

History

Jazz is a uniquely American art form, and continues to influence today's popular music. It developed in the 20th century when black musicians began combining African and European musical styles. "Dixieland" was a popular early jazz form, and the first jazz recording was made during World War I by the Original Dixieland Band in New Orleans. *That's A Plenty* is a famous Dixieland song.

Director Play jazz recordings as students are entering the classroom. Select from dixieland, be-bop, standards and modern day influences, and briefly discuss the elements of different jazz styles.

NEW NOTES INTRODUCED ON 44. THAT'S A PLENTY

44. THAT'S A PLENTY

Lew Pollack

Easy "2" feel

45. CHROMATIC TECHNIQUE

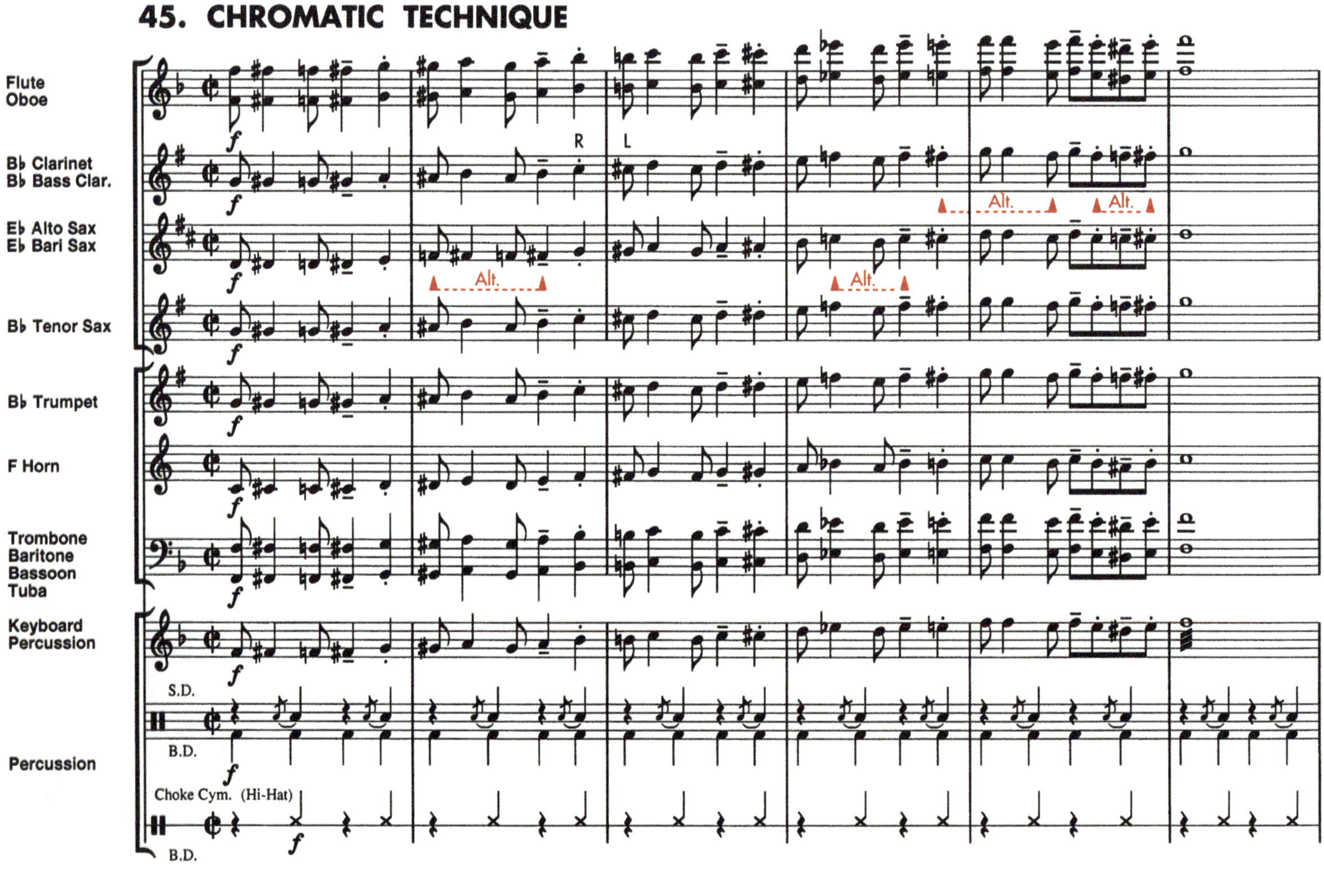

Flute
Oboe
B♭ Clarinet
B♭ Bass Clar.
L R L R L
L R
E♭ Alto Sax
E♭ Bari Sax
B♭ Tenor Sax
B♭ Trumpet
F Horn
Trombone
Baritone
Bassoon
Tuba
Keyboard
Percussion
Percussion

History Composers often use traditional folk songs within their music. Band composer John Barnes Chance used this simple tune in his *Variations On A Korean Folk Song,* now a famous work for concert band. The melody uses only the 1st, 2nd, 3rd, 5th and 6th notes from the Concert B♭ major scale. This type of scale is called a pentatonic scale. "Penta" is the Latin word for "five."

Director The history of band literature is an important part of playing in band. Play a recording of *Variations on a Korean Folk Song* for your band. Discuss the theme and variation form, and textural changes found throughout this significant work.

46. KOREAN FOLK SONG THEME

Korean Folk Song

Flute
Oboe
B♭ Clarinet
B♭ Bass Clar.
E♭ Alto Sax
E♭ Bari Sax
B♭ Tenor Sax
B♭ Trumpet
F Horn
Trombone
Baritone
Bassoon
Tuba
Keyboard
Percussion
Percussion
Timpani
mf
p
(4)

Divisi Tells players to "divide" and play the two (or more) notes written on the same staff. Be sure to decide who plays upper and lower notes before playing the piece. *Divisi* is usually abbreviated *div.* *Unis.*, or unison, tells performers to play the same note.

NEW NOTES INTRODUCED ON 47. MINUET

Bb Trumpet — F Horn — Trombone — Baritone B.C. — Baritone T.C. — Tuba

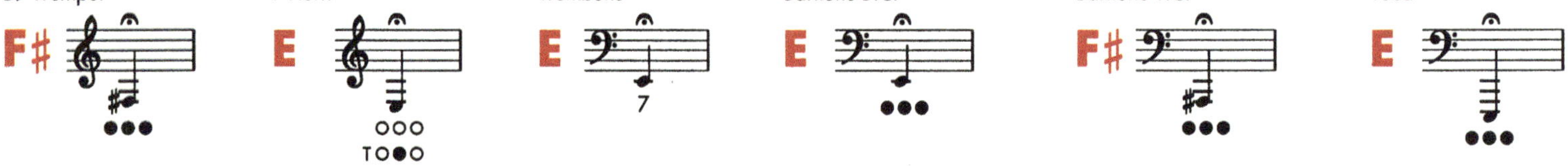

Eb Instruments: E-sharp is played with the same fingering as F-natural.

47. MINUET

Ludwig van Beethoven

Flute
Oboe
Bb Clarinet
Bb Bass Clar.
Eb Alto Sax
Eb Bari Sax
Bb Tenor Sax
Bb Trumpet
F Horn
Trombone
Baritone
Bassoon
Tuba
Keyboard
Percussion
Percussion
unis.
div.
(6)

Flute
Oboe
B♭ Clarinet
B♭ Bass Clar.
E♭ Alto Sax
E♭ Bari Sax
B♭ Tenor Sax
B♭ Trumpet
F Horn
Trombone
Baritone
Bassoon
Tuba
Keyboard
Percussion
Percussion
mf
f
p

Marcato Accent ^ A loud accented note of short duration.

48. ESSENTIAL TECHNIQUE QUIZ - RHYTHM CHALLENGE

Sixteenth Rest

𝄿 = 1/4 silent beat

𝄿 = 1/4 silent beat
𝄾 = 1/2 silent beat
𝄽 = 1 silent beat

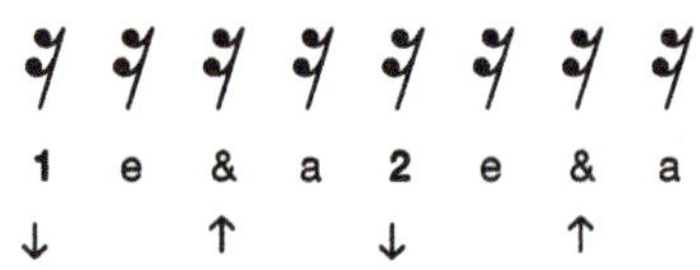

A sixteenth rest has two flags on the stem.

▼ Flags 𝄿

Director The rhythms in *49. Rhythm Rap* and *50. Count Carefully* are identical. *Rhythm Rap* teaching sequence: Entire band claps • Add percussion accompaniment • Clap as a round • Sing on "tah."

49. RHYTHM RAP

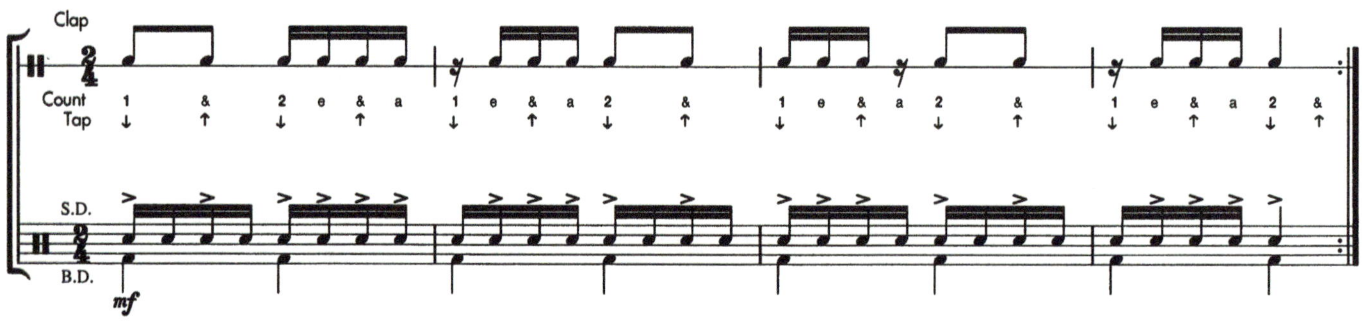

50. COUNT CAREFULLY

Moderato

51. ARTICULATION WORK - OUT

52. CHROMATIC TECHNIQUE

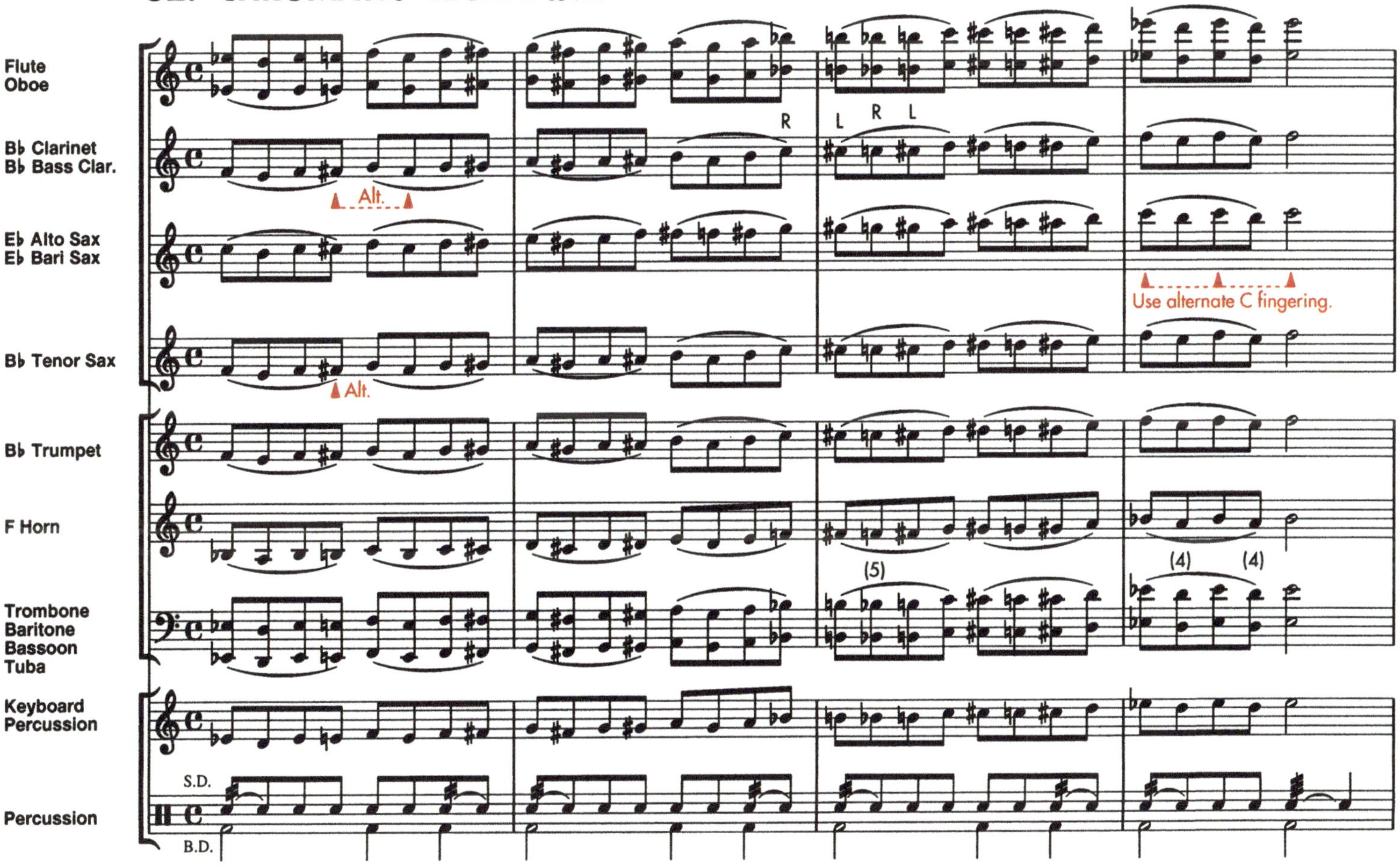

Flute
Oboe
L
L R L
B♭ Clarinet
B♭ Bass Clar.
Alt.
E♭ Alto Sax
E♭ Bari Sax
Alt.
B♭ Tenor Sax
Alt.
B♭ Trumpet
F Horn
(6)
Trombone
Baritone
Bassoon
Tuba
Keyboard
Percussion
Percussion

NEW NOTES INTRODUCED ON 53. FRENCH NATIONAL ANTHEM (LA MARSEILLAISE)

B♭ Clarinet

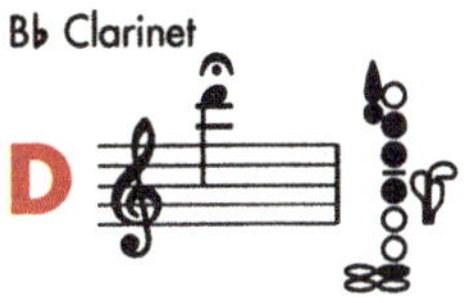

53. FRENCH NATIONAL ANTHEM (LA MARSEILLAISE)

Rouget De L'Isle

Flute
Oboe
B♭ Clarinet
B♭ Bass Clar.
E♭ Alto Sax
E♭ Bari Sax
B♭ Tenor Sax
B♭ Trumpet
F Horn
Trombone
Baritone
Bassoon
Tuba
Keyboard
Percussion
Percussion
Timpani

Flute
Oboe
B♭ Clarinet
B♭ Bass Clar.
E♭ Alto Sax
E♭ Bari Sax
B♭ Tenor Sax
B♭ Trumpet
F Horn
Trombone
Baritone
Bassoon
Tuba
Keyboard
Percussion
Percussion
Timpani

Flute
Oboe
B♭ Clarinet
B♭ Bass Clar.
E♭ Alto Sax
E♭ Bari Sax
B♭ Tenor Sax
B♭ Trumpet
F Horn
Trombone
Baritone
Bassoon
Tuba
Keyboard
Percussion
Percussion
Timpani

After 1755, a group of French-speaking Canadians living in what is now Nova Scotia migrated to southern Louisiana, calling themselves "Acadians." Their music is called **Cajun music**, and remains a significant part of American culture. Today's Cajun bands are usually made up of a fiddle, accordion, electric guitar, bass and drum set. The first Cajun recording was made in 1928, one year after the first television transmission.

Director Play recordings of Cajun music for your band, and other diverse styles of music. Ask students to describe the sounds and possible influences of Cajun music.

NEW NOTES INTRODUCED ON 54. ACADIAN DANCE

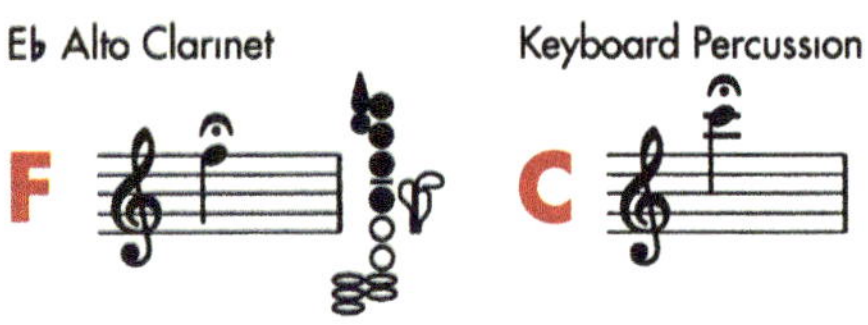

54. ACADIAN DANCE

Fine
D.C. al Fine
Flute
Oboe
B♭ Clarinet
B♭ Bass Clar.
E♭ Alto Sax
E♭ Bari Sax
B♭ Tenor Sax
B♭ Trumpet
F Horn
Trombone
Baritone
Bassoon
Tuba
Keyboard
Percussion
Percussion
Timpani

Sixteenth Notes in 

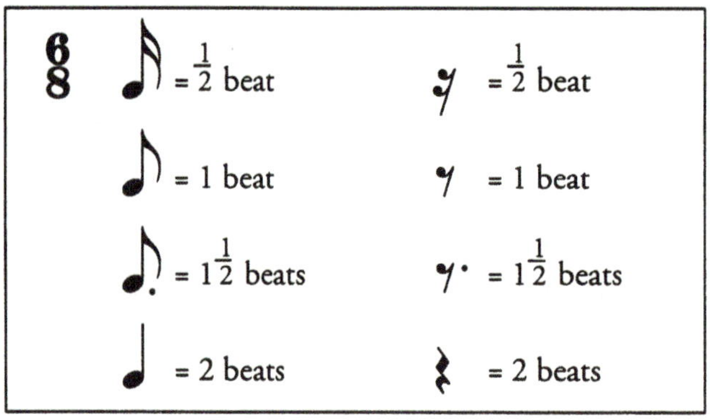

2 sixteenths = 1 beat in 6/8 meter.

Director The rhythm of *55. Rhythm Rap* and *56. Articulation Work-Out* are identical. *Rhythm Rap* teaching sequence: Entire band claps • Add percussion accompaniment • Clap as a round • Sing on "tah."

55. RHYTHM RAP

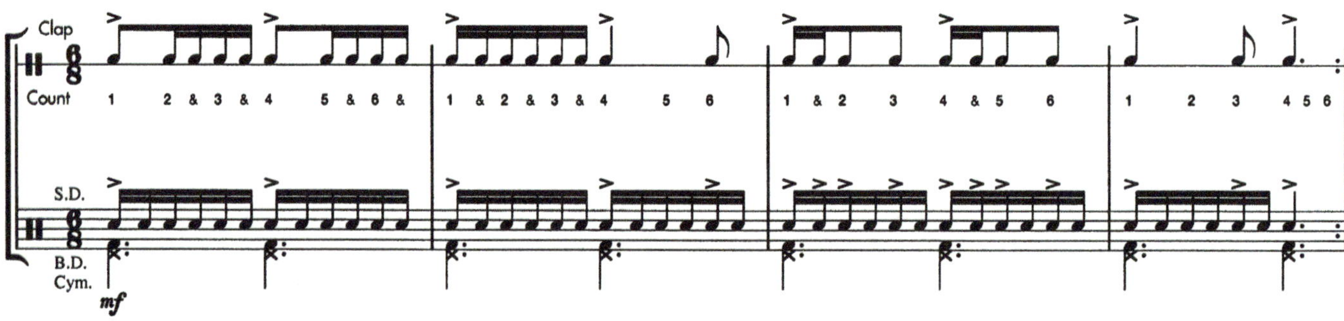

56. ARTICULATION WORK - OUT

Moderato

Director The rhythms of *57. Rhythm Rap* and *58. The Dot Always Counts Half* are identical. *Rhythm Rap* teaching sequence: Entire band claps • Add percussion accompaniment • Clap as a round • Sing on "tah."

57. RHYTHM RAP

NEW NOTES INTRODUCED ON 58. THE DOT ALWAYS COUNTS HALF

E♭ Alto Clarinet

G

58. THE DOT ALWAYS COUNTS HALF

Conducting

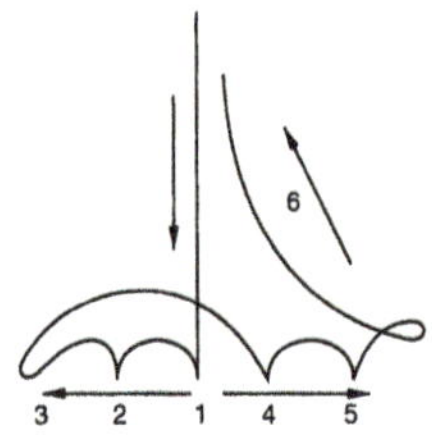

The six-beat pattern is used for pieces written in 6/8 meter. 6/8 pieces can also be conducted with a two-beat pattern, emphasizing beats 1 and 4. Practice conducting this six-beat pattern.

Director Former *Essential Elements* Book 1 students may remember that Austrian composer Wolfgang Amadeus Mozart (1756-1791) lived during the American Revolution (1775-1783). Mozart first performed in concert at age six. His music is melodic and imaginative. Play an excerpt of Mozart's music for the band. Discuss the elements of style and texture which make Mozart's music so unique. This melody is from *Piano Sonata in A, K. 331.*

59. SONATA

Wolfgang Amadeus Mozart

2
Flute
Oboe
B♭ Clarinet
B♭ Bass Clar.
E♭ Alto Sax
E♭ Bari Sax
B♭ Tenor Sax
B♭ Trumpet
F Horn
Trombone
Baritone
Bassoon
Tuba
Keyboard
Percussion
Percussion
mp
mf
(4)
rit.
p a tempo
pp
Alt.
p
a tempo

NEW NOTES INTRODUCED ON 60. ARPEGGIO EXTENSION

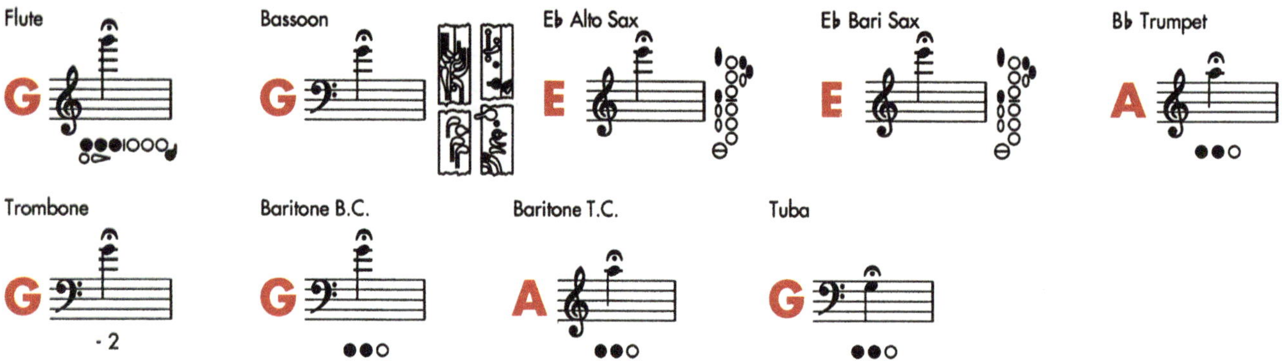

60. ARPEGGIO EXTENSION

Moderato

History Music written during the Renaissance era (1430-1600) was often upbeat and dance-like. *Wolsey's Wilde* was originally written for the lute, an ancestor to the guitar and the most popular instrument of the Renaissance era. Modern day concert band composer Gordon Jacob used this popular song in his *William Byrd Suite*, written as a tribute to English composer William Byrd (1543-1623).

Director Play excerpts of Gordon Jacob's *William Byrd Suite* and other Renaissance pieces for the band. Discuss how the contrapuntal style differs from the chorales found throughout this book.

61. WOLSEY'S WILDE

Anonymous

Animato ◂ Animated, lively

Flute
Oboe
B♭ Clarinet
B♭ Bass Clar.
E♭ Alto Sax
E♭ Bari Sax
B♭ Tenor Sax
▲Alt.
B♭ Trumpet
F Horn
Trombone
Baritone
Bassoon
Tuba
Keyboard
Percussion
Percussion
Flute
Oboe
B♭ Clarinet
B♭ Bass Clar.
E♭ Alto Sax
E♭ Bari Sax
B♭ Tenor Sax
B♭ Trumpet
F Horn
Trombone
Baritone
Bassoon
Tuba
Keyboard
Percussion
Percussion

Flute
Oboe
B♭ Clarinet
B♭ Bass Clar.
E♭ Alto Sax
E♭ Bari Sax
B♭ Tenor Sax
Alt.
Alt.
B♭ Trumpet
F Horn
Trombone
Baritone
Bassoon
Tuba
Keyboard
Percussion
Percussion

Flute
Oboe
B♭ Clarinet
B♭ Bass Clar.
E♭ Alto Sax
E♭ Bari Sax
B♭ Tenor Sax
Alt.
Alt.
B♭ Trumpet
F Horn
Trombone
Baritone
Bassoon
Tuba
Keyboard
Percussion
Percussion

Theory — Minor Scales

A **Minor Scale** is a series of eight notes which follow a definite pattern of whole steps and half steps. The three forms of the minor scale are natural minor, harmonic minor and melodic minor

Director All three forms of the minor scale are transposed on exercises 62, 63 and 64 so they can be played by the full band. A full page of minor scales appears on student book page 44 (score pages 239-240).

62. NATURAL MINOR - Follows the key signature. Half steps appear only between scale steps 2-3 and 5-6.

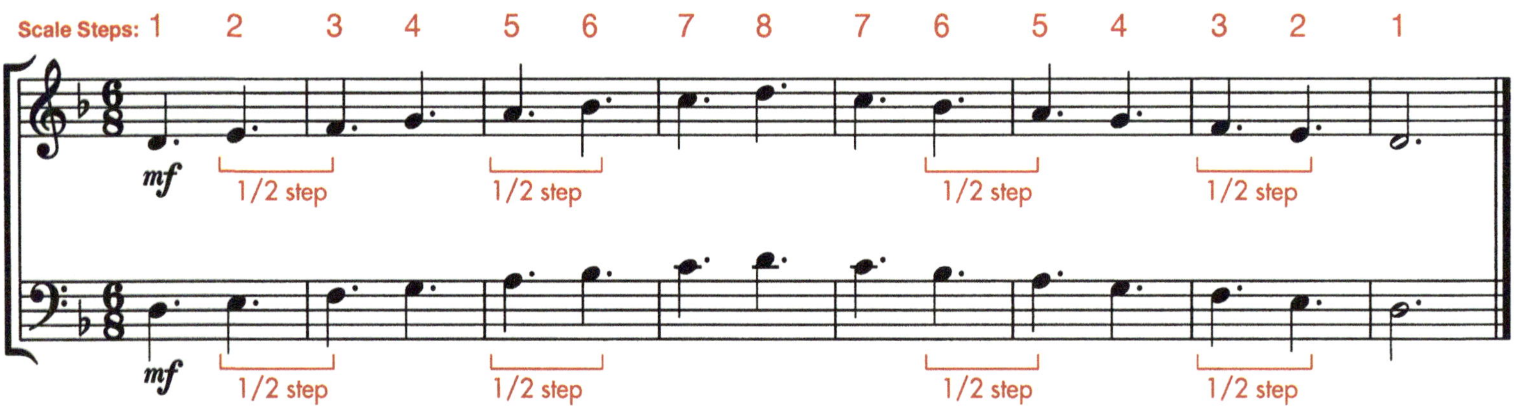

63. HARMONIC MINOR - Like natural minor, except the 7th scale step is raised one-half step.

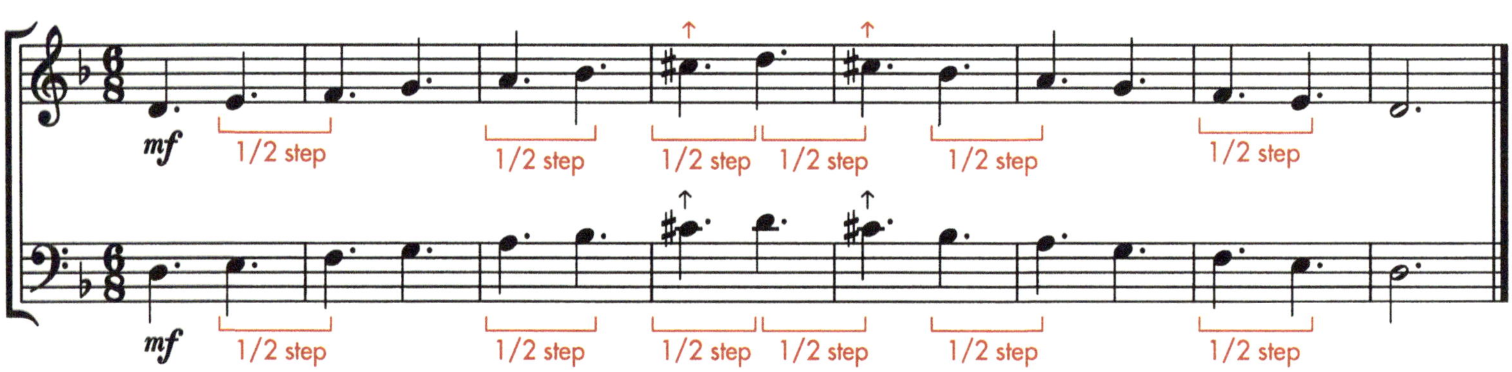

64. MELODIC MINOR

Ascending - Like natural minor, except the 6th and 7th scale steps are raised one-half step.
Descending - Just like natural minor.

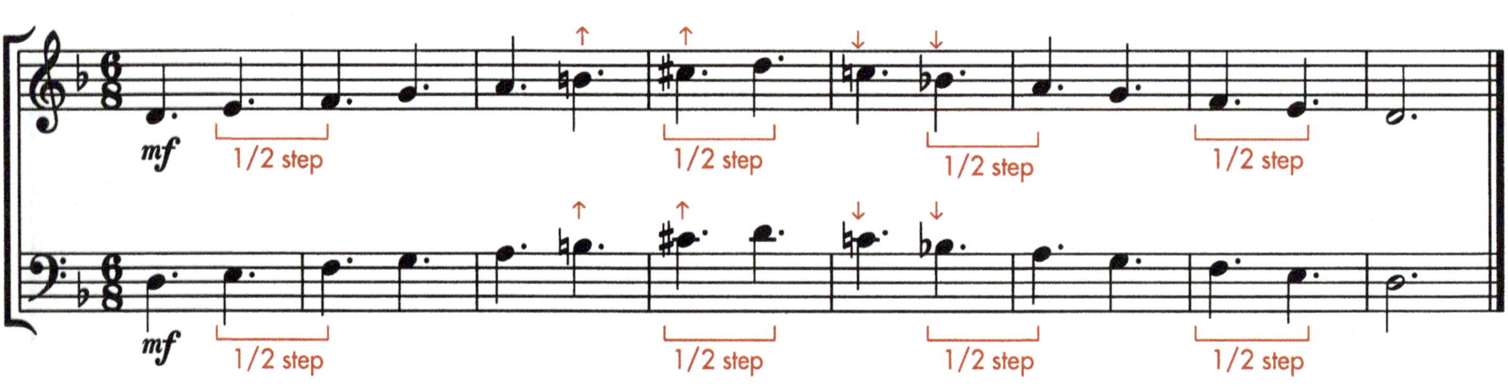

NEW NOTES INTRODUCED ON 65. CHORALE - Full Band Arrangement

Bassoon
C♯/D♭

65. CHORALE - Full Band Arrangement (Based on a Theme by Tchaikovsky)

Arr. by John Higgins

5
Flute
Oboe
Bassoon
B♭ Clarinet
E♭ Alto Clar.
R
L
B♭ Bass Clar.
E♭ Alto Sax.
B♭ Ten. Sax.
E♭ Bari. Sax.
5
B♭ Trumpet
F Horn
Trombone
Baritone
Tuba
Keyboard Percussion
Percussion
pp
Timpani

Flute
Oboe
Bassoon
B♭ Clarinet
E♭ Alto Clar.
B♭ Bass Clar.
E♭ Alto Sax.
B♭ Ten. Sax.
E♭ Bari. Sax.
B♭ Trumpet
F Horn
Trombone
Baritone
Tuba
Keyboard Percussion
Percussion
Timpani
10
rall.
Alt.

NEW NOTES INTRODUCED ON 66. CONCERT D MELODIC MINOR TECHNIQUE

B♭ Tenor Sax

D♯/E♭

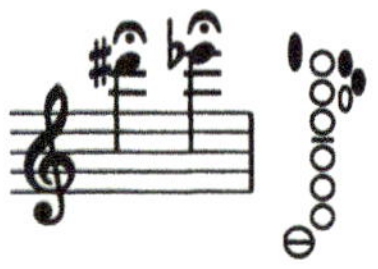

66. CONCERT D MELODIC MINOR TECHNIQUE

Scale in Thirds

Arpeggio

Director The first five notes of the concert D minor scale and complete tonic chord are transposed in each student book on this exercise. Ask students to select a chord tone and play the chord. Singing before playing improves aural awareness and intonation.

Minor Chords

Here is a chord from the D Minor scale. It is made up of the 1st, 3rd and 5th scale steps.

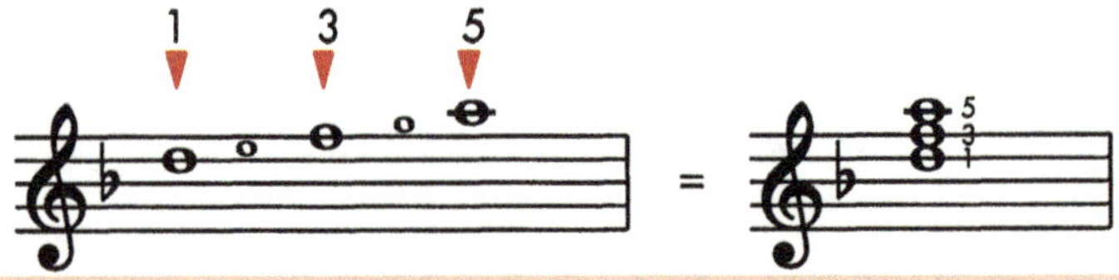

Director This exercise is transposed in each student book. The numbers inside the note heads reinforce scale steps and chord notes. You may wish to have a few students play or sing the root, then add band members singing the third and fifth before playing.

A single tone appears in the final measure. The chord voicings function as a teaching exercise. Play the chord, and ask students to identify their chord tone. Substitute different chord tones throughout the band, and experiment with balance and textural sounds.

67. EAR TRAINING TECHNIQUE

Play each exercise below, then sing it in your natural voice range
Make sure you can hear all the notes of the chord in the last measure.

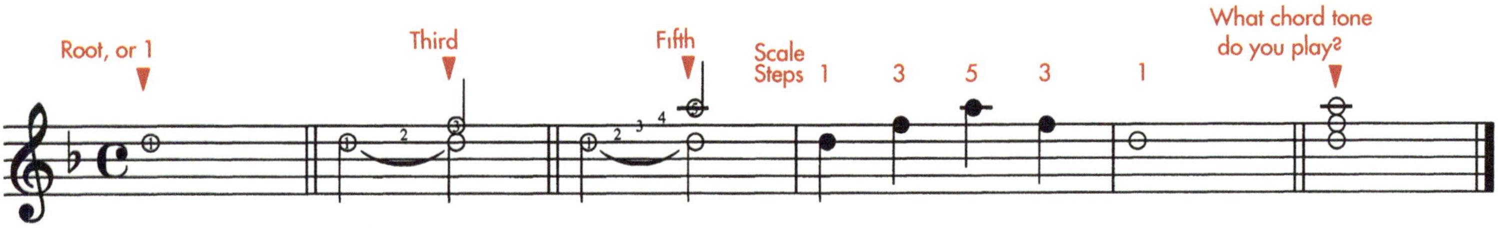

NEW NOTES INTRODUCED ON 68. GREENSLEEVES

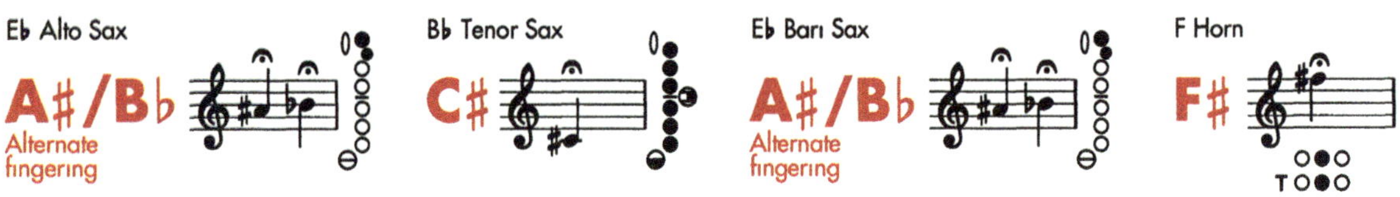

68. GREENSLEEVES

English Folk Song

Flute
Oboe
B♭ Clarinet
B♭ Bass Clar.
E♭ Alto Sax
E♭ Bari Sax
B♭ Tenor Sax
B♭ Trumpet
F Horn
Trombone
Baritone
Bassoon
Tuba
Keyboard
Percussion
Percussion
R L
Alt.

69. INTERVAL TECHNIQUE

Review the **STARS** guidelines before sightreading.

- **S** — Sharps or flats in the key signature
- **T** — Time signature and tempos
- **A** — Accidentals
- **R** — Rhythm
- **S** — Signs

70. SIGHTREADING CHALLENGE #3 - TARANTELLA

Director

Concert keys in **Essential Technique** are introduced in the following format:

Balance Builder
- A, B and C parts for all students

Chorale - Full Band Arrangement
- Rehearse woodwinds alone, brass alone and full band

Scale
- Marked articulations
- Scale in Thirds
- Arpeggio

Articulation Work-Out
- Focus on accuracy

If you wish to warm-up in specific key(s), ask students to turn to the indicated pages:

Concert Key	Score Pg.	Student Pg.
Bb Major	14	2
Eb Major	36	6
F Major	61	11
D Minor	100	18
Ab Major	110	20
C Major	132	23
G Minor	144	25
G Major	200	36
D Major	212	38
Db Major	224	40
Gb Major	230	41

Tune and shape each note on *Balance Builder* exercises, and experiment with different instrument combinations. Rehearse brass alone, woodwinds alone and the full band on each *Chorale* to improve balance and intonation. Include various dynamic levels on each *Scale* and *Articulation Work-Out*, including ***mf***, ***f***, ***p*** and < >.

Additional scale studies are found on score pages 234 - 240 (student book pages 42 - 44). All scale studies are transposed for group or individual practice. *Chromatic Technique* studies are found throughout the book, in addition to multicultural songs, rhythm reinforcement and theory exercises.

NEW NOTES INTRODUCED ON 71. BALANCE BUILDER

Bb Tenor Sax

Bb

Ear Training

Concert Ab Major Play each line below, then sing it in your natural voice range. Make sure all chord tones are heard equally well, and are in "balance." Begin tuning with lower instruments of the band.

71. BALANCE BUILDER

72. CHORALE - Full Band Arrangement (Erhalt Uns In Der Wahrheit)

Johann Sebastian Bach
Arr. by John Higgins

5
Flute
Oboe
Bassoon
B♭ Clarinet
E♭ Alto Clar.
B♭ Bass Clar.
E♭ Alto Sax.
B♭ Ten. Sax.
E♭ Bari. Sax.
5
B♭ Trumpet
F Horn
Trombone
Baritone
Tuba
Keyboard Percussion
Percussion
Sus. Cym.
pp
mf
Timpani

9
Flute
Oboe
Bassoon
B♭ Clarinet
E♭ Alto Clar.
B♭ Bass Clar.
E♭ Alto Sax.
B♭ Ten. Sax.
Alt.
E♭ Bari. Sax.
9
B♭ Trumpet
F Horn
Trombone
Baritone
Tuba
Keyboard Percussion
Percussion
pp
mf
Timpani

13
Flute
Oboe
Bassoon
B♭ Clarinet
E♭ Alto Clar.
B♭ Bass Clar.
E♭ Alto Sax.
B♭ Ten. Sax.
E♭ Bari. Sax.
B♭ Trumpet
F Horn
Trombone
Baritone
Tuba
Keyboard Percussion
Percussion
Timpani
rit.
Alt.
pp
mf

NEW NOTES INTRODUCED ON 73. CONCERT A♭ MAJOR SCALE TECHNIQUE

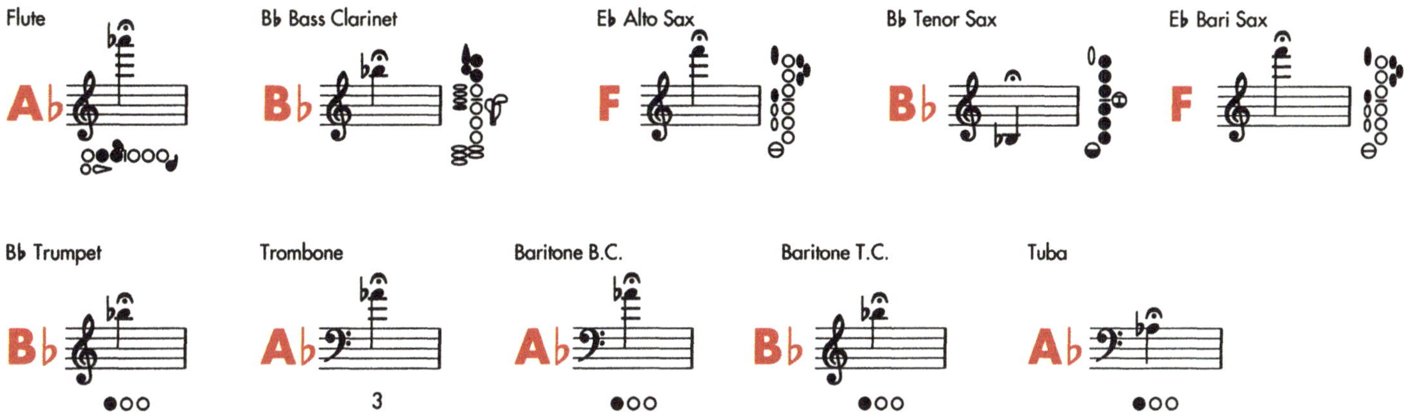

73. CONCERT A♭ MAJOR SCALE TECHNIQUE

Scale in Thirds

Arpeggio

74. ARTICULATION WORK - OUT

Play even rhythms at all tempos.

► Practice this exercise as a wrist builder with RRRR and LLLL sticking.

The Star Spangled Banner is the national anthem of the United States of America. Francis Scott Key wrote the words during the 1814 battle at Fort McHenry. He listened to the sounds of the fighting throughout the night while being detained on a ship. At dawn, he saw the American flag still flying over the fort. He was inspired to write these words, which were later set to the melody of a popular English song.

75. THE STAR SPANGLED BANNER

Words by Francis Scott Key
Music by John Stafford Smith

Allegro maestoso

Flute
Oboe
twi - light's last gleam - ing? Whose broad stripes and bright stars, through the per - il - ous fight, o'er the ram - parts we
B♭ Clarinet
B♭ Bass Clar.
E♭ Alto Sax
E♭ Bari Sax
B♭ Tenor Sax
B♭ Trumpet
F Horn
Trombone
Baritone
Bassoon
Tuba
Keyboard
Percussion
Percussion
f
Flute
Oboe
watched were so gal - lant - ly stream - ing? And the rock - et's red glare, the bombs burst - ing in air, gave
mf
B♭ Clarinet
B♭ Bass Clar.
E♭ Alto Sax
E♭ Bari Sax
B♭ Tenor Sax
B♭ Trumpet
F Horn
Trombone
Baritone
Bassoon
Tuba
Keyboard
Percussion
Percussion

Flute
Oboe
Bb Clarinet
Bb Bass Clar.
Eb Alto Sax
Eb Bari Sax
Bb Tenor Sax
Bb Trumpet
F Horn
Trombone
Baritone
Bassoon
Tuba
Keyboard
Percussion
Percussion
proof through the night that our flag was still there. Oh say does that Star Span - gled
Ban - ner yet wave o'er the land of the free and the home of the brave?

76. TRIPLET TECHNIQUE

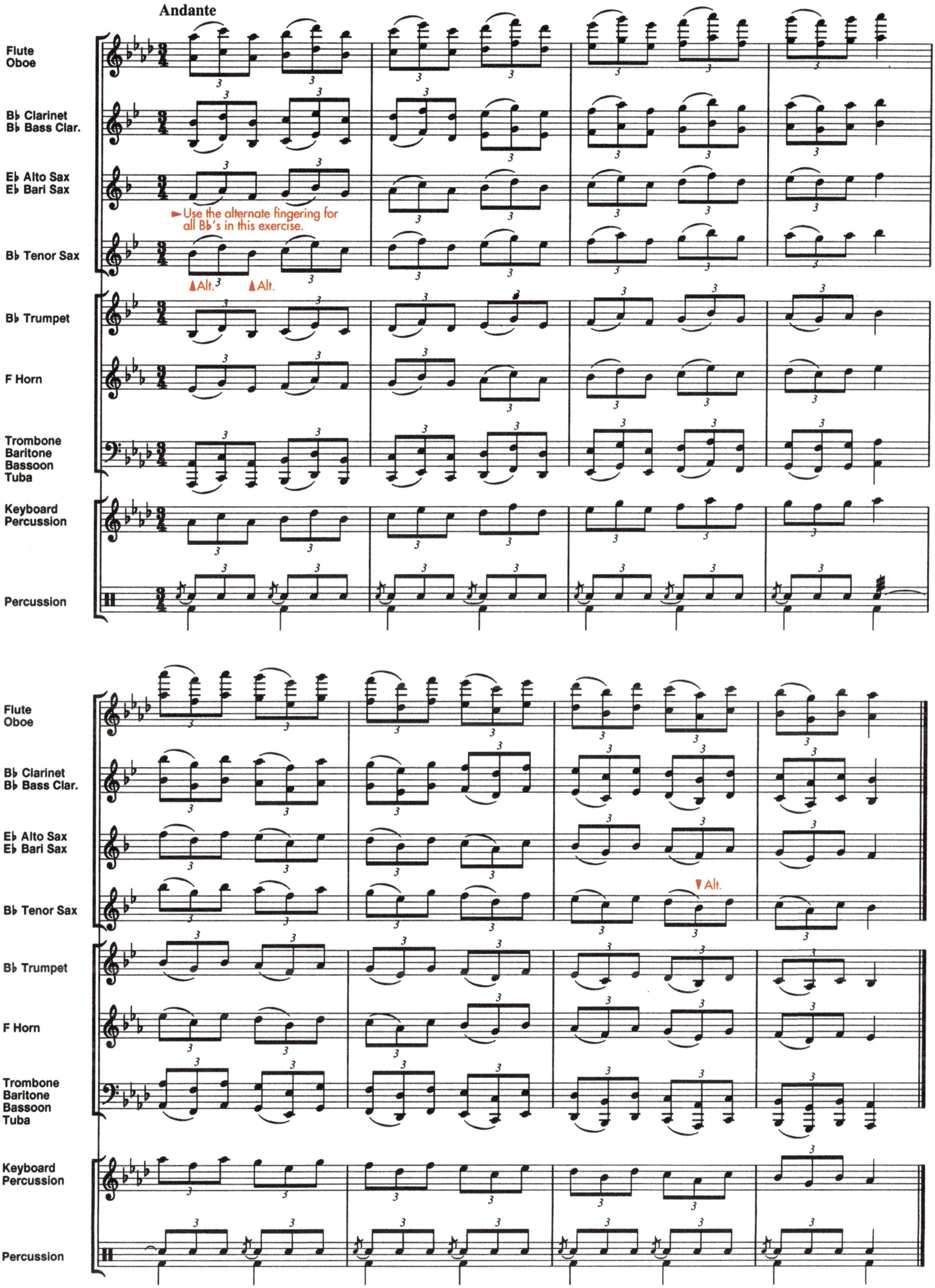

SPECIAL PERCUSSION EXERCISE

Roll exercise with triplets.

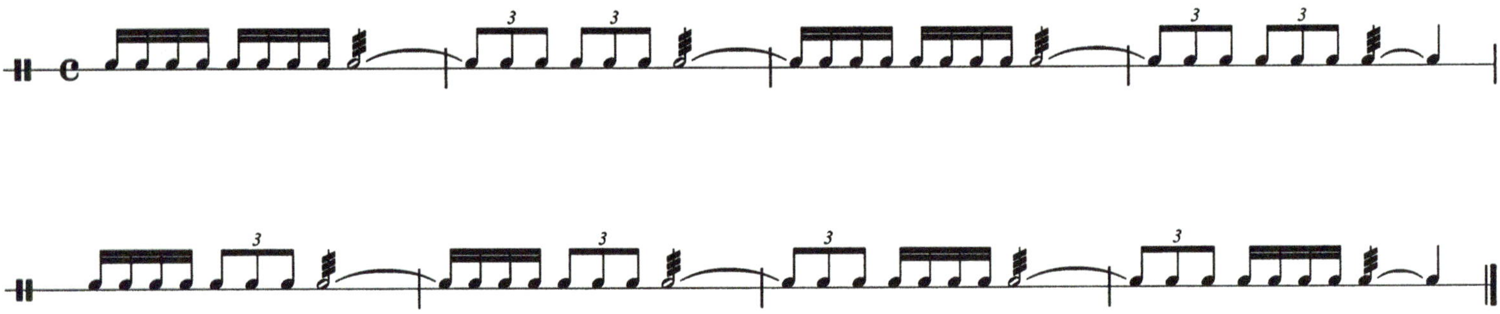

Percussion: Many instrumental compositions have very limited percussion parts. The percussion section is responsible for counting rests and carefully performing the written music. Proper attitude and behavior are the key attributes of the outstanding percussion section.

77. PAVANNE

Maurice Ravel

Flute
Oboe
B♭ Clarinet
B♭ Bass Clar.
E♭ Alto Sax
E♭ Bari Sax
B♭ Tenor Sax
Alt.
B♭ Trumpet
F Horn
Trombone
Baritone
Bassoon
Tuba
Keyboard
Percussion
Percussion
p
mf

Director Special exercises for each instrument appear on student book page 22. Trills are introduced in all woodwind books. Brass players learn to double tongue, and basic drum set patterns appear in the percussion books. Keyboard percussion players are asked to name all notes found on the bells. In addition, a color trill fingering chart appears on page 45 of each corresponding woodwind book (score pages 241-248). There is a full page of lip slur studies on page 45 of all brass books (score pages 249-254). Encourage players to use these exercises in their daily warm-ups.

SPECIAL WOODWIND EXERCISES

Trill *tr*

Rapidly alternate between a note and the note above (or below). *tr* and *tr~~~* are common trill abbreviations. Always trill to the note above the written note (in the key signature) unless the music indicates another trill note. You may need to use alternate fingerings when playing trills. Move the trill key (or keys) as quickly as possible. Trills should be played smoothly.

Flute **Oboe** **B♭ Clarinet** **All Saxes**

Bassoon trills from F→G.

Alto and Bass Clarinet trills are written one octave below clarinet.

Flute

Whole Step Trills

Practice these trills with the indicated fingerings:

Half Step Trills

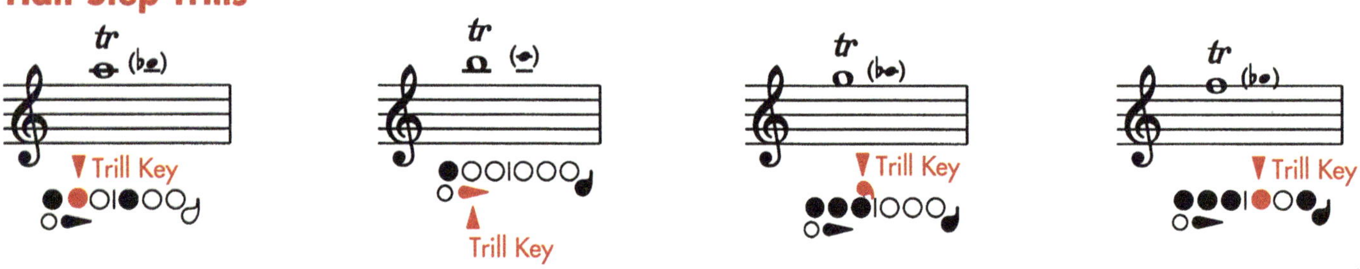

Oboe

Whole Step Trills

Practice these trills with the indicated fingerings:

Half Step Trills

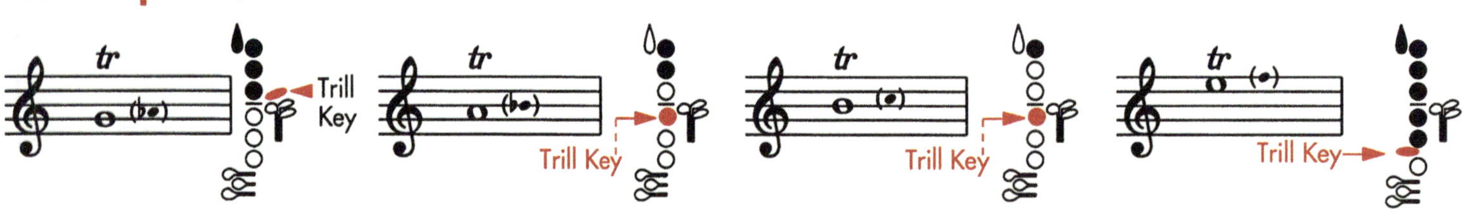

Bassoon

Whole Step Trills

Practice these trills with the indicated fingerings:

Half Step Trills

B♭ Clarinet

Whole Step Trills

Practice these trills with the indicated fingerings:

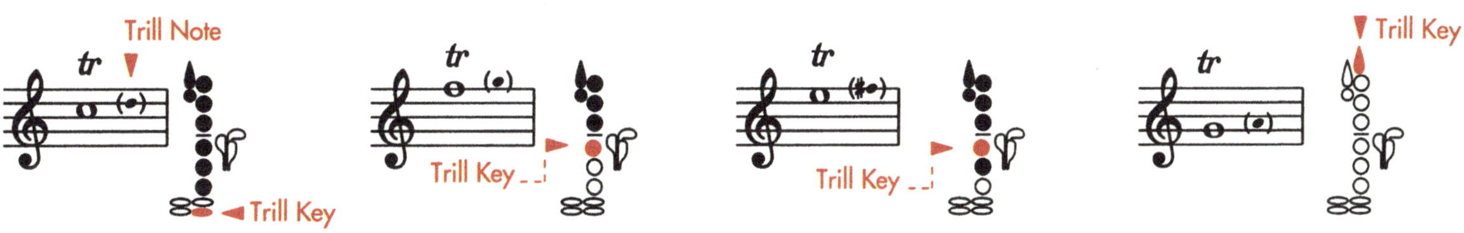

Half Step Trills

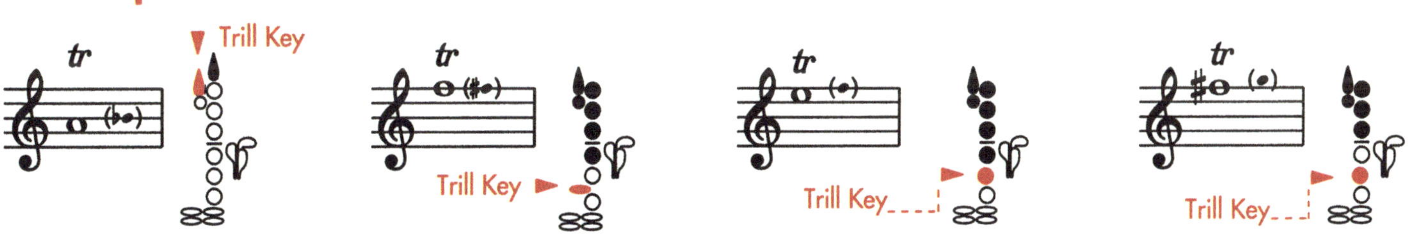

E♭ Alto Clarinet

Whole Step Trills

Practice these trills with the indicated fingerings:

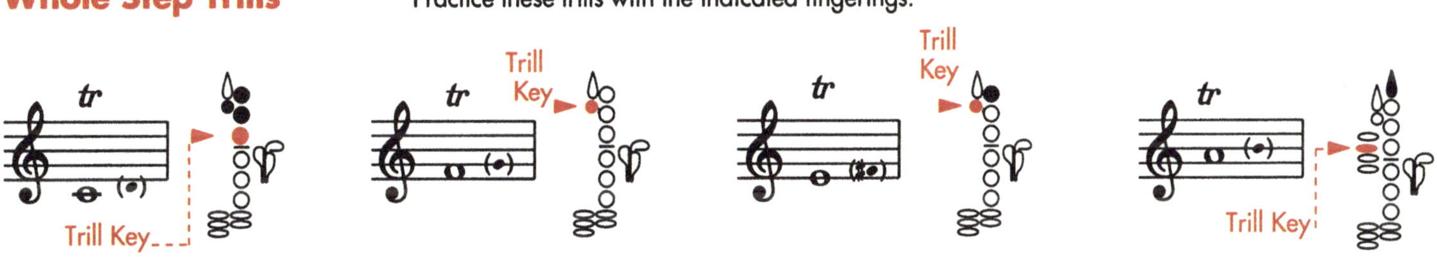

Half Step Trills

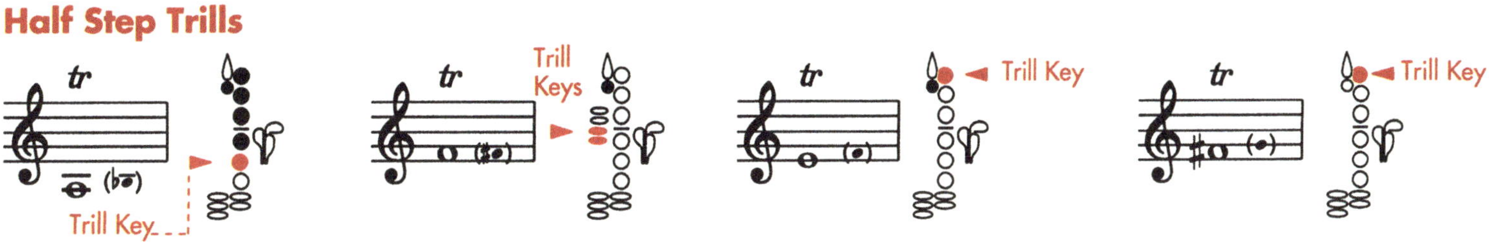

B♭ Bass Clarinet

Whole Step Trills

Practice these trills with the indicated fingerings:

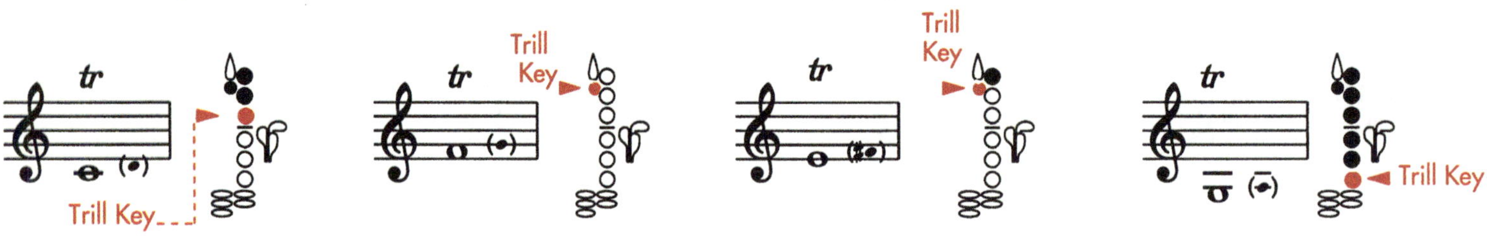

Half Step Trills

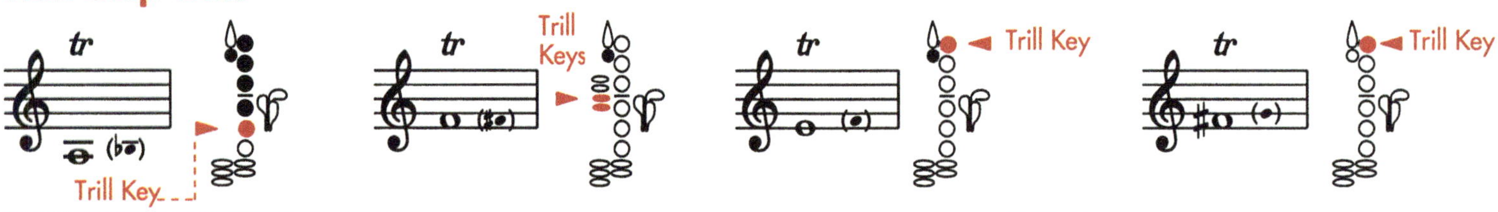

E♭ Alto Saxophone/E♭ Baritone Saxophone

Whole Step Trills

Practice these trills with the indicated fingerings:

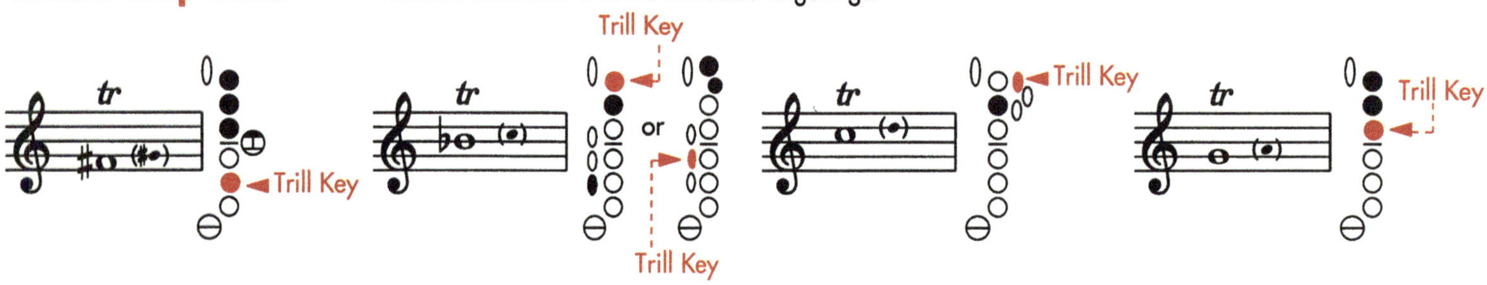

Half Step Trills

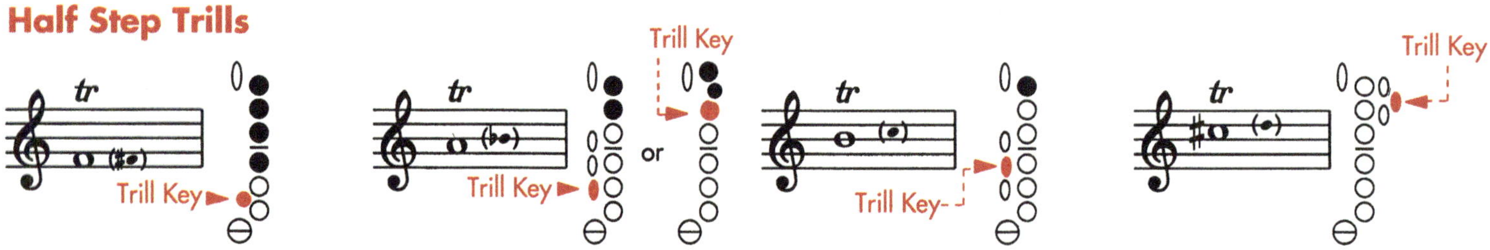

B♭ Tenor Saxophone

Whole Step Trills

Practice these trills with the indicated fingerings:

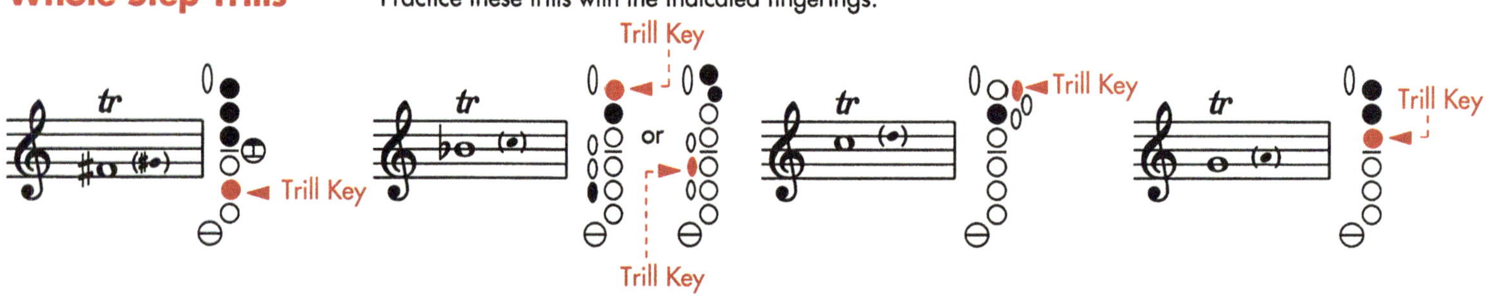

Half Step Trills

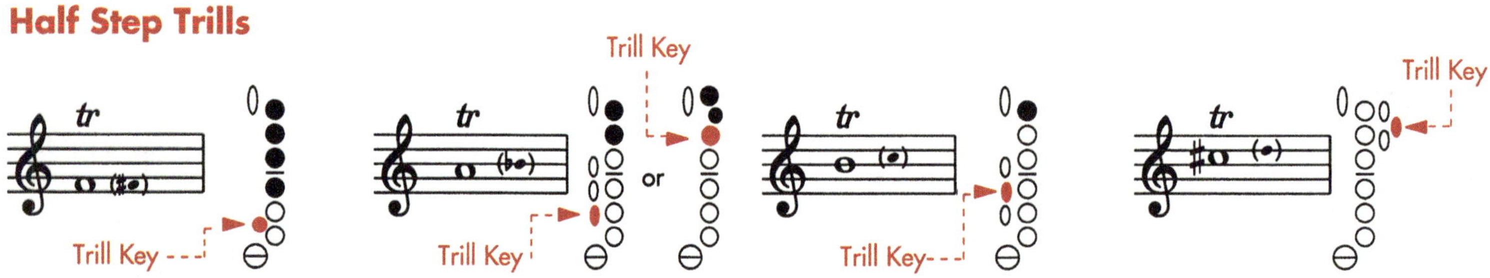

Director Exercises A, B, C and D are in unison (Concert F) for all brass players. Assign other pitches using these exercises, and implement your own suggestions for teaching double tonguing.

SPECIAL BRASS EXERCISES

Double Tonguing

Technique used by brass players to tongue repeated notes in fast tempos. Use the tonguing syllables "tah-kah" or "too-koo" when double tonguing. The accents written in the slower rhythms will help you develop double tonguing technique with equal dynamic emphasis on all notes.

Play and speak exercises A, B, C and D in a moderate tempo Gradually increase the speed
Be sure all notes have the same volume and that rhythms are played accurately

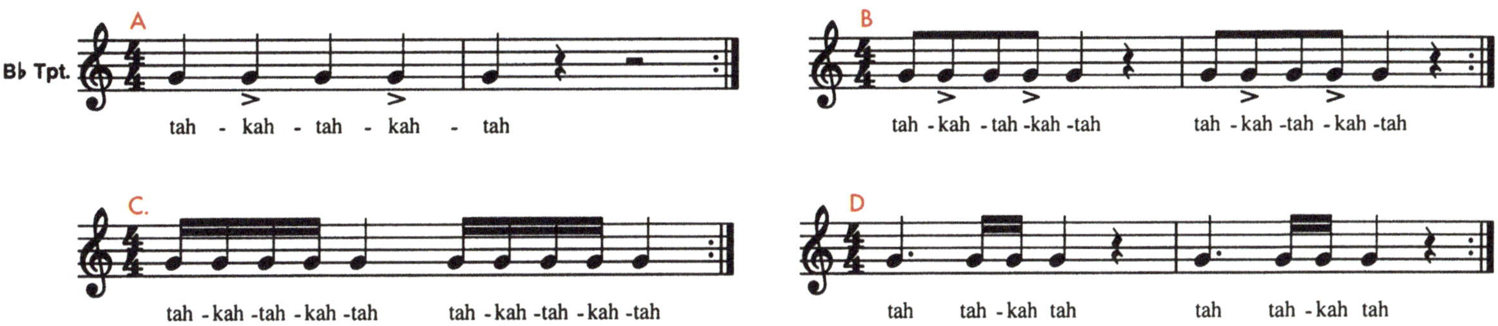

FANFARE FOR BRASS

SPECIAL PERCUSSION EXERCISES

Drum Set

The drum set accompanies bands, choirs, orchestras and small groups by playing diverse styles of music. Drum set performance requires independent movement of both hands and both feet. Be sure your drum set is assembled properly. Drum set parts are often written on a single staff line, as shown:

Instrument	Played with
Sus. or Ride Cym.	Right or left hand
S.D.	Right or left hand
B.D.	Right foot
Cr. Cym. or Hi-hat	Left foot

If a drum set is not available, use the exercises below to develop hand independence. Begin slowly, increasing speed gradually. Practice with a metronome if possible. Start with the right hand on the Suspended Cymbal and the left hand on the Snare Drum. Switch hands whenever possible.

A. BASIC PATTERN

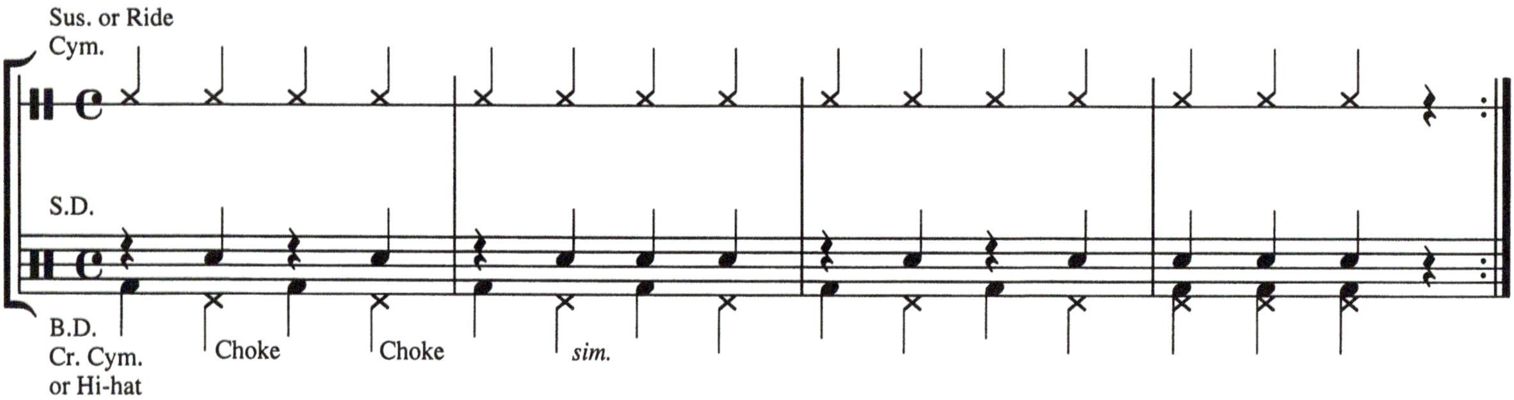

B. ROCK PATTERN

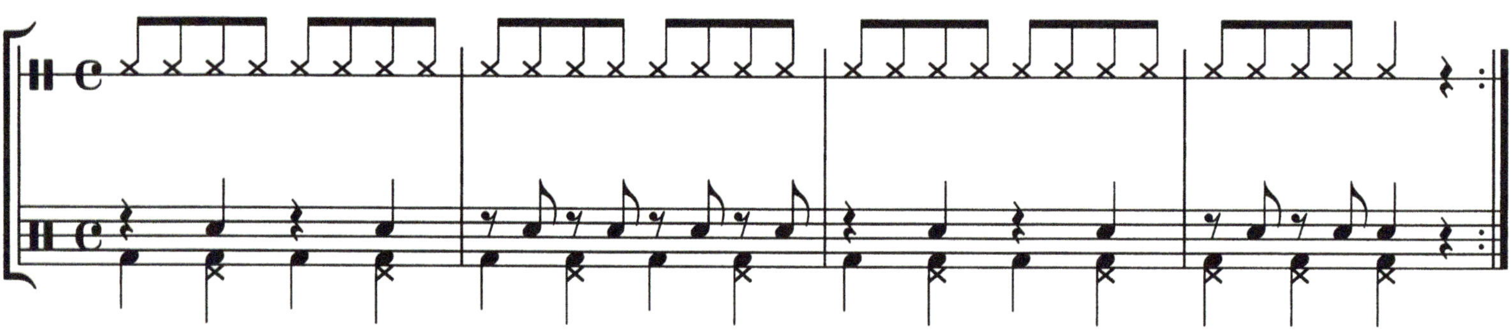

C. LATIN PATTERN

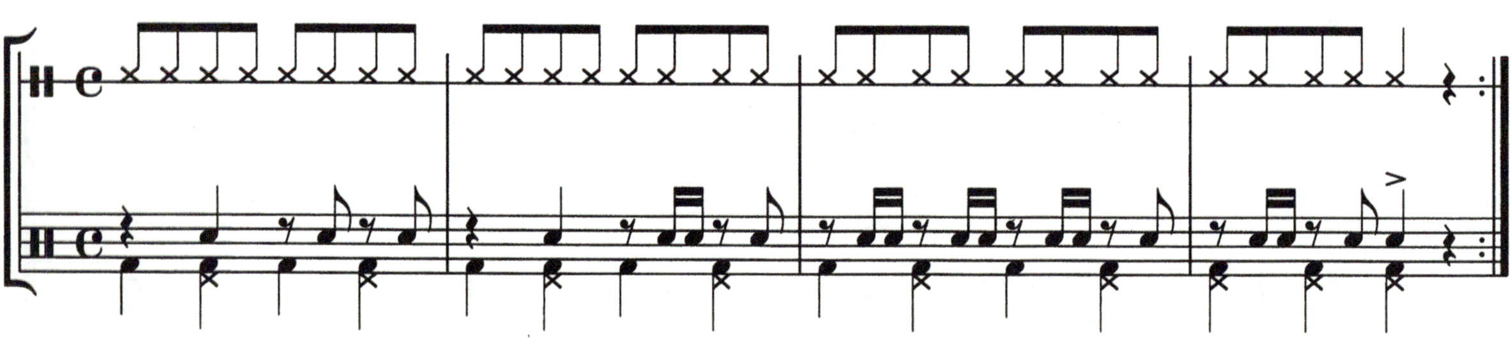

SPECIAL KEYBOARD PERCUSSION EXERCISES

Complete the note names on the chart below. Be sure to write in both enharmonic notes on the top row.

Note
Names: G♯/A♭ A♯/B♭ ___ ___ ___ ___ ___ ___ ___ ___ ___ ___

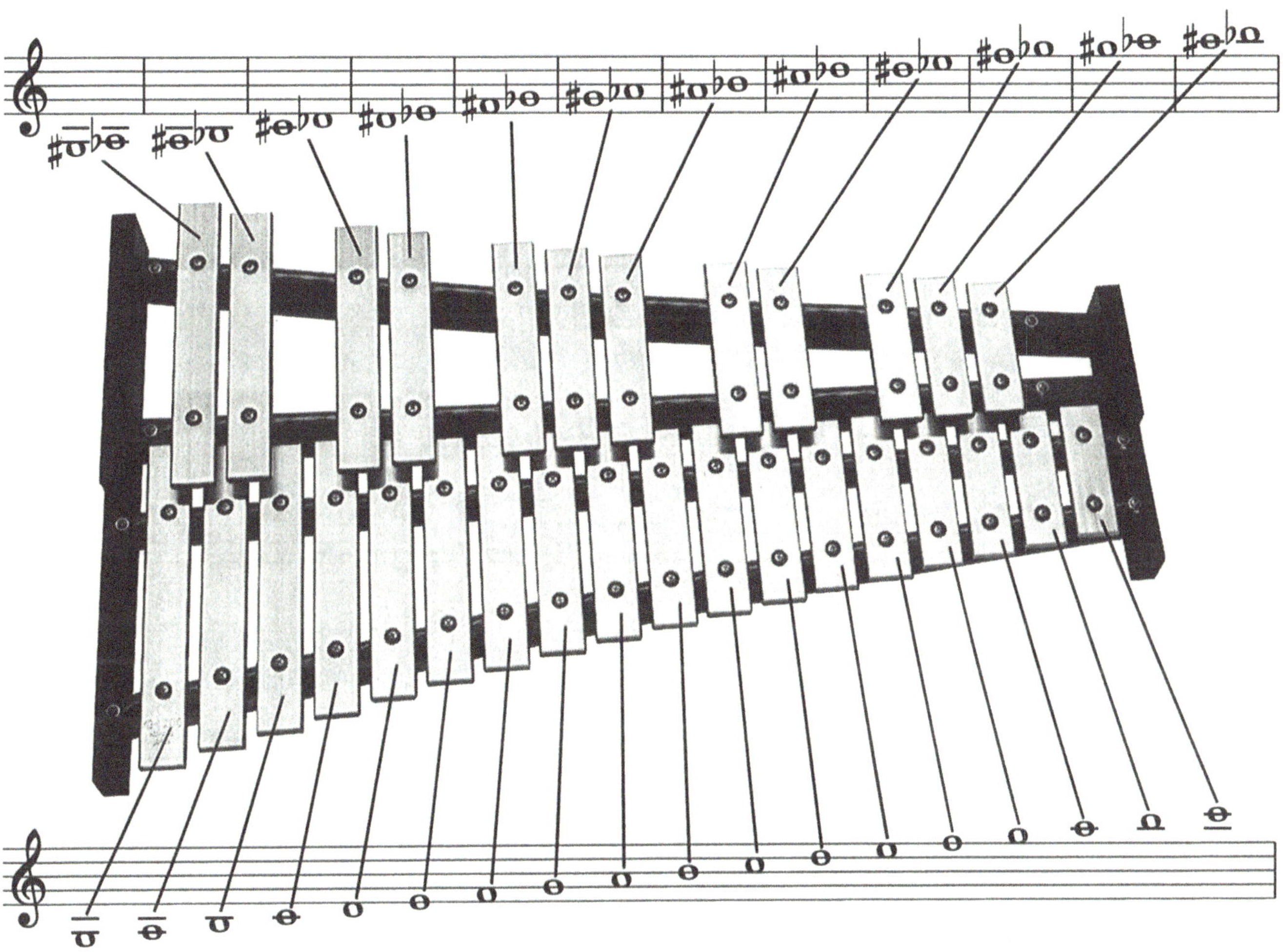

Note
Names: G A ___ ___ ___ ___ ___ ___ ___ ___ ___ ___ ___ ___ ___ ___ ___ ___ ___

Italian composer **Antonio Vivaldi** (1678-1741) lived during the Baroque era (1600-1750). Vivaldi completed *The Four Seasons* in 1726, just a few years before Benjamin Franklin discovered electricity. *The Four Seasons* was written to describe autumn, winter, spring and summer. This is the theme from the first movement, "Spring."

78. THEME FROM THE FOUR SEASONS

Antonio Vivaldi

Flute
Oboe
B♭ Clarinet
B♭ Bass Clar.
E♭ Alto Sax
E♭ Bari Sax
B♭ Tenor Sax
Alt.
B♭ Trumpet
F Horn
Trombone
Baritone
Bassoon
Tuba
Keyboard
Percussion
Percussion
Timpani

Director

Concert keys in **Essential Technique** are introduced in the following format:

Balance Builder
- A, B and C parts for all students

Chorale - Full Band Arrangement
- Rehearse woodwinds alone, brass alone and full band

Scale
- Marked articulations
- Scale in Thirds
- Arpeggio

Articulation Work-Out
- Focus on accuracy

If you wish to warm-up in specific key(s), ask students to turn to the indicated pages:

Concert Key	Score Pg.	Student Pg.
B♭ Major	14	2
E♭ Major	36	6
F Major	61	11
D Minor	100	18
A♭ Major	110	20
C Major	132	23
G Minor	144	25
G Major	200	36
D Major	212	38
D♭ Major	224	40
G♭ Major	230	41

Tune and shape each note on *Balance Builder* exercises, and experiment with different instrument combinations. Rehearse brass alone, woodwinds alone and the full band on each *Chorale* to improve balance and intonation. Include various dynamic levels on each *Scale* and *Articulation Work-Out*, including ***mf***, ***f***, ***p*** and cresc. decresc.

Additional scale studies are found on score pages 234 - 240 (student book pages 42 - 44). All scale studies are transposed for group or individual practice. *Chromatic Technique* studies are found throughout the book, in addition to multicultural songs, rhythm reinforcement and theory exercises.

NEW NOTES INTRODUCED ON 79. BALANCE BUILDER

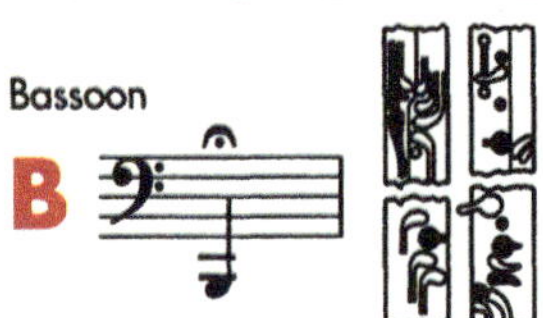

Ear Training

Concert C Major

Concert C Major challenges players to listen and tune very carefully. After warming up, you may need to adjust your instrument and/or embouchure to play all notes in tune. Play each line below, then sing it in your natural voice range. Make sure all chord tones are heard equally well, and are in "balance."

79. BALANCE BUILDER

80. CHORALE - Full Band Arrangement (Navy Hymn)

John Dykes
Arr. by John Higgins

5
Flute
Oboe
Bassoon
B♭ Clarinet
E♭ Alto Clar.
Alt.
B♭ Bass Clar.
E♭ Alto Sax.
B♭ Ten. Sax.
E♭ Bari. Sax.
5
B♭ Trumpet
F Horn
Trombone
Baritone
Tuba
Tri.
p
Percussion
Timpani

9
Flute
Oboe
Bassoon
B♭ Clarinet
E♭ Alto Clar.
B♭ Bass Clar.
E♭ Alto Sax.
B♭ Ten. Sax.
E♭ Bari. Sax.
B♭ Trumpet
F Horn
Trombone
Baritone
Tuba
Keyboard Percussion
Percussion
Timpani
cresc.
mf rall.
Sus. Cym.
pp cresc.
rall.

NEW NOTES INTRODUCED ON 81. CONCERT C MAJOR TECHNIQUE

Oboe

D

B♭ Clarinet

C♯/D♭

81. CONCERT C MAJOR TECHNIQUE

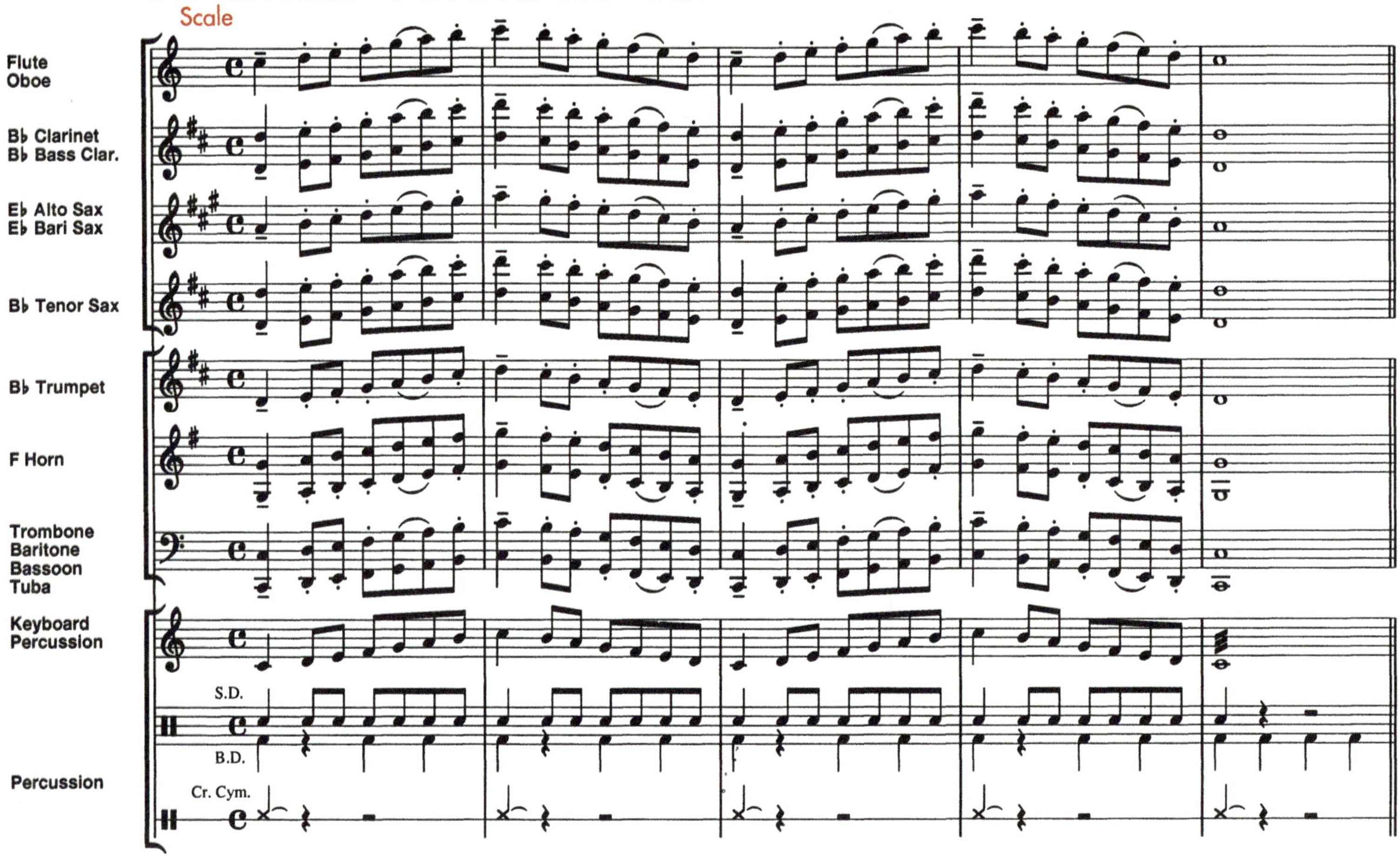

Arpeggio

82. ARTICULATION WORK - OUT

Play even rhythms at all tempos.

Moderato

83. CHILD OF THE RAINBOW

Chinese Folk Song

Flute
Oboe
B♭ Clarinet
B♭ Bass Clar.
E♭ Alto Sax
E♭ Bari Sax
B♭ Tenor Sax
B♭ Trumpet
F Horn
Trombone
Baritone
Bassoon
Tuba
Keyboard
Percussion
Percussion

Black American spirituals originated in the 1700's. As one of the largest categories of true American folk music, these melodies were sung and passed on for generations without being written down. Black and white people worked together to publish the first spiritual collection in 1867, four years after The Emancipation Proclamation was signed into law.

Director Play recordings of spirituals for the band. Explain the "call and response" style of performing American spirituals. A leader sings the verses often improvising to enhance the text. The chorus follows with the response.

84. SIT DOWN, SISTER

Black American Spiritual

Fine
Flute
Oboe
B♭ Clarinet
B♭ Bass Clar.
E♭ Alto Sax
E♭ Bari Sax
B♭ Tenor Sax
B♭ Trumpet
F Horn
Trombone
Baritone
Bassoon
Tuba
Keyboard
Percussion
Percussion
mp
D.S. al Fine
f

SPECIAL PERCUSSION EXERCISE

Mixed Meters.

85. ESSENTIAL TECHNIQUE QUIZ - METER MANIA #1

Flute
Oboe
B♭ Clarinet
B♭ Bass Clar.
E♭ Alto Sax
E♭ Bari Sax
B♭ Tenor Sax
B♭ Trumpet
F Horn
Trombone
Baritone
Bassoon
Tuba
Keyboard
Percussion
Percussion

Flute
Oboe
B♭ Clarinet
B♭ Bass Clar.
E♭ Alto Sax
E♭ Bari Sax
B♭ Tenor Sax
B♭ Trumpet
F Horn
Trombone
Baritone
Bassoon
Tuba
Keyboard
Percussion
Percussion

Director

Concert keys in **Essential Technique** are introduced in the following format:

Balance Builder
- A, B and C parts for all students

Chorale - Full Band Arrangement
- Rehearse woodwinds alone, brass alone and full band

Scale
- Marked articulations
- Scale in Thirds
- Arpeggio

Articulation Work-Out
- Focus on accuracy

If you wish to warm-up in specific key(s), ask students to turn to the indicated pages:

Concert Key	Score Pg.	Student Pg.
B♭ Major	14	2
E♭ Major	36	6
F Major	61	11
D Minor	100	18
A♭ Major	110	20
C Major	132	23
G Minor	144	25
G Major	200	36
D Major	212	38
D♭ Major	224	40
G♭ Major	230	41

Tune and shape each note on *Balance Builder* exercises, and experiment with different instrument combinations. Rehearse brass alone, woodwinds alone and the full band on each *Chorale* to improve balance and intonation. Include various dynamic levels on each *Scale* and *Articulation Work-Out*, including ***mf***, ***f***, ***p*** and < >.

Additional scale studies are found on score pages 234 - 240 (student book pages 42 - 44). All scale studies are transposed for group or individual practice. *Chromatic Technique* studies are found throughout the book, in addition to multicultural songs, rhythm reinforcement and theory exercises.

Ear Training **Concert G Minor** Compare the sounds of these minor chords with the major chords found in other *Balance Builders.* Which chord tone creates the unique sound of a minor chord?

86. BALANCE BUILDER

87. CHORALE - Full Band Arrangement (Prelude)

Frederic Chopin
Arr. by John Higgins

Flute
Oboe
Bassoon
B♭ Clarinet
E♭ Alto Clar.
B♭ Bass Clar.
E♭ Alto Sax.
B♭ Ten. Sax.
Alt.
E♭ Bari. Sax.
B♭ Trumpet
F Horn
Trombone
Baritone
Tuba
Keyboard Percussion
Tri.
Sus. Cym.
Percussion
Timpani

NEW NOTES INTRODUCED ON 88. CONCERT G MELODIC MINOR TECHNIQUE

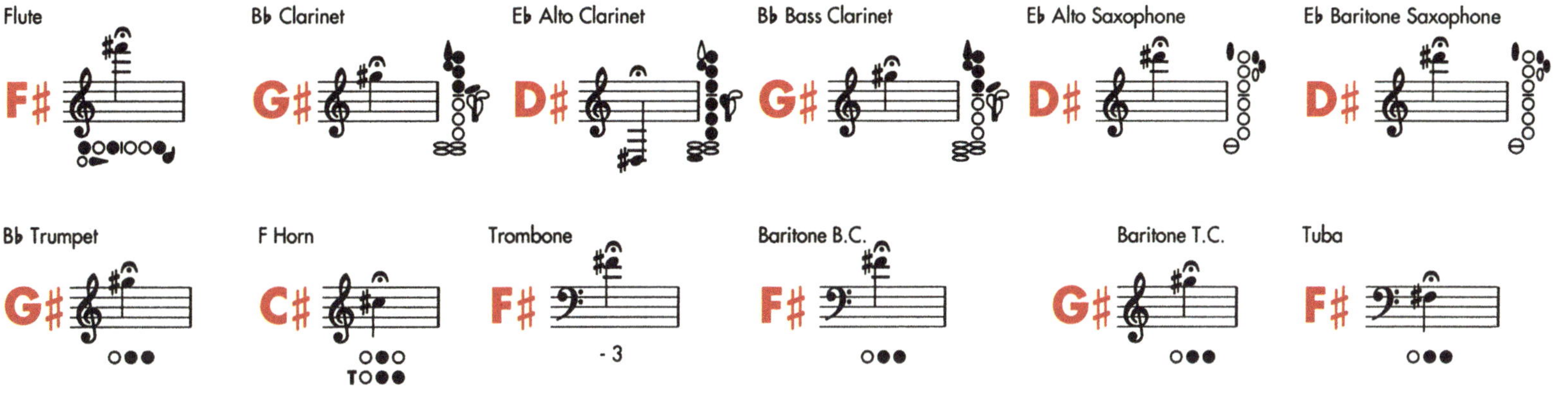

88. CONCERT G MELODIC MINOR TECHNIQUE

Scale in Thirds

Arpeggio

NEW NOTES INTRODUCED ON 89. ARTICULATION WORK - OUT

E♭ Alto Clarinet

A

89. ARTICULATION WORK - OUT

Play even rhythms at all tempos.

► Practice this exercise as a wrist builder with RRRR and LLLL sticking.

NEW NOTES INTRODUCED ON 90. SONG OF THE SHAKUHACHI

E♭ Alto Saxophone

B 

E♭ Bari Saxophone

B 

History **Native Japanese instruments** include the *shakuhachi,* a bamboo flute played pointing downward; the *koto,* a long zither with movable frets played sitting down; and the *gakubiwa,* a pear-shaped lute with strings that are plucked. These instruments have been an important part of Japanese culture since the 8th century. *Kabuki,* a Japanese theatrical form that originated in 1603, remains popular in Japan. Performers play native Japanese instruments during Kabuki performances.

90. SONG OF THE SHAKUHACHI

Japanese Folk Song

Flute
Oboe
B♭ Clarinet
B♭ Bass Clar.
E♭ Alto Sax
E♭ Bari Sax
B♭ Tenor Sax
B♭ Trumpet
F Horn
Trombone
Baritone
Bassoon
Tuba
Keyboard
Percussion
Percussion
(5)
(6)
mf
mp
p

NEW NOTES INTRODUCED ON 91. CONCERT B♭ SCALE IN FOURTHS

Oboe

D

91. CONCERT B♭ SCALE IN FOURTHS

Important French composers of the late 19th century include **Claude Debussy** (1862-1918), **Gabriel Fauré** (1845-1924), **Erik Satie** (1866-1925), **César Franck** (1822-1890), **Camille Saint-Saëns** (1835-1921) and **Paul Dukas** (1865-1935). Their works continue to have influence on the music of modern day composers. Gabriel Fauré wrote *Pavanne* (originally for orchestra) in 1887, two years before the Eiffel Tower was completed in Paris.

92. PAVANNE

Gabriel Fauré

Flute
Oboe
Bb Clarinet
Bb Bass Clar.
Eb Alto Sax
Eb Bari Sax
Bb Tenor Sax
Bb Trumpet
F Horn
Trombone
Baritone
Bassoon
Tuba
Keyboard
Percussion
Percussion
div.
Tuba 8vb

Flute
Oboe
Bb Clarinet
Bb Bass Clar.
Eb Alto Sax
Eb Bari Sax
Bb Tenor Sax
Bb Trumpet
F Horn
Trombone
Baritone
Bassoon
Tuba
Keyboard
Percussion
Percussion
unis.
Alt.
Tuba

Flute
Oboe
B♭ Clarinet
B♭ Bass Clar.
E♭ Alto Sax
E♭ Bari Sax
B♭ Tenor Sax
B♭ Trumpet
F Horn
Trombone
Baritone
Bassoon
Tuba
Keyboard
Percussion
Percussion
div.
unis.
rit.
pp

Enharmonics

Notes that have different note names, but sound the same and are played with the same fingering. Enharmonics often appear in chromatic patterns. **Woodwinds:** Alternate fingerings make it easier to play certain chromatic passages. Practice this exercise slowly, and carefully follow the indicated fingerings. Be sure to use alternate fingerings when these chromatic patterns appear in your band exercise. **Brass:** Here are some common enharmonic notes that you will need to know to play the following exercise. **Percussion and Keyboard Percussion:** Notes that have different note names, but share the same bar on the keyboard percussion instruments. Enharmonics often appear in chromatic patterns. Here are some common enharmonic notes that you will need to know to play the following exercise.

Flute

Oboe

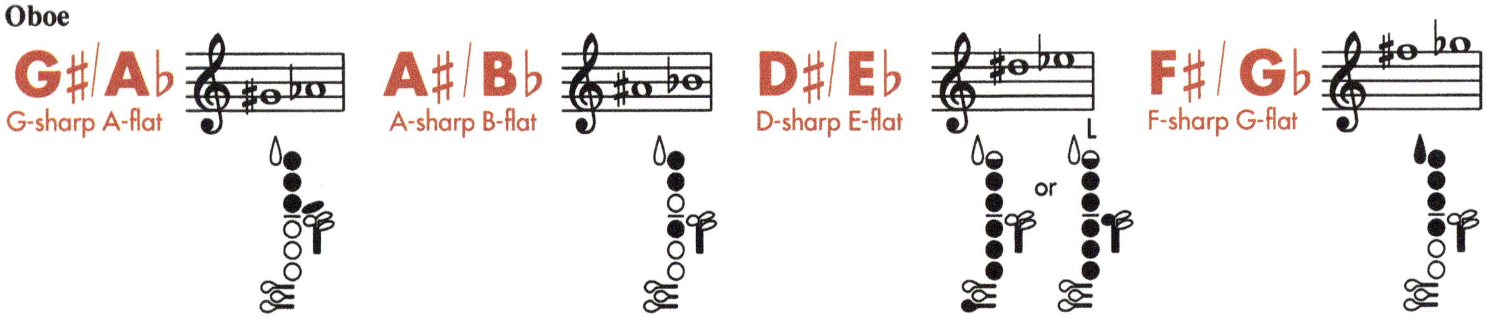

Bassoon

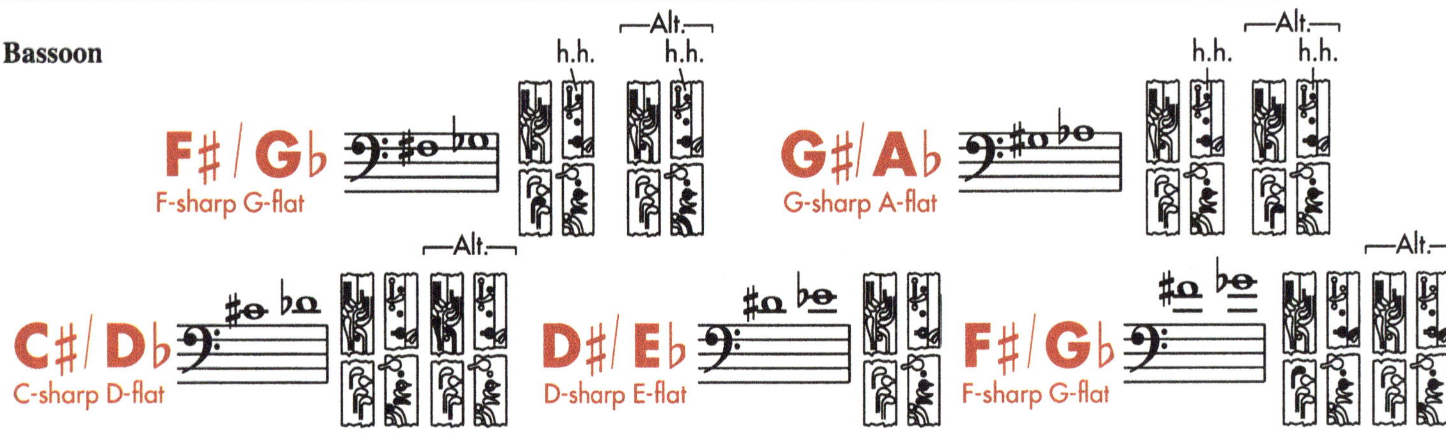

B♭ Clarinet

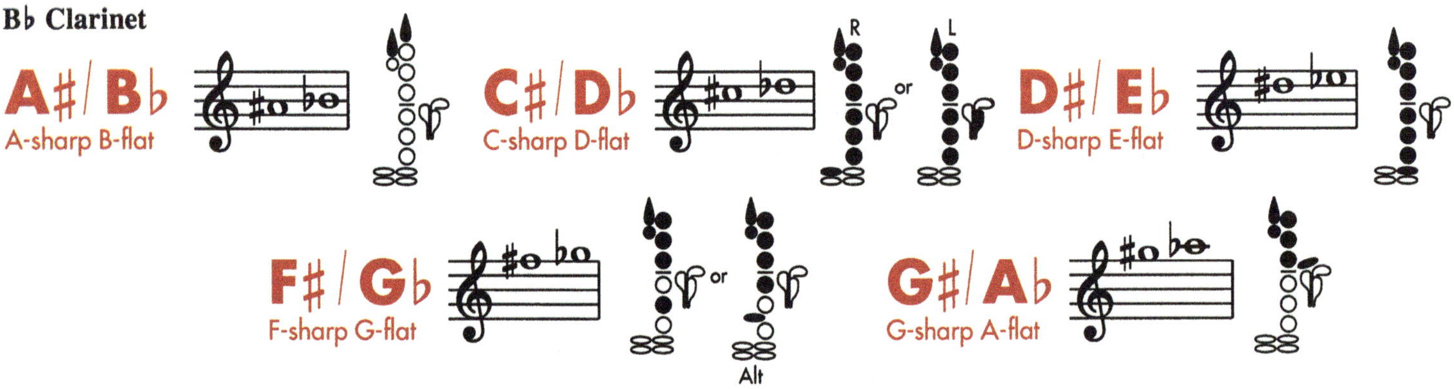

E♭ Alto Clarinet

B♭ Bass Clarinet

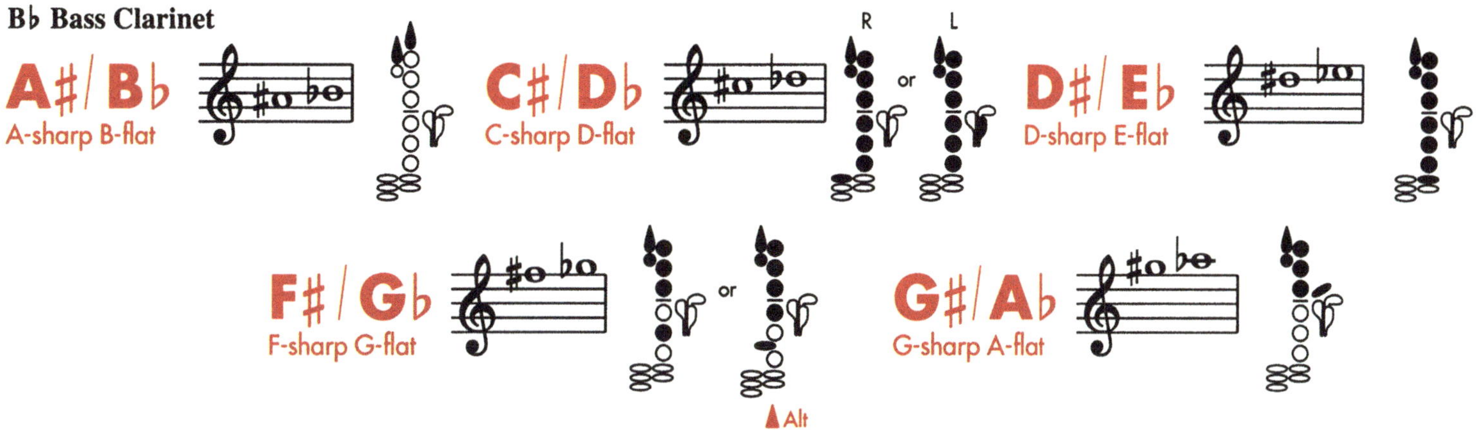

E♭ Alto Saxophone

B♭ Tenor Saxophone

E♭ Baritone Saxophone

B♭ Trumpet

A♯/B♭ A-sharp B-flat

C♯/D♭ C-sharp D-flat

D♯/E♭ D-sharp E-flat

F♯/G♭ F-sharp G-flat

G♯/A♭ G-sharp A-flat

F Horn

D♯/E♭ D-sharp E-flat

F♯/G♭ F-sharp G-flat

G♯/A♭ G-sharp A-flat

A♯/B♭ A-sharp B-flat

C♯/D♭ C-sharp D-flat

Trombone

F♯/G♭ F-sharp G-flat
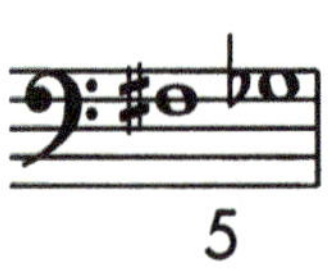

G♯/A♭ G-sharp A-flat
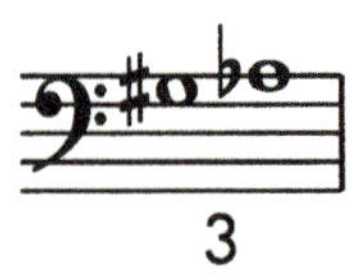

C♯/D♭ C-sharp D-flat
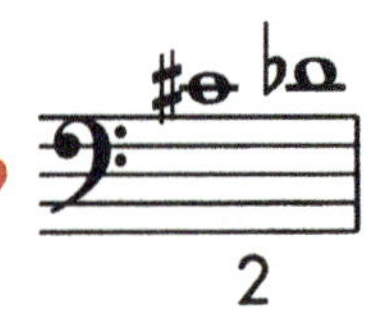

D♯/E♭ D-sharp E-flat

F♯/G♭ F-sharp G-flat

Baritone B.C.

F♯/G♭ F-sharp G-flat

G♯/A♭ G-sharp A-flat

C♯/D♭ C-sharp D-flat

D♯/E♭ D-sharp E-flat

F♯/G♭ F-sharp G-flat

Baritone T.C.

A♯/B♭ A-sharp B-flat

C♯/D♭ C-sharp D-flat

D♯/E♭ D-sharp E-flat

F♯/G♭ F-sharp G-flat

G♯/A♭ G-sharp A-flat

Tuba

F♯/G♭
F-sharp G-flat

G♯/A♭
G-sharp A-flat

C♯/D♭
C-sharp D-flat

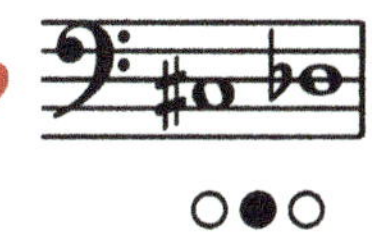

D♯/E♭
D-sharp E-flat

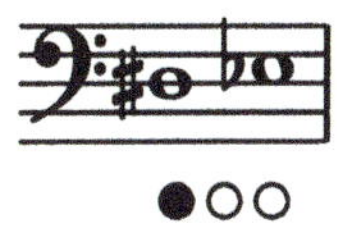

F♯/G♭
F-sharp G-flat

Percussion/Keyboard Percussion

G♯/A♭
G-sharp A-flat

A♯/B♭
A-sharp B-flat

C♯/D♭
C-sharp D-flat

D♯/E♭
D-sharp E-flat

93. CHROMATIC TECHNIQUE

Alt.
Use regular fingering.
Flute
Oboe
L R L
L L L R
B♭ Clarinet
B♭ Bass Clar.
E♭ Alto Sax
E♭ Bari Sax
Alt.
B♭ Tenor Sax
B♭ Trumpet
F Horn
(4)
Trombone
Baritone
Bassoon
Tuba
Keyboard
Percussion
Percussion

Flute
Oboe
B♭ Clarinet
B♭ Bass Clar.
Use regular fingering.
Alt.
Alt.
Alt.
E♭ Alto Sax
E♭ Bari Sax
B♭ Tenor Sax
Use regular fingering.
Alt.
Alt.
Alt.
B♭ Trumpet
F Horn
Trombone
Baritone
Bassoon
Tuba
Keyboard
Percussion
Percussion

Time Signature (Meter)

3 - 3 beats per measure
8 - ♪ or 𝄾 gets one beat

There are two ways to count 3/8 meter:

3 beats to a measure with the eighth note receiving one beat.	OR	1 beat to a measure with 3 eighth notes (or the equivalent) receiving one beat.

Director *Rhythm Rap* teaching sequence: Entire band claps • Add percussion accompaniment • Clap as a round • Sing on "tah."

94. RHYTHM RAP

95. THE SORCERER'S APPRENTICE

Paul Dukas

Flute
Oboe
B♭ Clarinet
B♭ Bass Clar.
E♭ Alto Sax
E♭ Bari Sax
Alt.
B♭ Tenor Sax
B♭ Trumpet
F Horn
(6)
(5)
(5)
(6)
Trombone
Baritone
Bassoon
Tuba
Keyboard
Percussion
Percussion

Flute
Oboe
B♭ Clarinet
B♭ Bass Clar.
E♭ Alto Sax
E♭ Bari Sax
B♭ Tenor Sax
B♭ Trumpet
F Horn
Trombone
Baritone
Bassoon
Tuba
Keyboard
Percussion
Percussion

96. BLOW YE WINDS, WESTERLY

English Sea Song

97. SANTA LUCIA

Teodore Cottrau

Flute
Oboe
B♭ Clarinet
B♭ Bass Clar.
E♭ Alto Sax
E♭ Bari Sax
B♭ Tenor Sax
B♭ Trumpet
F Horn
Trombone
Baritone
Bassoon
Tuba
Keyboard
Percussion
Percussion
f
(6)
(6)
2

Flute
Oboe
B♭ Clarinet
B♭ Bass Clar.
E♭ Alto Sax
E♭ Bari Sax
B♭ Tenor Sax
B♭ Trumpet
F Horn
Trombone
Baritone
Bassoon
Tuba
Keyboard
Percussion
Percussion
(6)
2

Director The following sixteen key signature examples are found in the percussion book. Woodwind and brass books each have eight key signature examples which match the corresponding clef of that instrument. Review key signature note names frequently.

98. ESSENTIAL TECHNIQUE QUIZ

Knowing the names of the sharps and flats is a very important part of learning to read key signatures. The names of several common key signatures are listed below Write the name of the sharps or flats on the line labeled "Play "

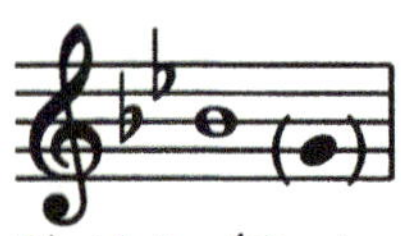

B♭ Major/G minor

Play B♭'s and E♭'s

F Major/D minor

Play ____________

E♭ Major/C minor

Play ____________

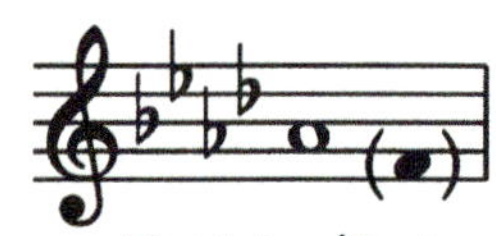

A♭ Major/F minor

Play ____________

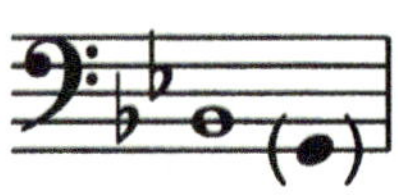

B♭ Major/G minor

Play B♭'s and E♭'s

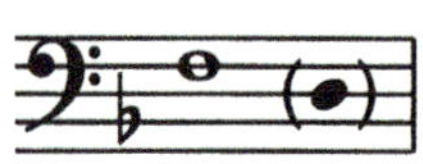

F Major/D minor

Play ____________

E♭ Major/C minor

Play ____________

A♭ Major/F minor

Play ____________

C Major/A minor

Play ____________

G Major/E minor

Play ____________

D Major/B minor

Play ____________

A Major/F♯ minor

Play ____________

C Major/A minor

Play ____________

G Major/E minor

Play ____________

D Major/B minor

Play ____________

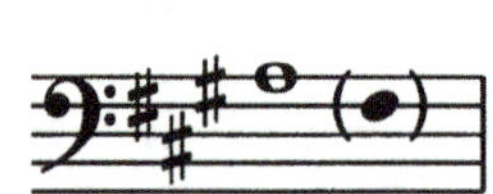

A Major/F♯ minor

Play ____________

NEW NOTES INTRODUCED ON 99. JULIET'S WALTZ

B♭ Clarinet

E

Grace Note A small note (or notes) which is played on or slightly before the beat.

99. JULIET'S WALTZ

Charles Gounod

Tempo di valse ◄ Waltz tempo

Flute
Oboe
B♭ Clarinet
B♭ Bass Clar.
E♭ Alto Sax
E♭ Bari Sax
B♭ Tenor Sax
B♭ Trumpet
F Horn
Trombone
Baritone
Bassoon
Tuba
Keyboard
Percussion
Percussion
1
2
f
dim.
p
Choke

Time Signature (Meter)

9 - 9 beats per measure
8 - ♪ or 𝄾 gets one beat

There are two ways to count 9/8 meter:

9 beats to a measure with the eighth note receiving one beat. OR 3 beats to a measure with 3 eighth notes (or the equivalent) receiving one beat.

Director *Rhythm Rap* teaching sequence: Entire band claps • Add percussion accompaniment • Clap as a round • Sing on "tah."

100. RHYTHM RAP

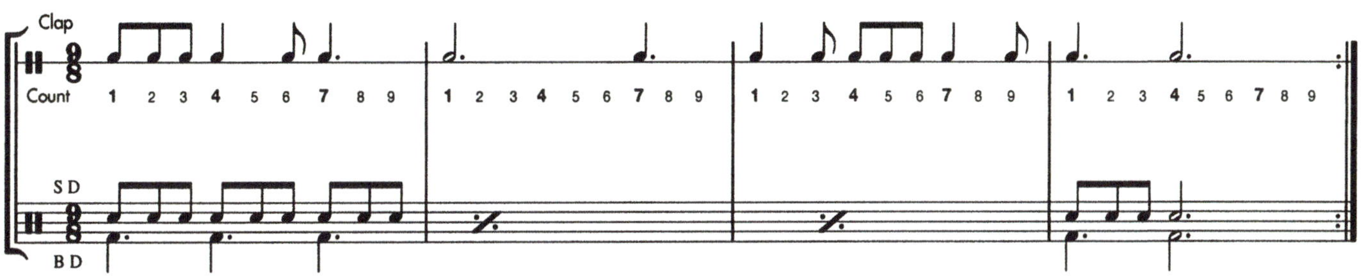

Director The rhythms of *100. Rhythm Rap* and *101. Elliot's Toys* are identical. Be sure to count, clap and tap all exercises before playing them.

101. ELLIOT'S TOYS

102. JOY

J.S. Bach

Andante espressivo ◂ Expressively

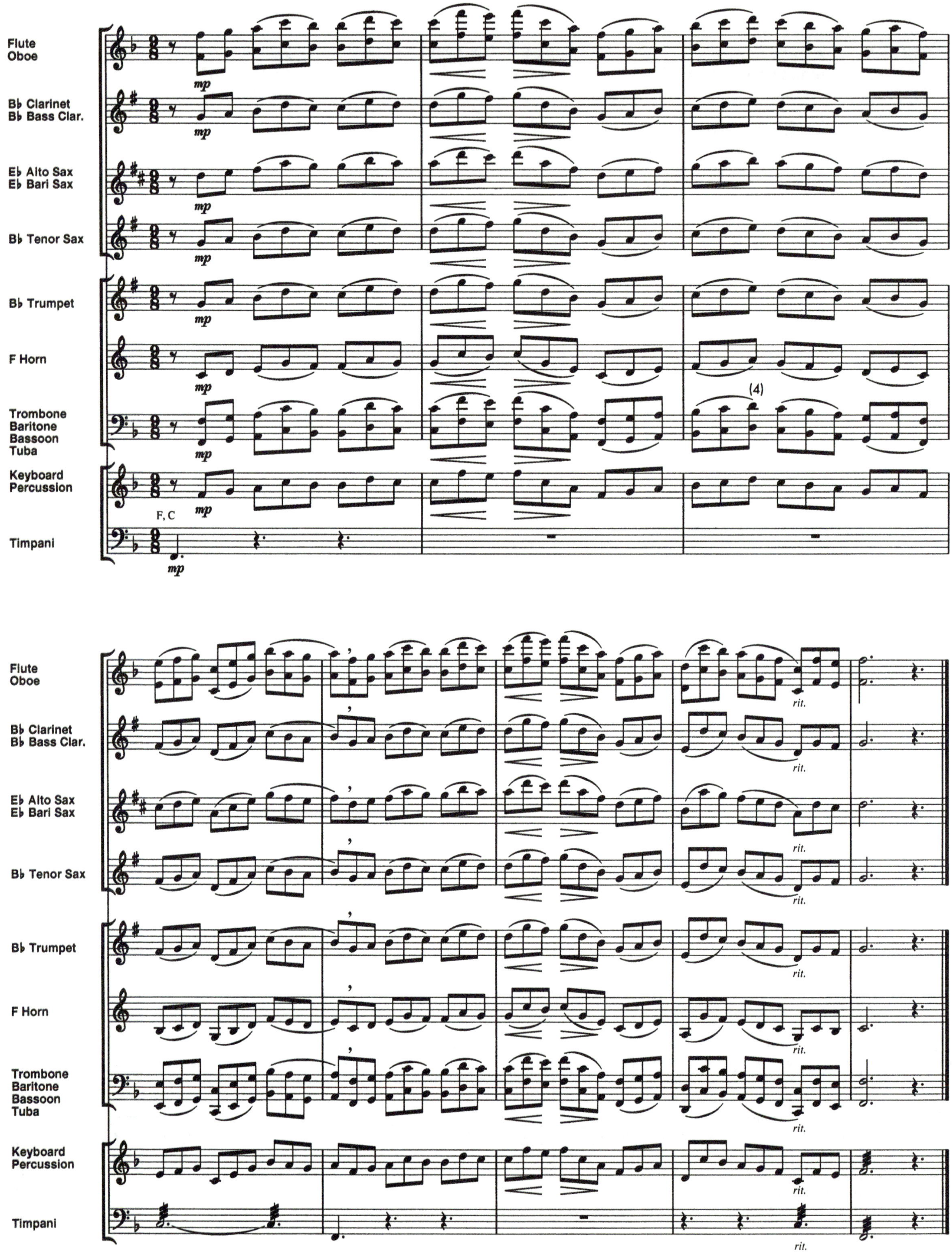

103. ESSENTIAL TECHNIQUE QUIZ - METER MANIA #2

Leggiero ◄ Lightly

Theory — Transposing Instruments

A note name is part of the complete name of many instruments, such as F Horn, B♭ Clarinet and E♭ Alto Saxophone. This note name is the actual sounding pitch heard when a written "C" is played on the instrument. The chart below tells you the actual sounding pitches heard when these common band instruments play a written "C."

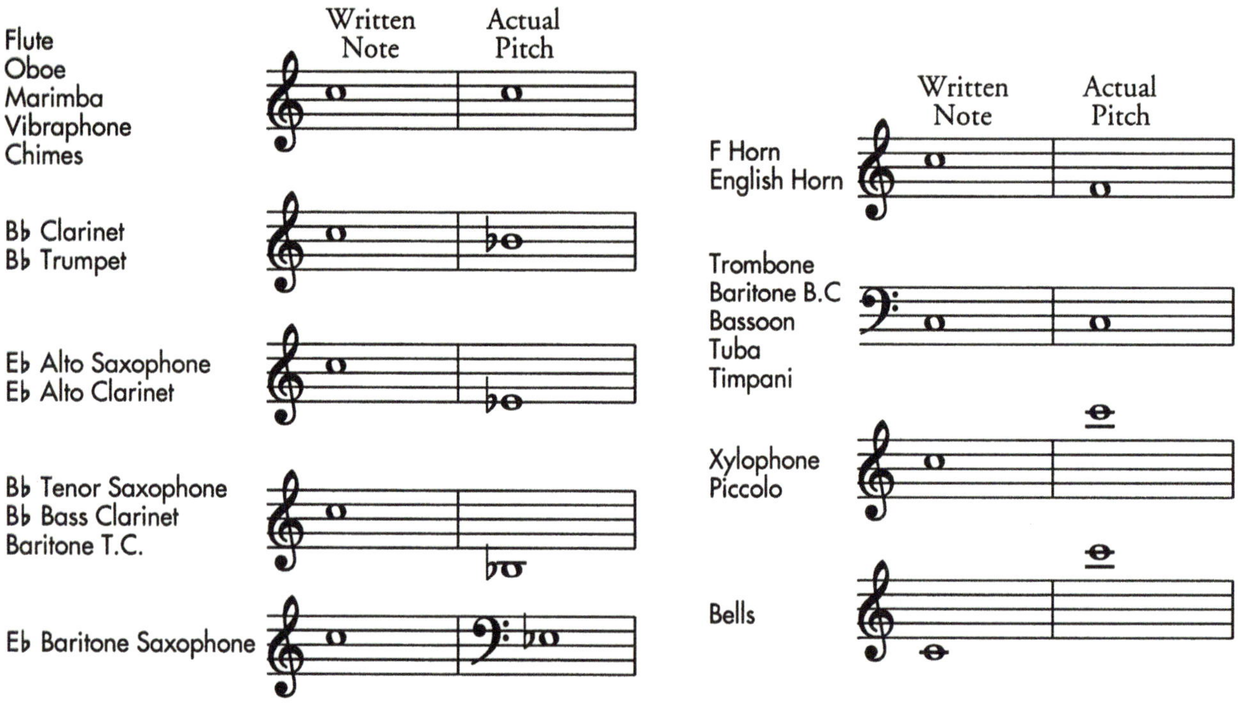

As you can see, many band instruments **sound lower** than their written pitches. Composers and arrangers must think of the actual note they want each instrument to play, and adjust the written note so it matches the intended pitch. This process is called **transposition.**

Transposing instruments allow woodwind players to use the same fingerings when playing instruments in the same family. For example, clarinet fingerings are virtually the same on all types of clarinets. Treble clef brass instrument transposition is based on the harmonic series where "C" is played with open valves. The actual sounding pitch is a B♭ for trumpets and an F for horns.

Director Each instrument's written "C" in exercise *104. What's Your Pitch?* matches the Written Note from the chart above. Percussion books include written "C" for bells, xylophone, timpani and chimes. Be certain students understand transposition and the concert key concept.

104. WHAT'S YOUR PITCH?

Find the name of your instrument on the chart above. Write the actual sounding pitch of your instrument when you play this written "C":

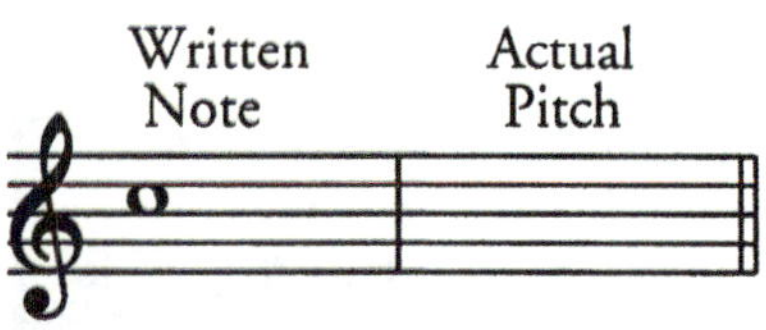

What is the name of this note? ____________

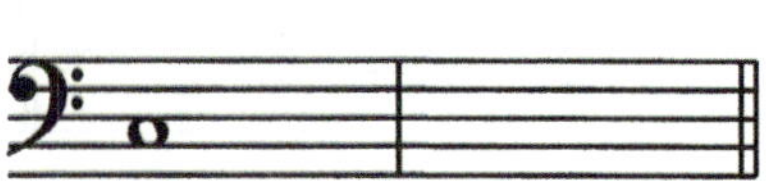

What is the name of this note? ____________

NEW NOTES INTRODUCED ON 105. TRUMPET TUNE

Oboe

A♭

Alternate fingering

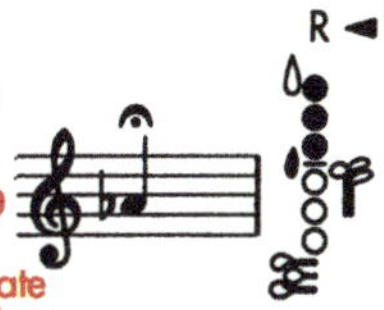

105. TRUMPET TUNE

Henry Purcell

Maestoso

Flute
Oboe
B♭ Clarinet
B♭ Bass Clar.
E♭ Alto Sax
E♭ Bari Sax
B♭ Tenor Sax
Alt.
B♭ Trumpet
F Horn
Trombone
Baritone
Bassoon
Tuba
Keyboard
Percussion
Percussion
Timpani
mf
rit. last time
tr
f

Russian composers **Alexander Borodin** (1833-1887), **Modest Mussorgsky** (1839-1881), and **Nicolas Rimsky-Korsakov** (1844-1908) used native folk songs in their music. Their work inspired the next generation of Russian writers, including **Sergei Prokofiev** (1891-1953) and **Mikhail Ippolitov-Ivanov** (1859-1935). Prokofiev's *March From The Love Of Three Oranges* and Ippolitov-Ivanov's *The Sadar's Procession* were both written around the same time as the Wright brothers' first successful airplane flight.

106. MARCH FROM THE LOVE OF THREE ORANGES

Sergei Prokofiev

107. THE SADAR'S PROCESSION

Mikhail Ippolitov-Ivanov

Allegro maestoso

Flute
Oboe
B♭ Clarinet
B♭ Bass Clar.
E♭ Alto Sax
E♭ Bari Sax
B♭ Tenor Sax
B♭ Trumpet
F Horn
Trombone
Baritone
Bassoon
Tuba
Keyboard
Percussion
Percussion
(6)
Flute
Oboe
B♭ Clarinet
B♭ Bass Clar.
E♭ Alto Sax
E♭ Bari Sax
B♭ Tenor Sax
B♭ Trumpet
F Horn
Trombone
Baritone
Bassoon
Tuba
Keyboard
Percussion
Percussion

108. CORONATION MARCH

Giacomo Meyerbeer

Alla marcia ◄ In a march style

Flute
Oboe
B♭ Clarinet
B♭ Bass Clar.
E♭ Alto Sax
E♭ Bari Sax
B♭ Tenor Sax
B♭ Trumpet
F Horn
Trombone
Baritone
Bassoon
Tuba
Keyboard
Percussion
Percussion
Chimes

Quarter Note Triplet

 = 2 beats

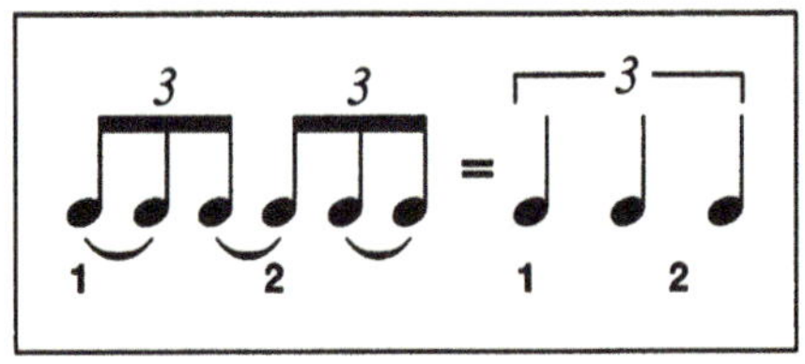

Quarter note triplet is 3 notes that equal 2 beats.

Director *Rhythm Rap* teaching sequence: Entire band claps • Add percussion accompaniment • Clap as a round • Sing on "tah."

109. RHYTHM RAP

Director The rhythms of *109. Rhythm Rap* and *110. Triplet Twisters* are identical. Be sure to count, clap and tap all exercises before playing them.

110. TRIPLET TWISTERS

111. SURIRAM'S SONG

Malaysian Folk Song

Africa is a large continent that is made up of many nations, and **African folk music** is as diverse as its many cultures. Folk songs from any country are expressions of work, love, war, sadness and joy. This song is from Tanzania. The words describe a rabbit hopping and running through a field. Listen to the percussion section play African-sounding drums and rhythms.

112. JIBULI (The Rabbit's Song)

Adapted Tanzanian Folk Song

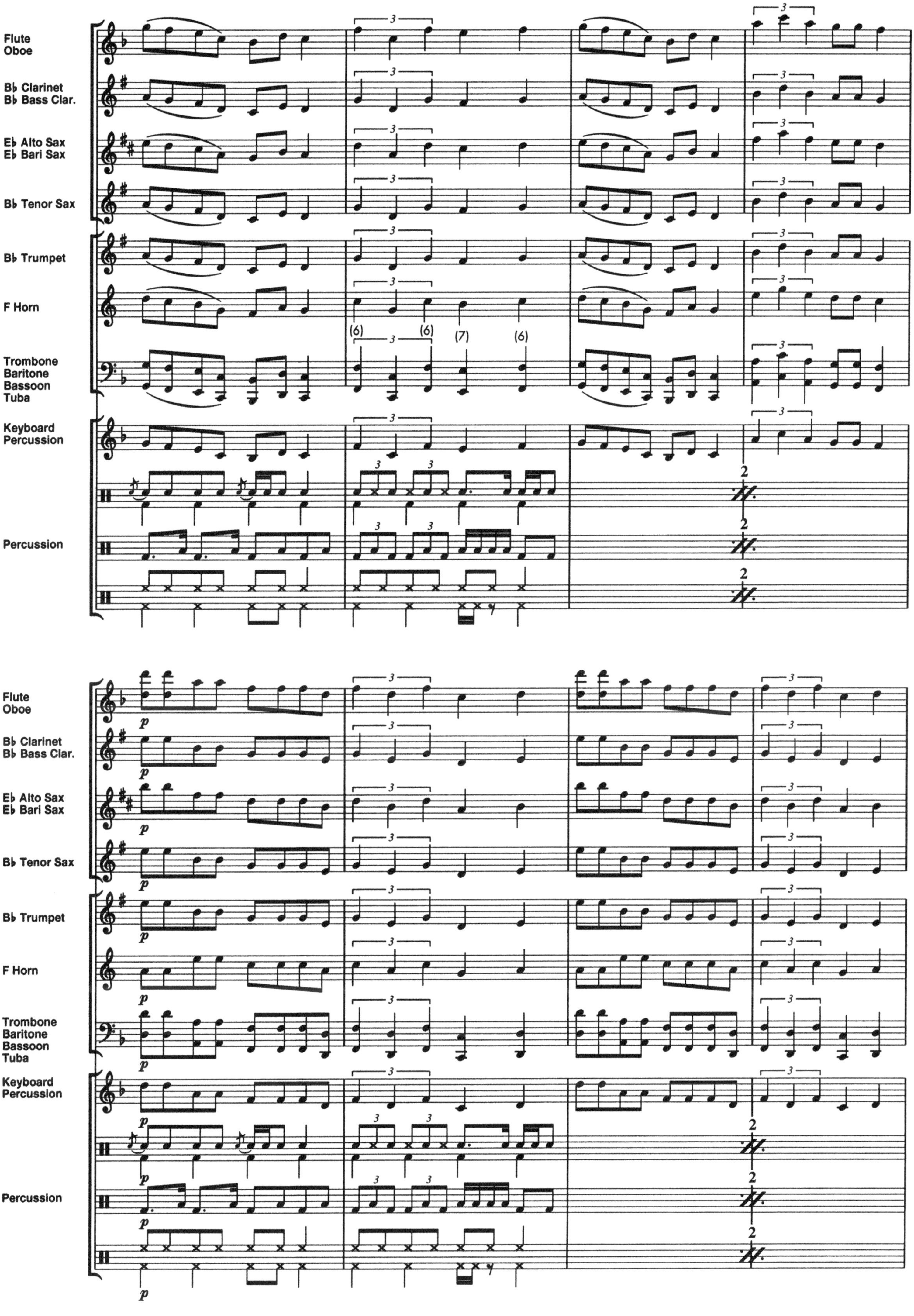
Flute
Oboe
B♭ Clarinet
B♭ Bass Clar.
E♭ Alto Sax
E♭ Bari Sax
B♭ Tenor Sax
B♭ Trumpet
F Horn
Trombone
Baritone
Bassoon
Tuba
Keyboard
Percussion
Percussion
(6) (6) (7) (6)
p

Flute
Oboe
B♭ Clarinet
B♭ Bass Clar.
E♭ Alto Sax
E♭ Bari Sax
B♭ Tenor Sax
B♭ Trumpet
F Horn
Trombone
Baritone
Bassoon
Tuba
(6) (6) (7) (6)
Keyboard
Percussion
Percussion
mf
f

Time Signature (Meter)

12 - 12 beats per measure
8 - ♪ or 𝄾 gets one beat

There are two ways to count 12/8 meter:

12 beats to a measure with the eighth note receiving one beat. OR 4 beats to a measure with 3 eighth notes (or the equivalent) receiving one beat.

Director *Rhythm Rap* teaching sequence: Entire band claps • Add percussion accompaniment • Clap as a round • Sing on "tah."

113. RHYTHM RAP

Director The rhythms of *113. Rhythm Rap* and *114. Count To Twelve* are identical. Be sure to count, clap and tap all exercises before playing them.

114. COUNT TO TWELVE

History

African-American composer **W. C. Handy** (1873-1958), the "Father of the Blues", was the first to publish popular blues songs. "Blues" is a term which describes scale notes and a style of music. Scale notes are altered (or "bent") to create "blue" notes. The blues style is a 12-bar chord progression that serves as the basis for improvisation. *St. Louis Blues* was written in 1914, the same year that World War I began. Blues artists include singers Ma Rainey and Bessie Smith, and instrumental performers Muddy Waters and B. B. King.

NEW NOTES INTRODUCED ON 115. ST. LOUIS BLUES

B♭ Clarinet

D♯/E♭

115. ST. LOUIS BLUES

W.C. Handy

Moderate blues tempo

Flute
Oboe
B♭ Clarinet
B♭ Bass Clar.
E♭ Alto Sax
E♭ Bari Sax
B♭ Tenor Sax
B♭ Trumpet
F Horn
Trombone
Baritone
Bassoon
Tuba
Keyboard
Percussion
Percussion
Choke
Choke
sim.
Solo

Flute
Oboe
B♭ Clarinet
B♭ Bass Clar.
E♭ Alto Sax
E♭ Bari Sax
B♭ Tenor Sax
B♭ Trumpet
F Horn
Trombone
Baritone
Bassoon
Tuba
Keyboard
Percussion
Percussion
Choke
Choke
sim.
Solo

Swing

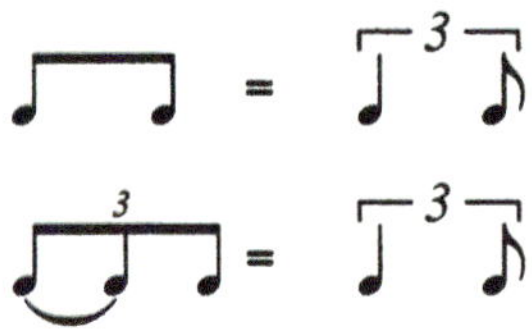

Swing eighth notes are played with an uneven division of the beat. When the style mark indicates "swing", play eighth notes as if they were written: ♩♪ (triplet)
Swing notation denotes a popular style often used in jazz music.

Director Exercises *115. St. Louis Blues* and *116. St. Louis Blues Swing* can be played together in unison. The rhythms are identical. Use 𝄵 meter to teach an introduction to swing style.

116. ST. LOUIS BLUES SWING

W C. Handy

Flute
Oboe
B♭ Clarinet
B♭ Bass Clar.
E♭ Alto Sax
E♭ Bari Sax
B♭ Tenor Sax
B♭ Trumpet
F Horn
Trombone
Baritone
Bassoon
Tuba
Keyboard
Percussion
Percussion
Choke
Choke
sim.
Solo
Flute
Oboe
B♭ Clarinet
B♭ Bass Clar.
E♭ Alto Sax
E♭ Bari Sax
B♭ Tenor Sax
B♭ Trumpet
F Horn
Trombone
Baritone
Bassoon
Tuba
Keyboard
Percussion
Percussion
Choke
Choke
sim.
Solo

Time Signature (Meter)

3/2 - 3 beats per measure
- 𝅗𝅥 or ▬ gets one beat

Use the three-beat conducting pattern for 3/2 pieces.

Director *Rhythm Rap* teaching sequence: Entire band claps • Add percussion accompaniment • Clap as a round • Sing on "tah."

117. RHYTHM RAP

NEW NOTES INTRODUCED ON 118. CONCERT A♭ STUDY

E♭ Alto Saxophone

B♭

Alternate fingering

E♭ Baritone Saxophone

B♭

Alternate fingering

Director The rhythms of *117. Rhythm Rap* and *118. Concert A♭ Study* are identical.

118. CONCERT A♭ STUDY

Flute
Oboe
B♭ Clarinet
B♭ Bass Clar.
E♭ Alto Sax
E♭ Bari Sax
Alt.
B♭ Tenor Sax
Alt.
B♭ Trumpet
F Horn
Trombone
Baritone
Bassoon
Tuba
Keyboard
Percussion
Percussion

Eighth Notes in $\frac{3}{2}$ meter

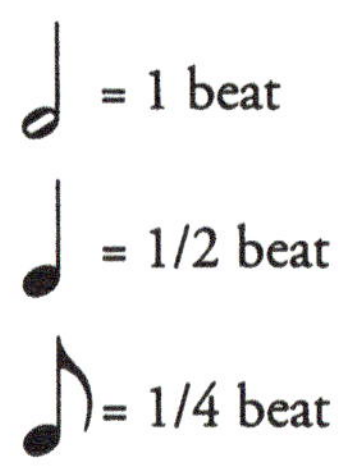

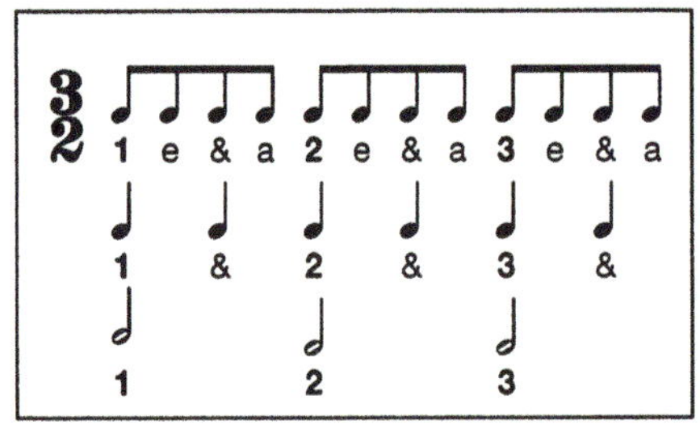

History

English composer **George Frideric Handel** (1685-1759) lived during the Baroque era (1600-1750). *Water Music* was written in honor of England's King George I. The first performance took place on the Thames River on July 17, 1717. Fifty musicians performed the work while floating on a barge. Handel lived during the same time as Johann Sebastian Bach, perhaps the most famous Baroque composer.

119. WATER MUSIC

George Frideric Handel

Allegro maestoso

Flute
Oboe
B♭ Clarinet
B♭ Bass Clar.
E♭ Alto Sax
E♭ Bari Sax
B♭ Tenor Sax
B♭ Trumpet
F Horn
Trombone
Baritone
Bassoon
Tuba
Keyboard
Percussion
Percussion
Timpani
div.

Flute
Oboe
B♭ Clarinet
B♭ Bass Clar.
E♭ Alto Sax
E♭ Bari Sax
B♭ Tenor Sax
B♭ Trumpet
F Horn
Trombone
Baritone
Bassoon
Tuba
Keyboard
Percussion
Percussion
Timpani
tr
mf

Flute
Oboe
B♭ Clarinet
B♭ Bass Clar.
E♭ Alto Sax
E♭ Bari Sax
B♭ Tenor Sax
B♭ Trumpet
F Horn
Trombone
Baritone
Bassoon
Tuba
Keyboard
Percussion
Percussion
Timpani
rit.

Time Signature (Meter)

5 - 5 beats per measure
4 - ♩ or 𝄽 gets one beat

Conducting

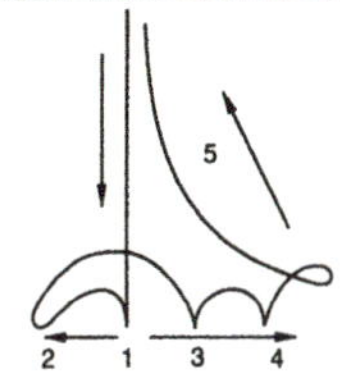

or

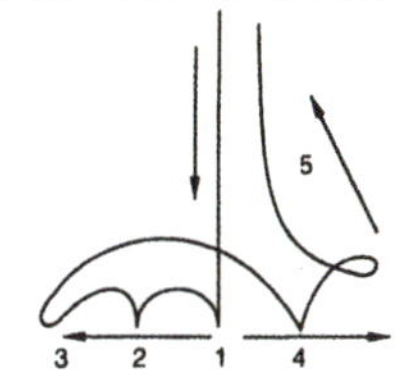

Practice conducting these five-beat patterns.

Director *Rhythm Rap* teaching sequence: Entire band claps • Add percussion accompaniment • Clap as a round • Sing on "tah."

120. RHYTHM RAP

Director The rhythms of *120. Rhythm Rap* and *121. Concert A♭ Review* are identical. Be sure to count, clap and tap all exercises before playing them.

121. CONCERT A♭ REVIEW

122. SUKURU ITO

African Folk Song

Moderato

123. CHROMATIC TECHNIQUE

124. ESSENTIAL TECHNIQUE QUIZ - PICTURES AT AN EXHIBITION

Modest Mussorgsky

Flute
Oboe
B♭ Clarinet
B♭ Bass Clar.
E♭ Alto Sax
E♭ Bari Sax
B♭ Tenor Sax
Alt.
B♭ Trumpet
F Horn
Trombone
Baritone
Bassoon
Tuba
Keyboard
Percussion
Percussion
mp

Flute
Oboe
B♭ Clarinet
B♭ Bass Clar.
E♭ Alto Sax
E♭ Bari Sax
Alt.
B♭ Tenor Sax
Alt.
Alt.
Alt.
B♭ Trumpet
F Horn
Trombone
Baritone
Bassoon
Tuba
Keyboard
Percussion
Percussion
f

Director

Concert keys in **Essential Technique** are introduced in the following format:

Balance Builder
- A, B and C parts for all students

Chorale - Full Band Arrangement
- Rehearse woodwinds alone, brass alone and full band

Scale
- Marked articulations
- Scale in Thirds
- Arpeggio

Articulation Work-Out
- Focus on accuracy

If you wish to warm-up in specific key(s), ask students to turn to the indicated pages:

Concert Key	Score Pg.	Student Pg.
B♭ Major	14	2
E♭ Major	36	6
F Major	61	11
D Minor	100	18
A♭ Major	110	20
C Major	132	23
G Minor	144	25
G Major	200	36
D Major	212	38
D♭ Major	224	40
G♭ Major	230	41

Tune and shape each note on *Balance Builder* exercises, and experiment with different instrument combinations. Rehearse brass alone, woodwinds alone and the full band on each *Chorale* to improve balance and intonation. Include various dynamic levels on each *Scale* and *Articulation Work-Out*, including ***mf***, ***f***, ***p*** and < >.

Additional scale studies are found on score pages 234 - 240 (student book pages 42 - 44). All scale studies are transposed for group or individual practice. *Chromatic Technique* studies are found throughout the book, in addition to multicultural songs, rhythm reinforcement and theory exercises.

Ear Training

Concert G Major

Play each exercise below, then sing it in your natural voice range. Make sure all chord tones are heard equally well, and are in "balance." Begin tuning with the lower instruments of the band.

125. BALANCE BUILDER

Woodwinds & Upper Brass

Low Brass, Woodwinds & Timpani

126. CHORALE - Full Band Arrangement (All Beautiful The March Of Days)

Ralph Vaughan Williams
Arr. John Higgins

Flute
Oboe
Bassoon
B♭ Clarinet
E♭ Alto Clar.
B♭ Bass Clar.
E♭ Alto Sax.
B♭ Ten. Sax.
E♭ Bari. Sax.
B♭ Trumpet
F Horn
Trombone
Baritone
Tuba
Keyboard Percussion
Tri.
S.D.
Percussion
mp
Timpani

9
Flute
Oboe
Bassoon
B♭ Clarinet
E♭ Alto Clar.
B♭ Bass Clar.
E♭ Alto Sax.
B♭ Ten. Sax.
E♭ Bari. Sax.
B♭ Trumpet
F Horn
Trombone
Baritone
Tuba
Keyboard Percussion
Percussion
B.D.
Timpani
mf

Flute
Oboe
Bassoon
B♭ Clarinet
E♭ Alto Clar.
B♭ Bass Clar.
E♭ Alto Sax.
B♭ Ten. Sax.
E♭ Bari. Sax.
B♭ Trumpet
F Horn
Trombone
Baritone
Tuba
Keyboard Percussion
Percussion
Timpani
mp
rit.

127. CONCERT G MAJOR TECHNIQUE

128. ARTICULATION WORK - OUT

Play even rhythms at all tempos.

► Practice this exercise as a wrist builder with RRRR and LLLL sticking.

NEW NOTES INTRODUCED ON 129. ENGLISH CHORALE - Duet

129. ENGLISH CHORALE - Duet

Franz Josef Haydn

Andante grazioso ► Gracefully

Flute
Oboe
Flute
Oboe
Bb Clarinet
Bb Bass Clar.
Bb Clarinet
Bb Bass Clar.
Eb Alto Sax
Eb Bari Sax
Eb Alto Sax
Eb Bari Sax
Bb Tenor Sax
Bb Tenor Sax
Bb Trumpet
Bb Trumpet
F Horn
F Horn
Trombone
Baritone
Bassoon
Tuba
Trombone
Baritone
Bassoon
Tuba
Keyboard
Percussion
Keyboard
Percussion
Percussion
Timpani

Norwegian composer **Edvard Grieg** (1843-1907) based much of his music on the folk songs and dances of Norway. During the late 19th century, composers often used melodies from their native land. This trend is called **nationalism.** Russian **Modest Mussorgsky** (1839-1881), Czech **Antonin Dvořák** (1841-1904) and Englishman **Sir Edward Elgar** (1857-1934) are other famous composers whose music was influenced by nationalism.

130. NORWEGIAN DANCE

Edvard Grieg

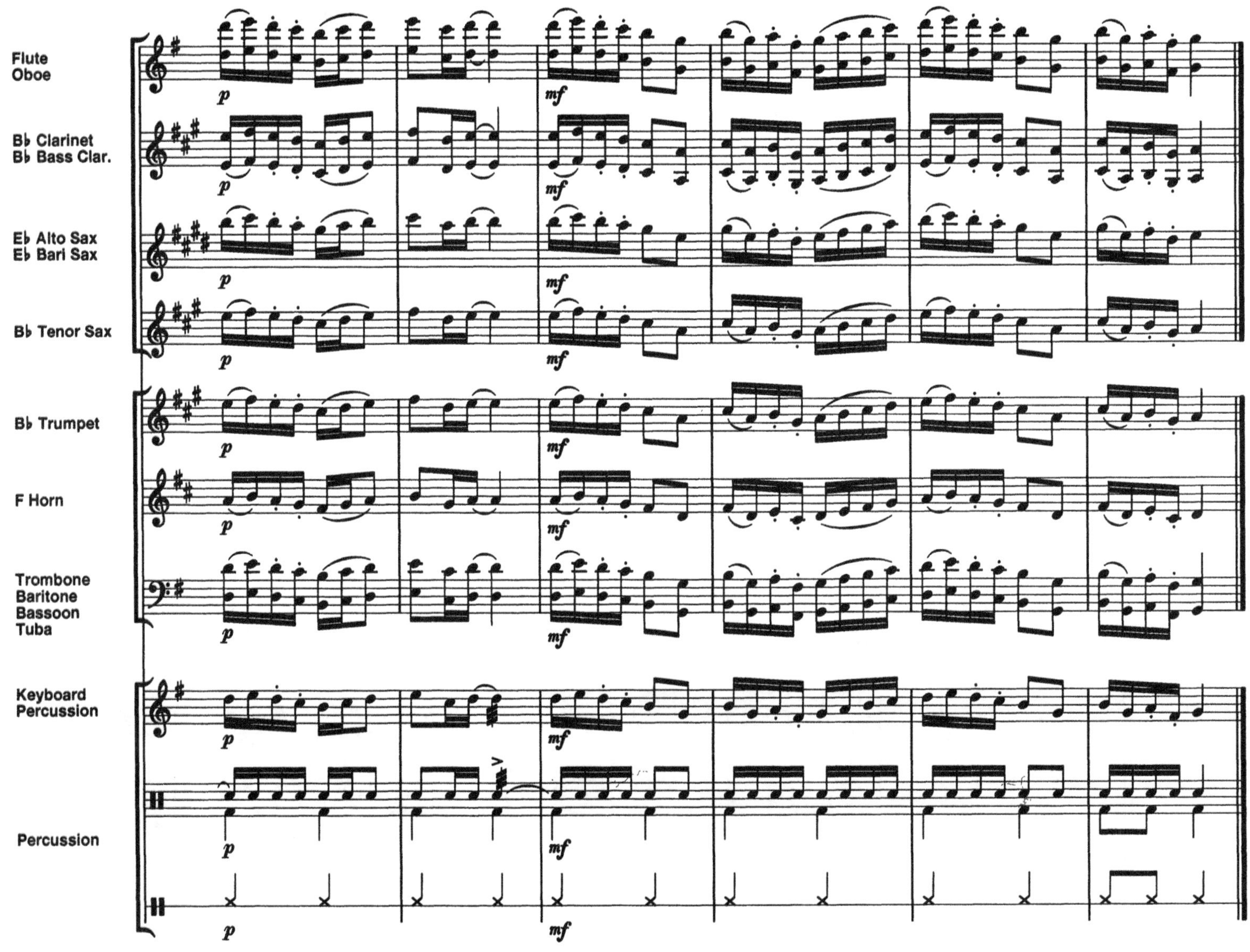
Flute
Oboe
B♭ Clarinet
B♭ Bass Clar.
E♭ Alto Sax
E♭ Bari Sax
B♭ Tenor Sax
B♭ Trumpet
F Horn
Trombone
Baritone
Bassoon
Tuba
Keyboard
Percussion
Percussion

History: Several twentieth century composers began to expand the traditional rules of music and harmony. **Arnold Schoenberg** (1874-1951) was the first composer to use a fixed sequence of twelve pitches. This technique is known as **serialism.** **Alban Berg** (1885-1935), **Igor Stravinsky** (1882-1971) and **Anton Webern** (1883-1945) also used serialism in their music. *Twelve Tones* is an example of this type of music. This melody does not have a key center, and includes some "dissonant" interval distances between notes.

131. TWELVE TONES

Director

Concert keys in **Essential Technique** are introduced in the following format:

Balance Builder
- A, B and C parts for all students

Chorale - Full Band Arrangement
- Rehearse woodwinds alone, brass alone and full band

Scale
- Marked articulations
- Scale in Thirds
- Arpeggio

Articulation Work-Out
- Focus on accuracy

If you wish to warm-up in specific key(s), ask students to turn to the indicated pages:

Concert Key	Score Pg.	Student Pg.
Bb Major	14	2
Eb Major	36	6
F Major	61	11
D Minor	100	18
Ab Major	110	20
C Major	132	23
G Minor	144	25
G Major	200	36
D Major	212	38
Db Major	224	40
Gb Major	230	41

Tune and shape each note on *Balance Builder* exercises, and experiment with different instrument combinations. Rehearse brass alone, woodwinds alone and the full band on each *Chorale* to improve balance and intonation. Include various dynamic levels on each *Scale* and *Articulation Work-Out*, including ***mf***, ***f***, ***p*** and < >.

Additional scale studies are found on score pages 234 - 240 (student book pages 42 - 44). All scale studies are transposed for group or individual practice. *Chromatic Technique* studies are found throughout the book, in addition to multicultural songs, rhythm reinforcement and theory exercises.

Ear Training

Concert D Major

Play each exercise below, then sing it in your natural voice range. Make sure all chord tones are heard equally well, and are in "balance." Begin tuning with the lower instruments of the band.

132. BALANCE BUILDER

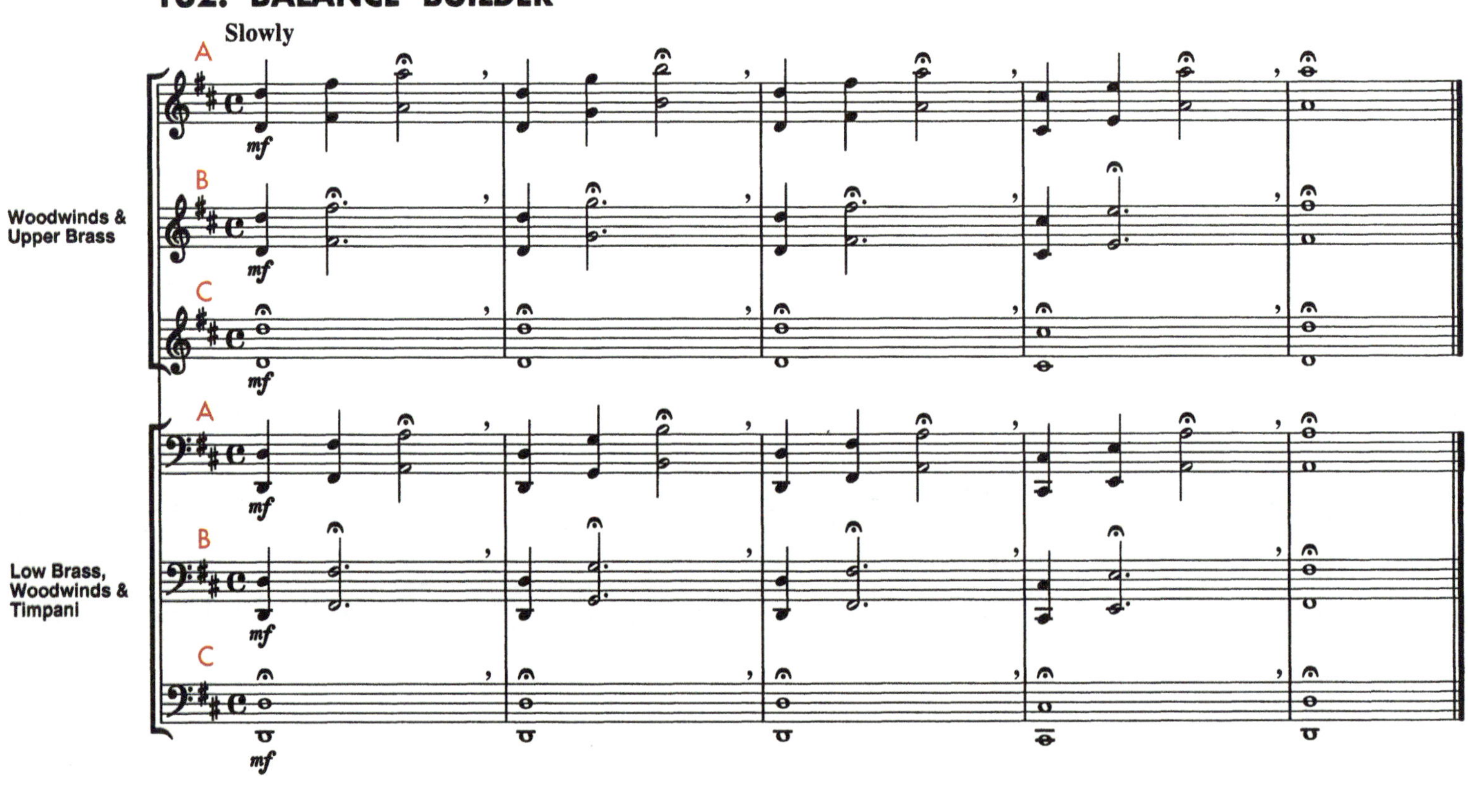

133. CHORALE - Full Band Arrangement (With One Voice)

John Higgins

9
Flute
Oboe
Bassoon
B♭ Clarinet
E♭ Alto Clar.
B♭ Bass Clar.
E♭ Alto Sax.
B♭ Ten. Sax.
E♭ Bari. Sax.
B♭ Trumpet
F Horn
Trombone
Baritone
Tuba
Keyboard Percussion
Percussion
Timpani
rit.
p a tempo

Flute
Oboe
Bassoon
B♭ Clarinet
E♭ Alto Clar.
B♭ Bass Clar.
E♭ Alto Sax.
B♭ Ten. Sax.
E♭ Bari. Sax.
B♭ Trumpet
F Horn
Trombone
Baritone
Tuba
Keyboard Percussion
Percussion
Timpani
decresc.
Tri.

NEW NOTES INTRODUCED ON 134. CONCERT D MAJOR TECHNIQUE

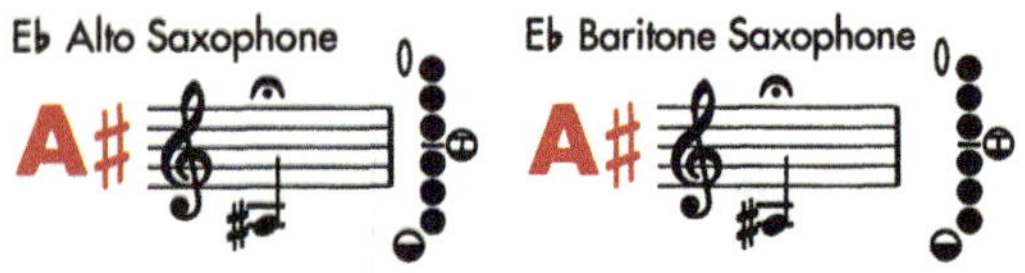

134. CONCERT D MAJOR TECHNIQUE

NEW NOTES INTRODUCED ON 135. ARTICULATION WORK - OUT

135. ARTICULATION WORK - OUT

Play even rhythms at all tempos.

► Practice this exercise as a wrist builder with RRRR and LLLL sticking.

136. BOUND FOR SOUTH AUSTRALIA

Australian Folk Song

Director This exercise is transposed in each student book. A single note appears in the final measure. The chord voicings function as a teaching exercise. Play the chord, and ask students to identify their chord tone. Substitute different chord tones throughout the band, and experiment with balance and textural sounds. You may wish to have a few students play or sing the root, then add band members singing the third and fifth before playing.

137. EAR TRAINING TECHNIQUE

Play each exercise below, then sing it in your natural voice range.
Make sure you can hear all the notes of the chord in the last measure.

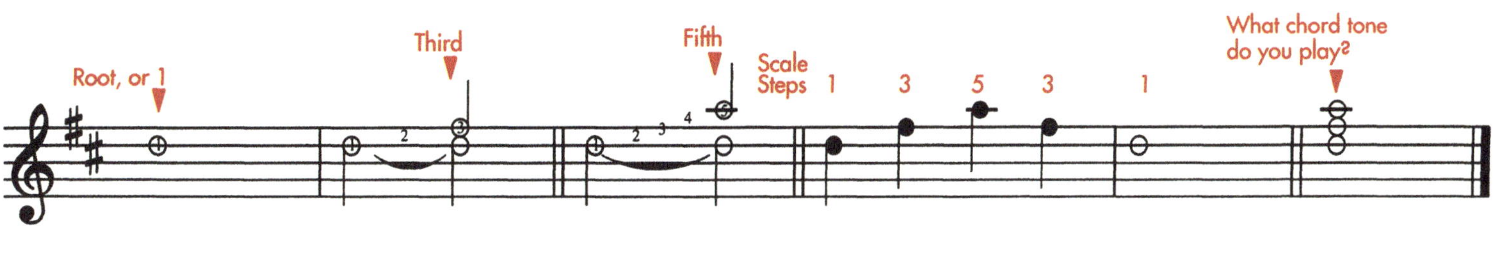

138. INTERVAL TECHNIQUE

Latin American music combines the folk music from South and Central America, the Caribbean Islands, American Indian, Spanish and Portuguese cultures. Melodies are often accompanied by drums, maracas and claves. Latin American music continues to influence jazz, classical and popular styles of music. *Cielito Lindo* is a Latin American love song.

139. CIELITO LINDO

C. Fernandez

Flute
Oboe
B♭ Clarinet
B♭ Bass Clar.
E♭ Alto Sax
E♭ Bari Sax
B♭ Tenor Sax
B♭ Trumpet
F Horn
Trombone
Baritone
Bassoon
Tuba
Keyboard
Percussion
Percussion

Flute
Oboe
B♭ Clarinet
B♭ Bass Clar.
E♭ Alto Sax
E♭ Bari Sax
B♭ Tenor Sax
B♭ Trumpet
F Horn
Trombone
Baritone
Bassoon
Tuba
Keyboard
Percussion
Percussion
1
2

Flute
Oboe
B♭ Clarinet
B♭ Bass Clar.
E♭ Alto Sax
E♭ Bari Sax
B♭ Tenor Sax
B♭ Trumpet
F Horn
Trombone
Baritone
Bassoon
Tuba
Keyboard Percussion
Percussion
Alt.

Director

Concert keys in **Essential Technique** are introduced in the following format:

Balance Builder
- A, B and C parts for all students

Chorale - Full Band Arrangement
- Rehearse woodwinds alone, brass alone and full band

Scale
- Marked articulations
- Scale in Thirds
- Arpeggio

Articulation Work-Out
- Focus on accuracy

If you wish to warm-up in specific key(s), ask students to turn to the indicated pages:

Concert Key	Score Pg.	Student Pg.
B♭ Major	14	2
E♭ Major	36	6
F Major	61	11
D Minor	100	18
A♭ Major	110	20
C Major	132	23
G Minor	144	25
G Major	200	36
D Major	212	38
D♭ Major	224	40
G♭ Major	230	41

Tune and shape each note on *Balance Builder* exercises, and experiment with different instrument combinations. Rehearse brass alone, woodwinds alone and the full band on each *Chorale* to improve balance and intonation. Include various dynamic levels on each *Scale* and *Articulation Work-Out*, including ***mf***, ***f***, ***p*** and <>.

Additional scale studies are found on score pages 234 - 240 (student book pages 42 - 44). All scale studies are transposed for group or individual practice. *Chromatic Technique* studies are found throughout the book, in addition to multicultural songs, rhythm reinforcement and theory exercises.

Ear Training

Concert D♭ Major Play each exercise below, then sing it in your natural voice range. Make sure all chord tones are heard equally well, and are in "balance." Begin tuning with the lower instruments of the band.

140. BALANCE BUILDER

NEW NOTES INTRODUCED ON 141. CONCERT D♭ MAJOR TECHNIQUE

B♭ Bass Clarinet

E♭ Alto Saxophone

E♭ Baritone Saxophone

141. CONCERT D♭ MAJOR TECHNIQUE

Scale in Thirds
Flute
Oboe
B♭ Clarinet
B♭ Bass Clar.
Alt.
E♭ Alto Sax
E♭ Bari Sax
Alt.
B♭ Tenor Sax
Alt.
Alt.
B♭ Trumpet
F Horn
(6)
(5)
(5)
Trombone
Baritone
Bassoon
Tuba
Keyboard
Percussion
Percussion

Arpeggio
Flute
Oboe
B♭ Clarinet
B♭ Bass Clar.
Use alternate fingering for all B♭'s.
E♭ Alto Sax
E♭ Bari Sax
Use alternate fingering for all B♭'s.
B♭ Tenor Sax
B♭ Trumpet
F Horn
Trombone
Baritone
Bassoon
Tuba
Keyboard
Percussion
Percussion

142. GERMAN NATIONAL ANTHEM

Franz Josef Haydn

Flute
Oboe
B♭ Clarinet
B♭ Bass Clar.
E♭ Alto Sax
E♭ Bari Sax
▲ Alt.
B♭ Tenor Sax
B♭ Trumpet
F Horn
(6)
(6)
(6)
Trombone
Baritone
Bassoon
Tuba
Keyboard
Percussion
Percussion
Chimes
Timpani

Flute
Oboe
B♭ Clarinet
B♭ Bass Clar.
E♭ Alto Sax
E♭ Bari Sax
B♭ Tenor Sax
B♭ Trumpet
F Horn
Trombone
Baritone
Bassoon
Tuba
Keyboard
Percussion
Percussion
Chimes
Timpani
▼Alt.
▲Alt.
(6)
(6)

Director

Concert keys in **Essential Technique** are introduced in the following format:

Balance Builder
- A, B and C parts for all students

Chorale - Full Band Arrangement
- Rehearse woodwinds alone, brass alone and full band

Scale
- Marked articulations
- Scale in Thirds
- Arpeggio

Articulation Work-Out
- Focus on accuracy

If you wish to warm-up in specific key(s), ask students to turn to the indicated pages:

Concert Key	Score Pg.	Student Pg.
Bb Major	14	2
Eb Major	36	6
F Major	61	11
D Minor	100	18
Ab Major	110	20
C Major	132	23
G Minor	144	25
G Major	200	36
D Major	212	38
Db Major	224	40
Gb Major	230	41

Tune and shape each note on *Balance Builder* exercises, and experiment with different instrument combinations. Rehearse brass alone, woodwinds alone and the full band on each *Chorale* to improve balance and intonation. Include various dynamic levels on each *Scale* and *Articulation Work-Out*, including ***mf***, ***f***, ***p*** and < >.

Additional scale studies are found on score pages 234 - 240 (student book pages 42 - 44). All scale studies are transposed for group or individual practice. *Chromatic Technique* studies are found throughout the book, in addition to multicultural songs, rhythm reinforcement and theory exercises.

Ear Training — Concert G♭ Major

Play each exercise below, then sing it in your natural voice range. Make sure all chord tones are heard equally well, and are in "balance." Begin tuning with the lower instruments of the band.

143. BALANCE BUILDER

C Instruments: C-flat is played with the same fingering as B-natural.

NEW NOTES INTRODUCED ON 144. CONCERT G♭ MAJOR TECHNIQUE

E♭ Alto Clarinet

E♭

144. CONCERT G♭ MAJOR TECHNIQUE

145. SPRING SONG

Felix Mendelssohn

Andante

Flute
Oboe
B♭ Clarinet
B♭ Bass Clar.
E♭ Alto Sax
E♭ Bari Sax
B♭ Tenor Sax
B♭ Trumpet
F Horn
Trombone
Baritone
Bassoon
Tuba
Keyboard
Percussion
Percussion
Alt.
Alt.
(6)
Flute
Oboe
B♭ Clarinet
B♭ Bass Clar.
E♭ Alto Sax
E♭ Bari Sax
B♭ Tenor Sax
B♭ Trumpet
F Horn
Trombone
Baritone
Bassoon
Tuba
Keyboard
Percussion
Percussion
(6)

Major Scales

Play major scales as part of your daily practice routine. Play all octaves, keys and arpeggios at various dynamic levels and tempos. Keep a steady pulse. Try different articulation patterns, such as:

A. B. C. D.

Percussion: Exercises 146-155 allow the band to practice several major scales. Be sure to follow the indicated sticking. You should also practice these scales using the keyboard percussion book.

146. CONCERT B♭ MAJOR SCALE

147. CONCERT E♭ MAJOR SCALE

148. CONCERT F MAJOR SCALE

149. CONCERT C MAJOR SCALE

150. CONCERT A♭ MAJOR SCALE

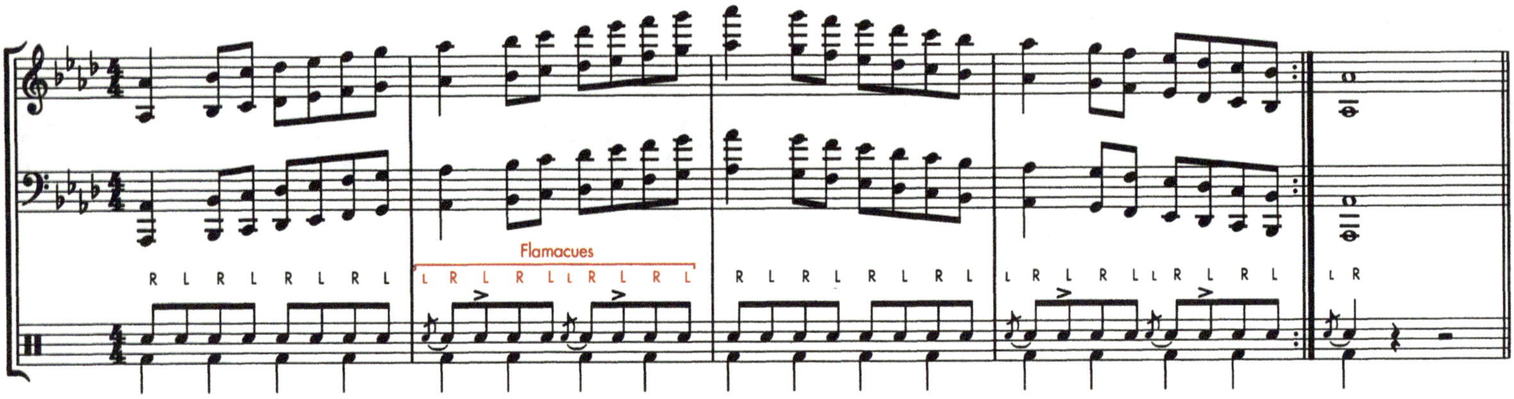

151. CONCERT D♭ MAJOR SCALE

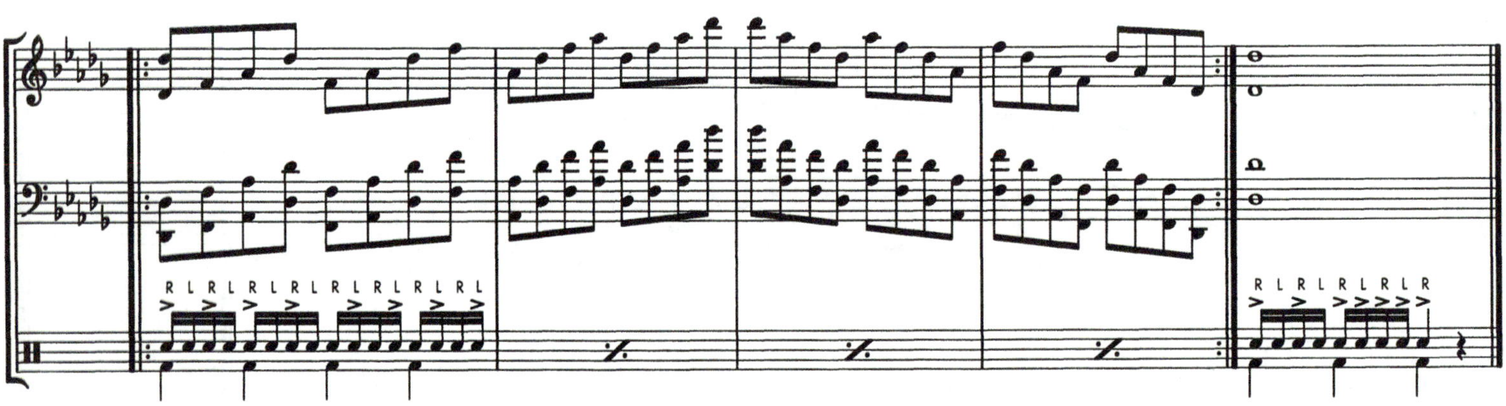

152. CONCERT G MAJOR SCALE

153. CONCERT D MAJOR SCALE

154. CONCERT A MAJOR SCALE

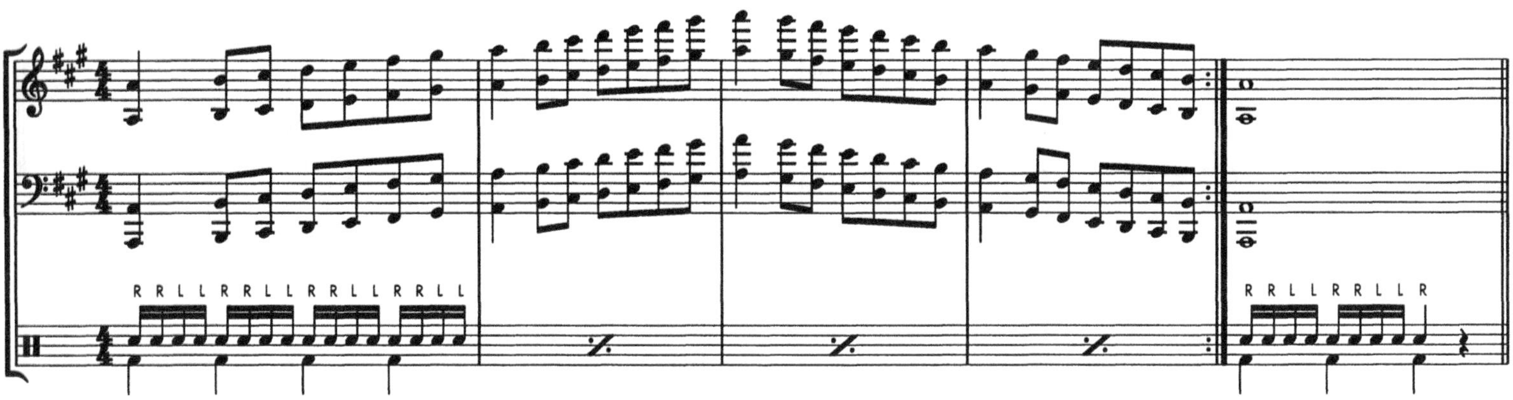

155. CONCERT G♭ MAJOR SCALE

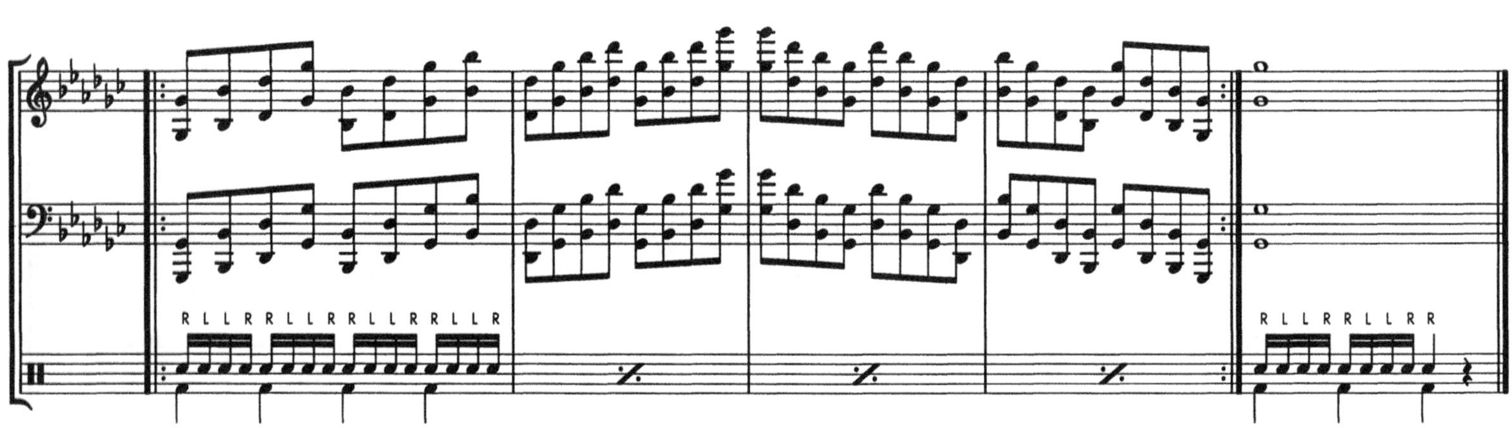

Minor Scales

Play minor scales as part of your daily practice routine. Play all octaves, all three forms and the arpeggios at various dynamic levels and tempos. Keep a steady pulse. Try different articulation patterns, such as:

Percussion: Exercises 156-159 allow the band to practice several minor scales. Be sure to follow the indicated sticking. You should also practice these scales using the keyboard percussion book.

156. CONCERT D MINOR SCALE

157. CONCERT G MINOR SCALE

158. CONCERT C MINOR SCALE

159. CONCERT F MINOR SCALE

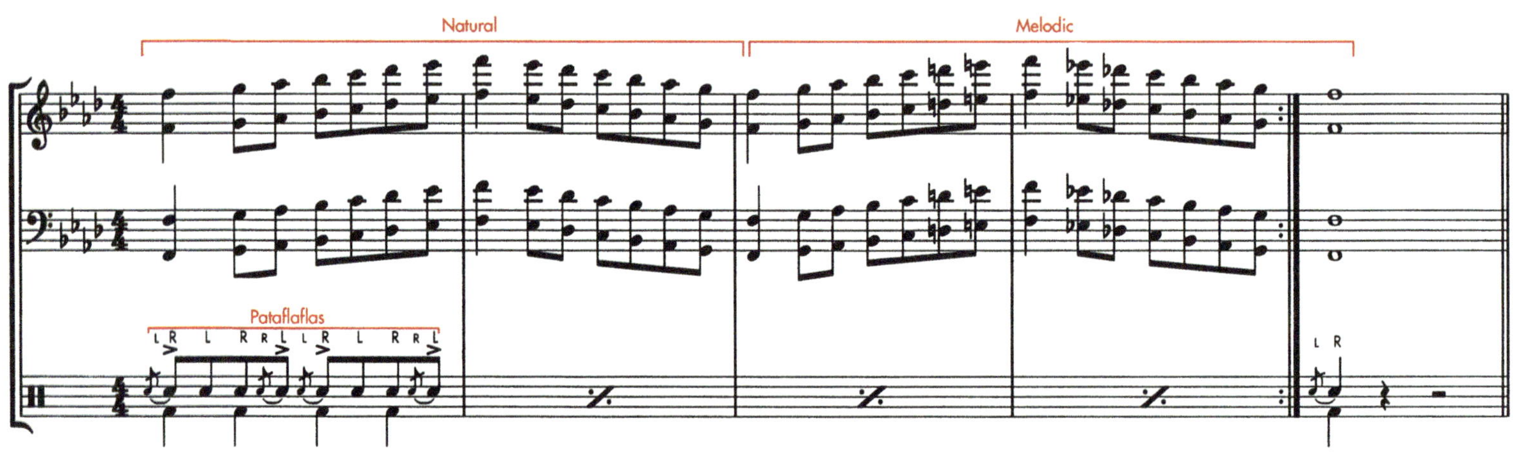

FLUTE TRILL CHART

Director The following Special Exercises are found on student book page 45. Fingering charts for all instruments appear on pages 258-293 (student book pages 46-47). The glossary on page 294 appears on student book page 48.

Here are some common trill fingerings. Trill key(s) appear in color.

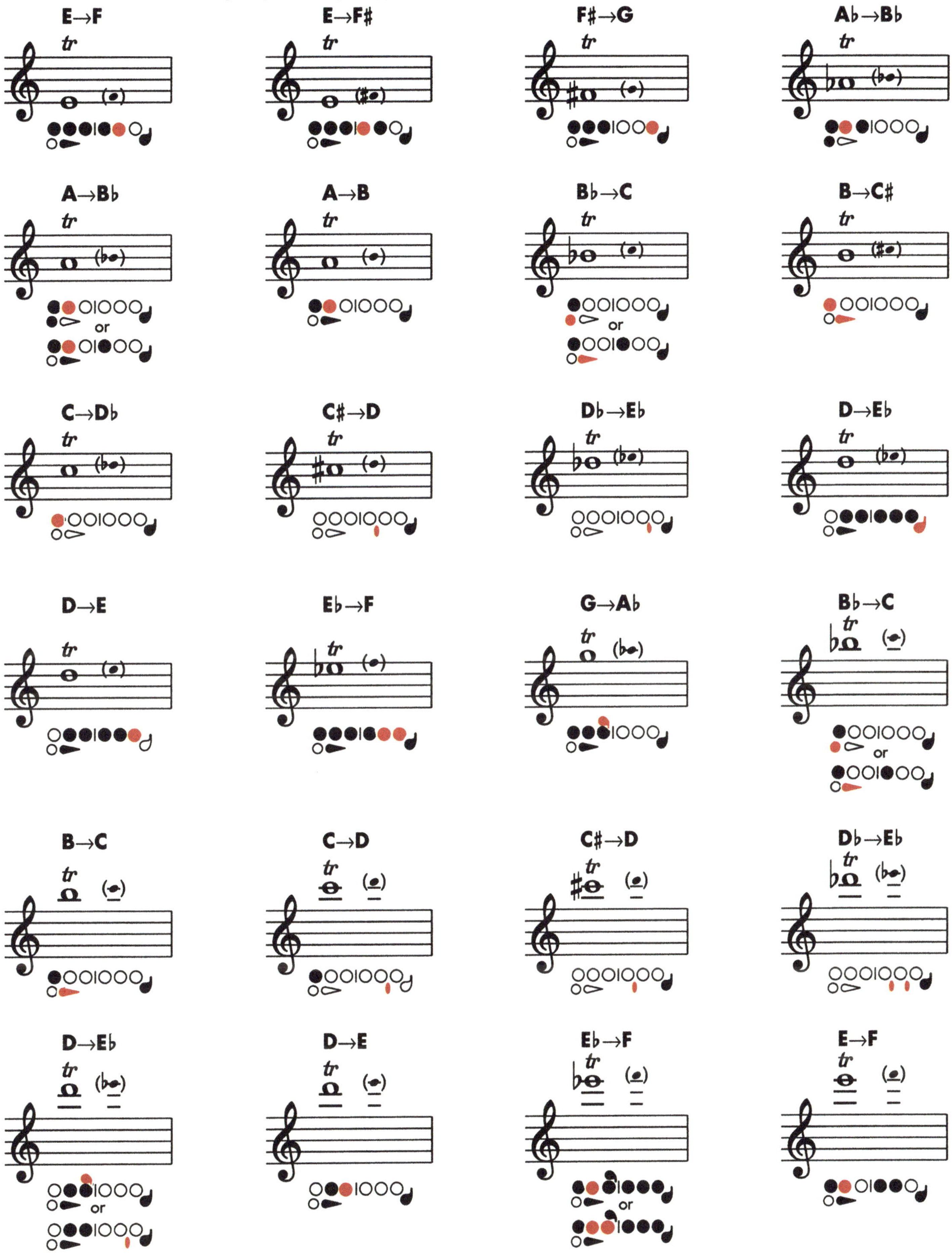

OBOE TRILL CHART

Here are some common trill fingerings. Trill key(s) appear in color.

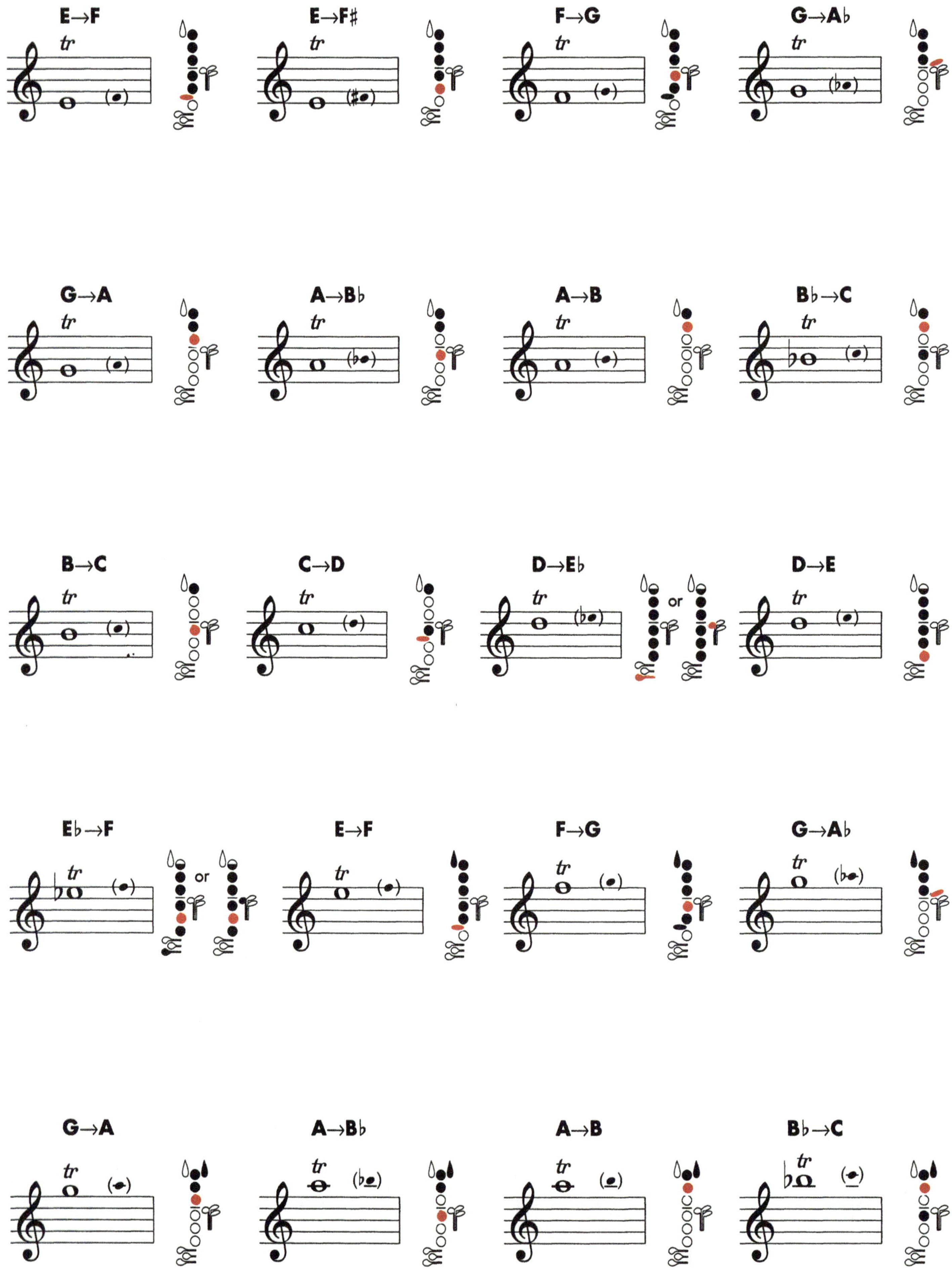

BASSOON TRILL CHART

Here are some common trill fingerings. Trill key(s) appear in color.

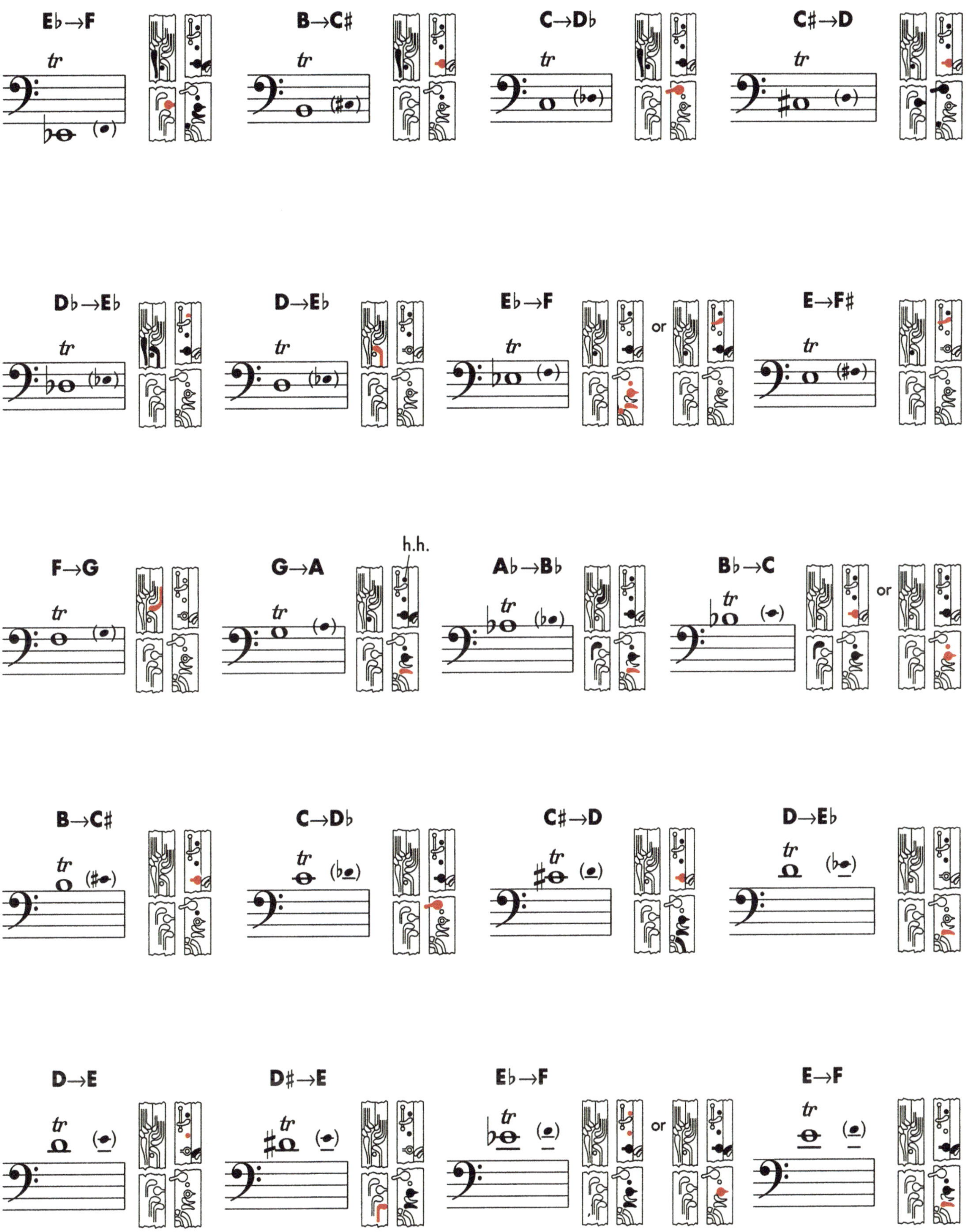

B♭ CLARINET TRILL CHART

Here are some common trill fingerings. Trill key(s) appear in color.

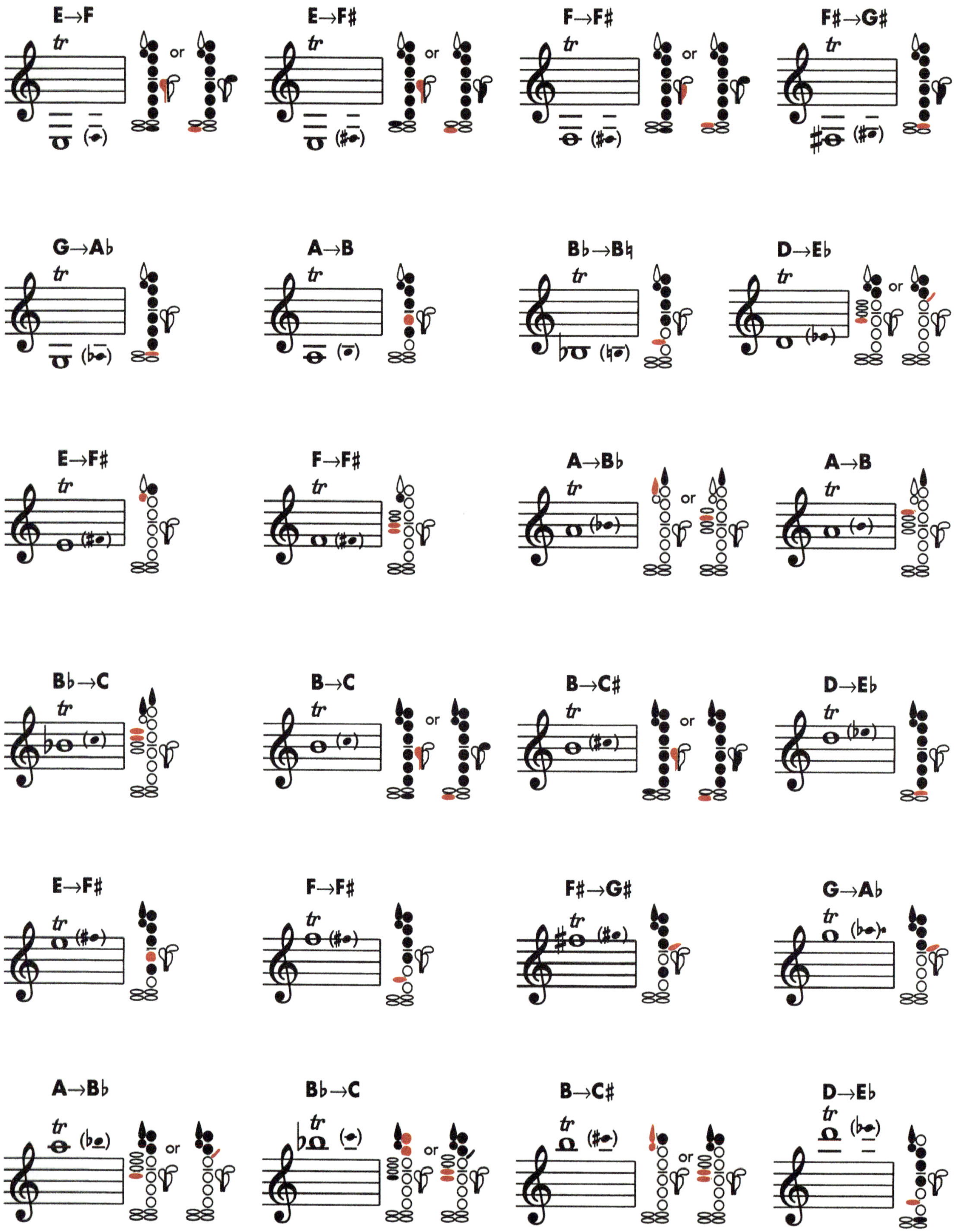

E♭ ALTO CLARINET TRILL CHART

Here are some common trill fingerings. Trill key(s) appear in color.

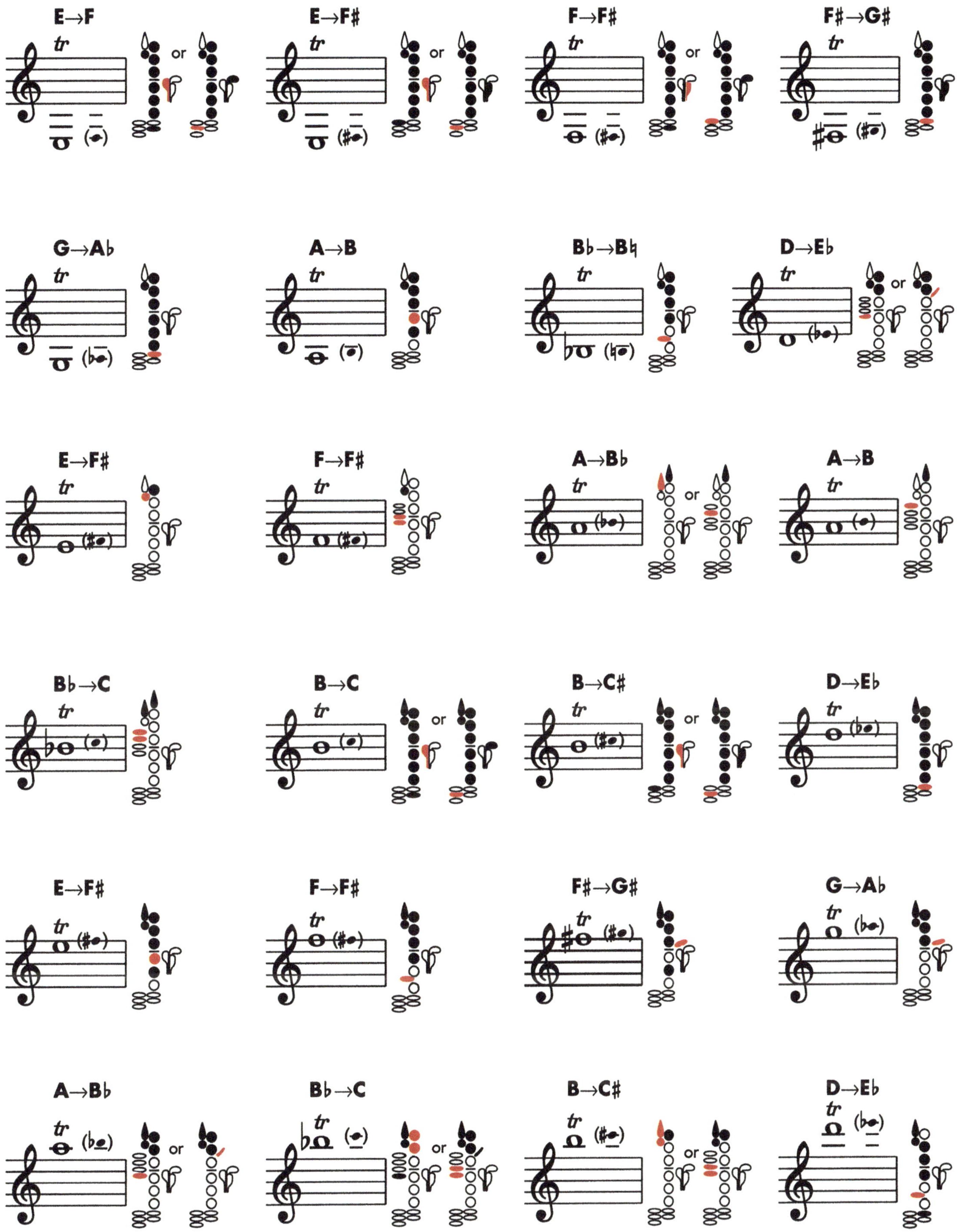

B♭ BASS CLARINET TRILL CHART

Here are some common trill fingerings. Trill key(s) appear in color.

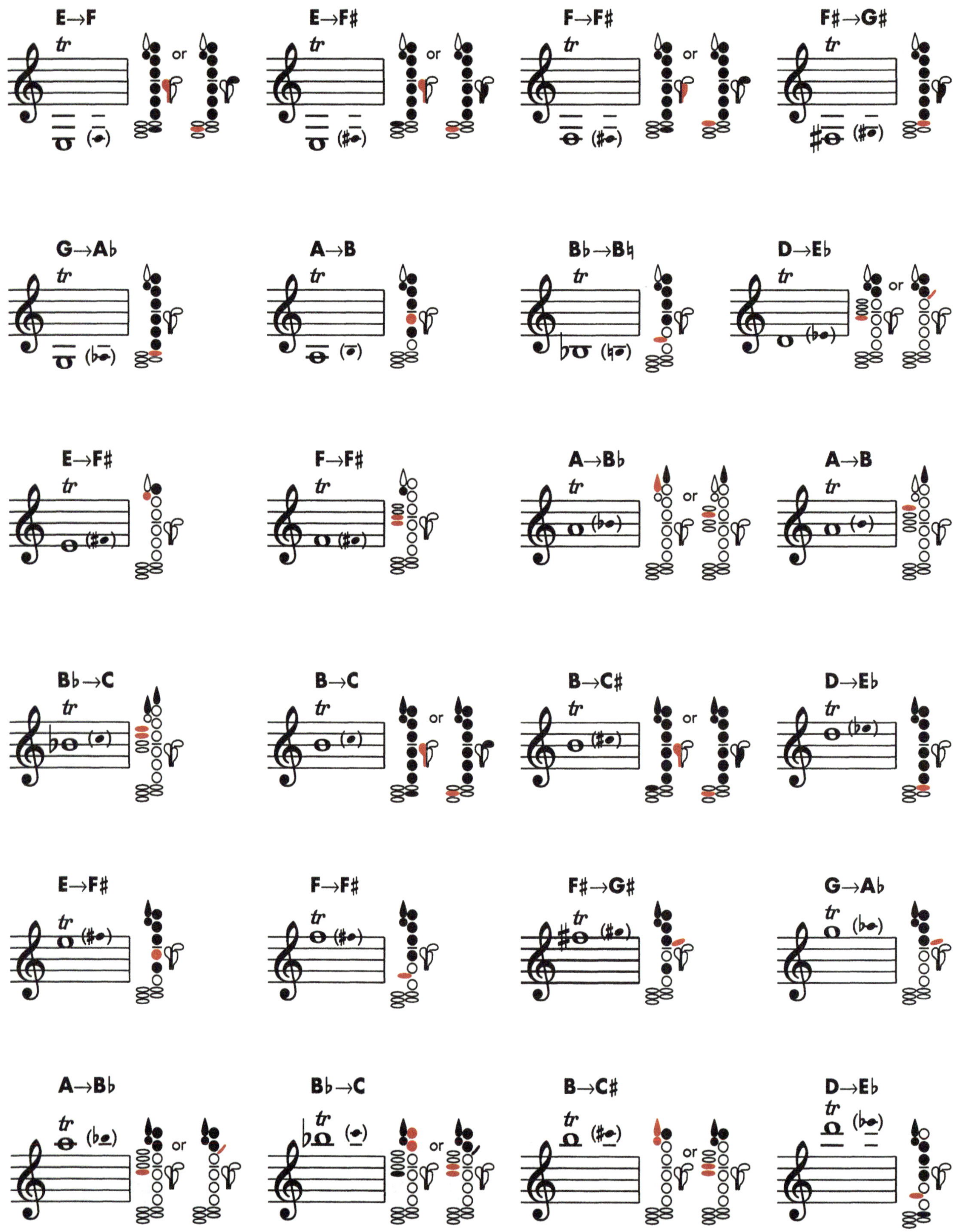

E♭ ALTO SAXOPHONE TRILL CHART

Here are some common trill fingerings. Trill key(s) appear in color.

E→F

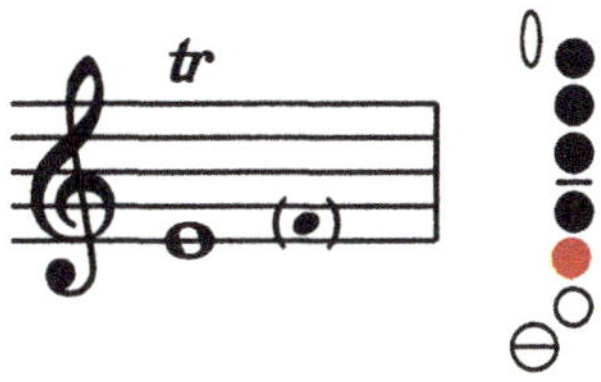

E→F♯

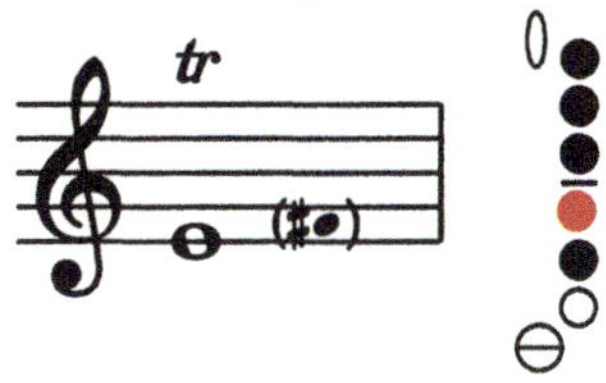

F→G

G→A♭

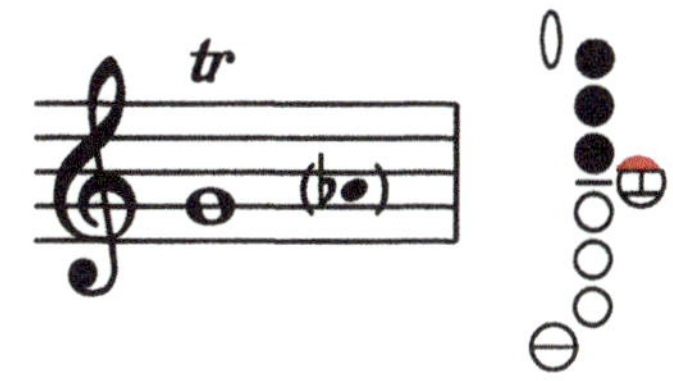

G→A

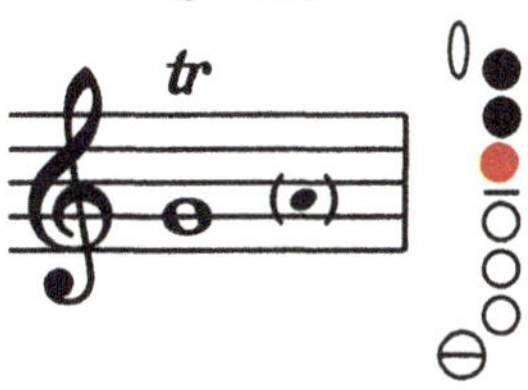

A→B♭

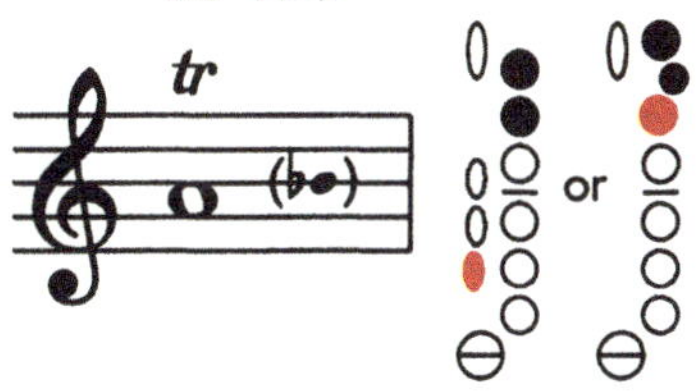

A→B

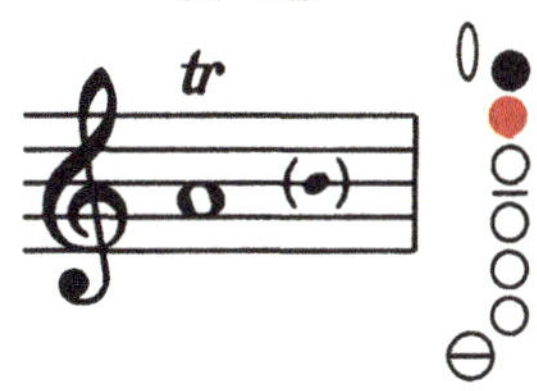

B♭→C

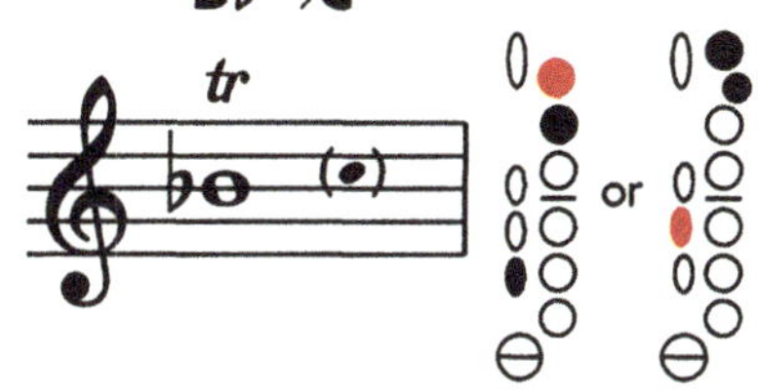

B→C

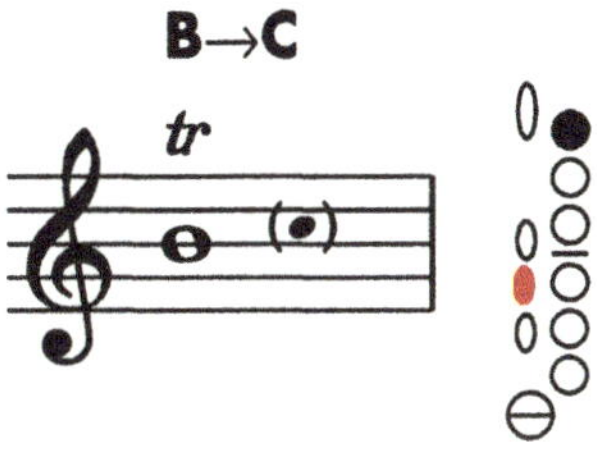

B→C♯

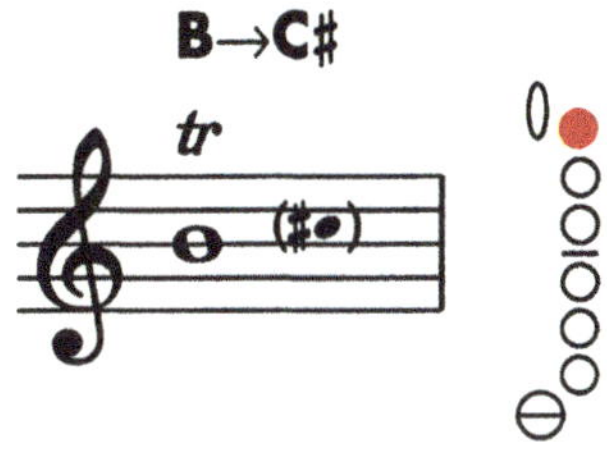

C→D

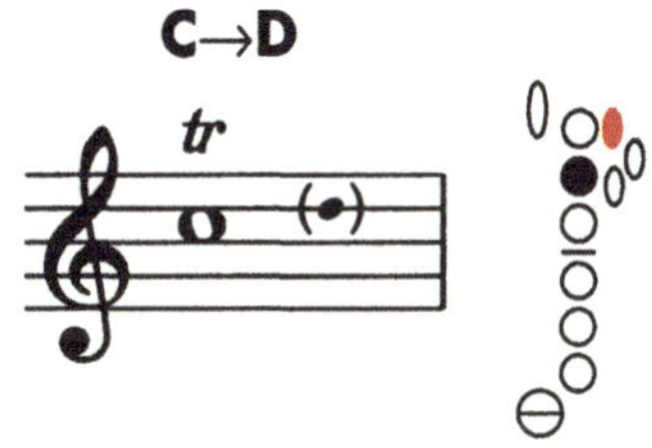

C♯→D

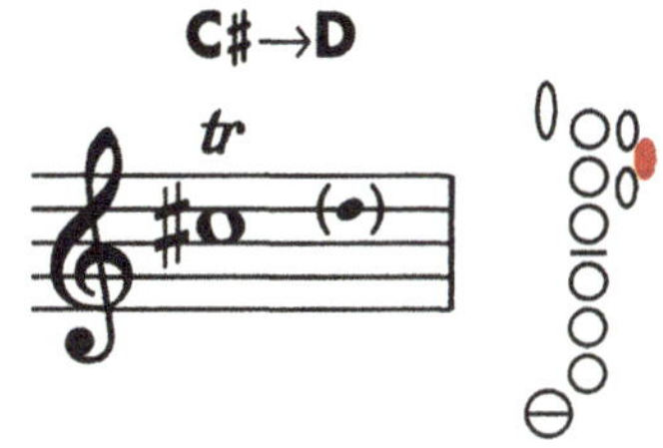

D→E♭

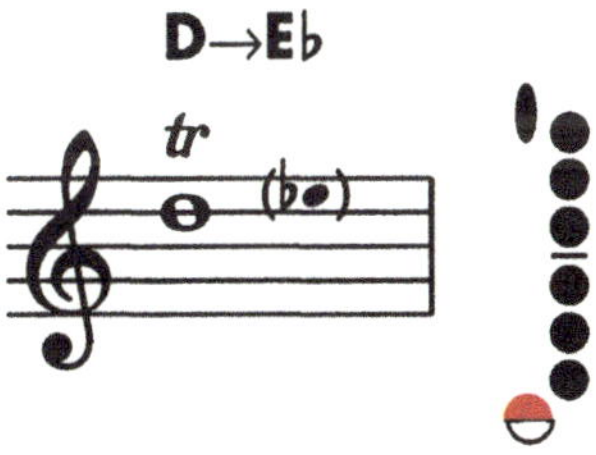

D→E

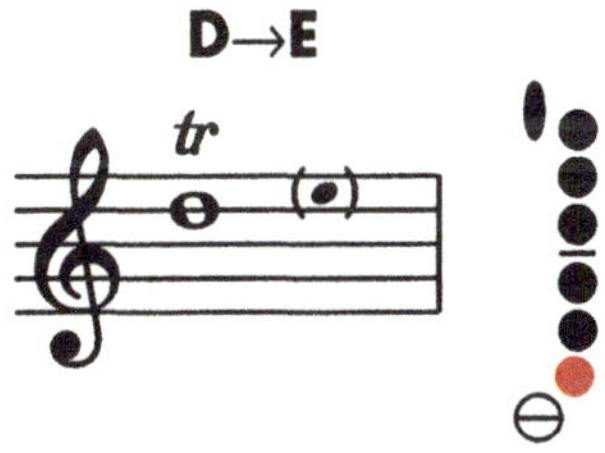

E♭→F

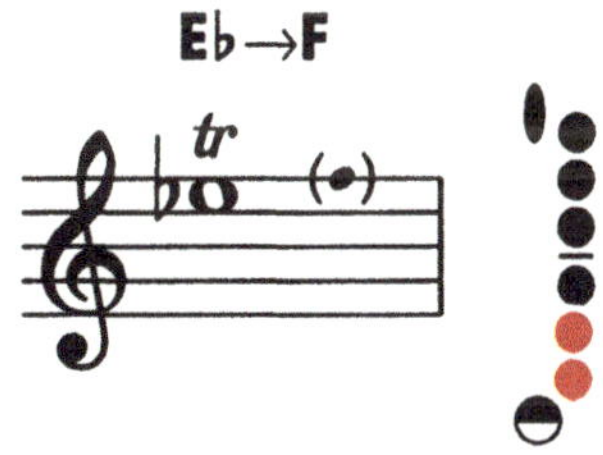

E→F

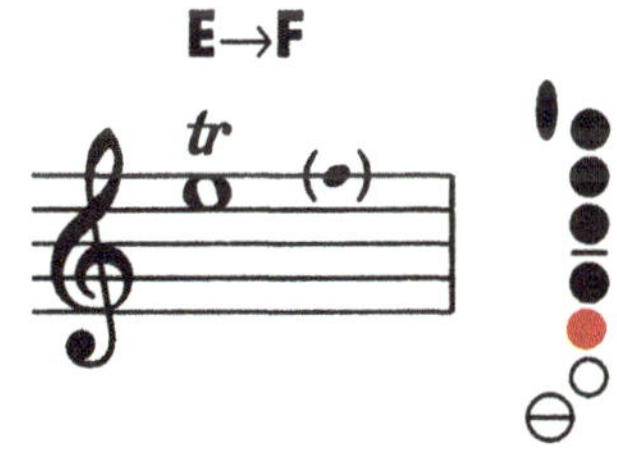

E→F♯

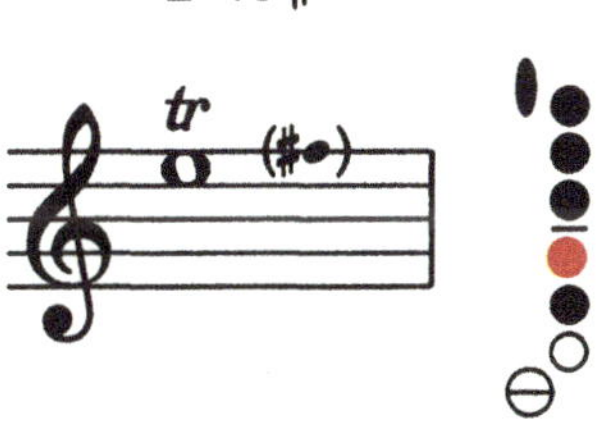

F→G

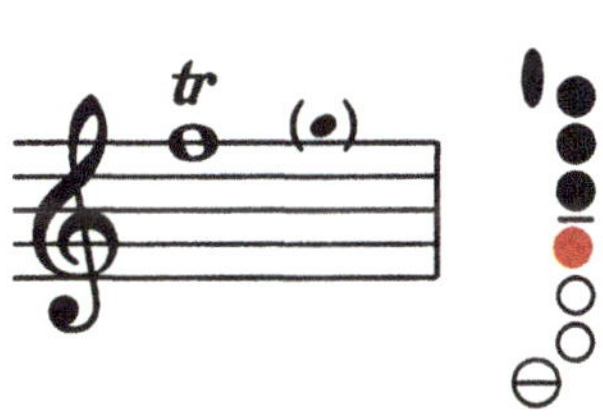

G→A

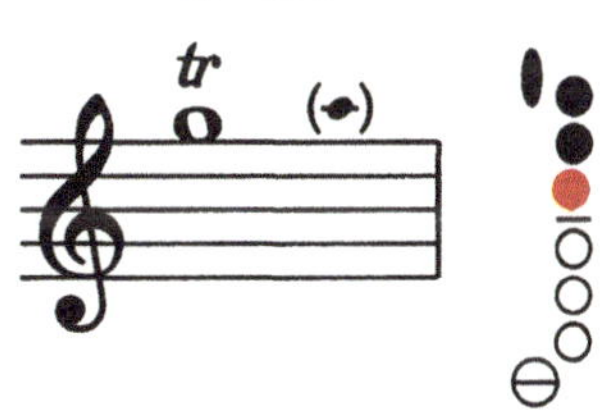

A→B♭

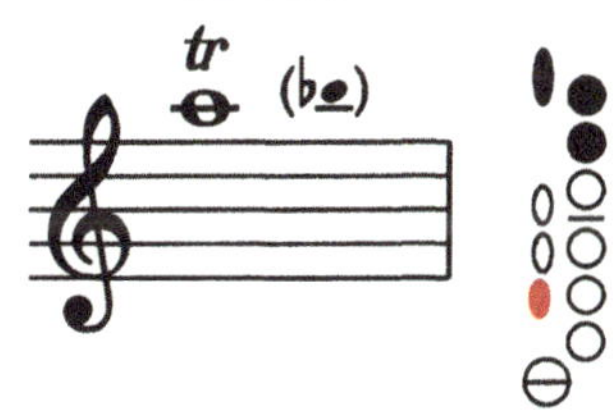

A→B

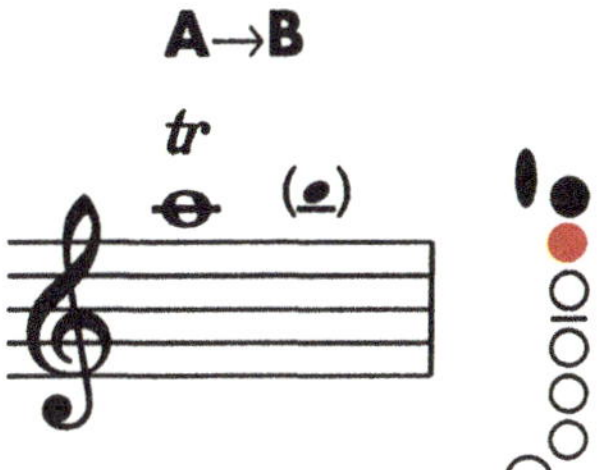

B→C

B→C♯

C→D

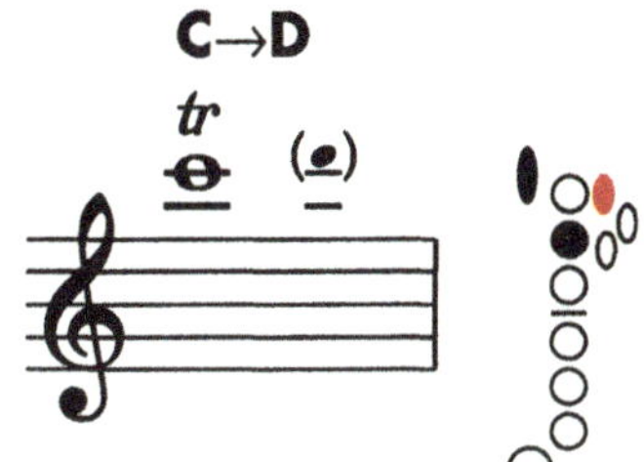

B♭ TENOR SAXOPHONE TRILL CHART

Here are some common trill fingerings. Trill key(s) appear in color.

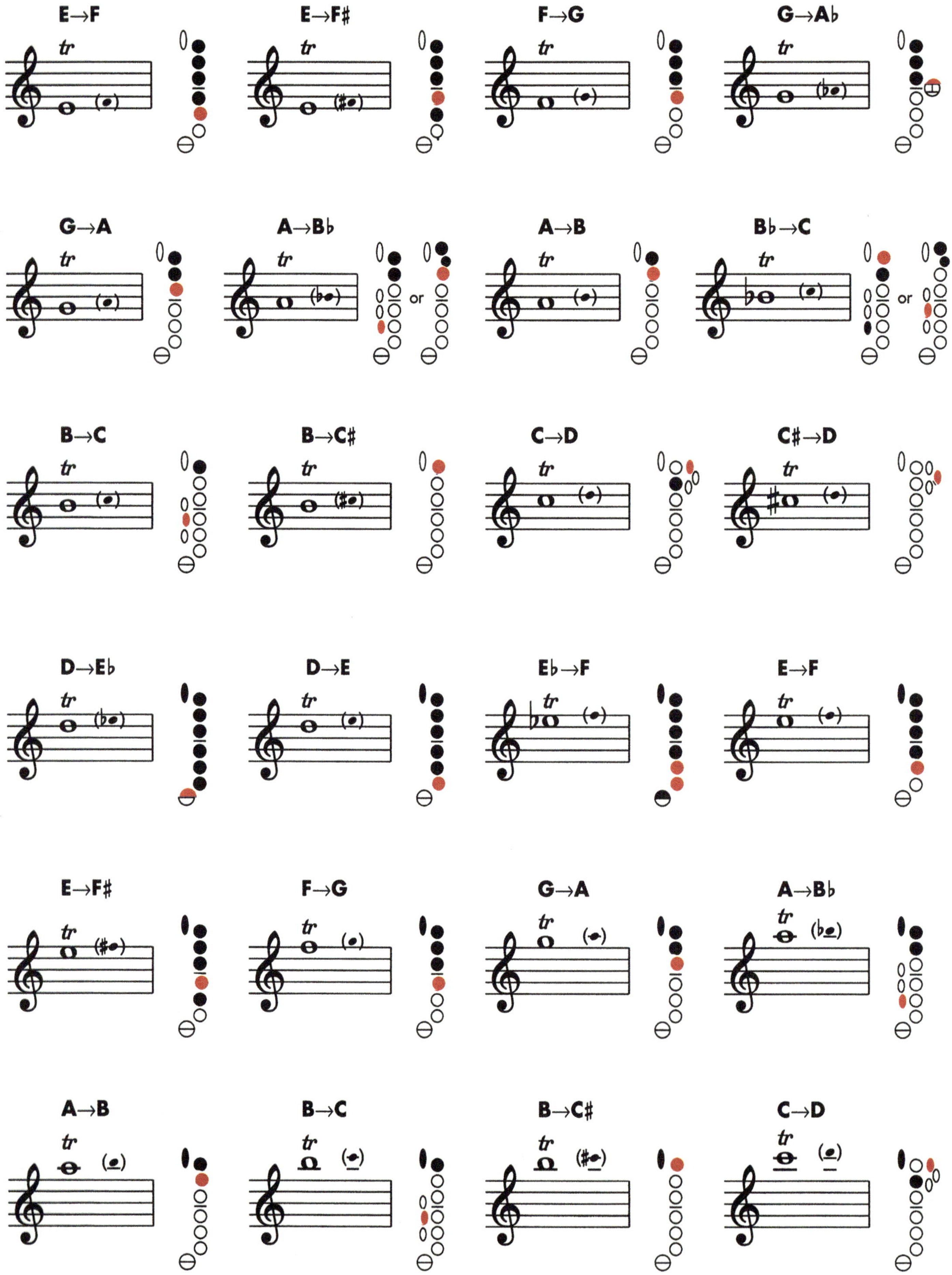

E♭ BARITONE SAXOPHONE TRILL CHART

Here are some common trill fingerings. Trill key(s) appear in color.

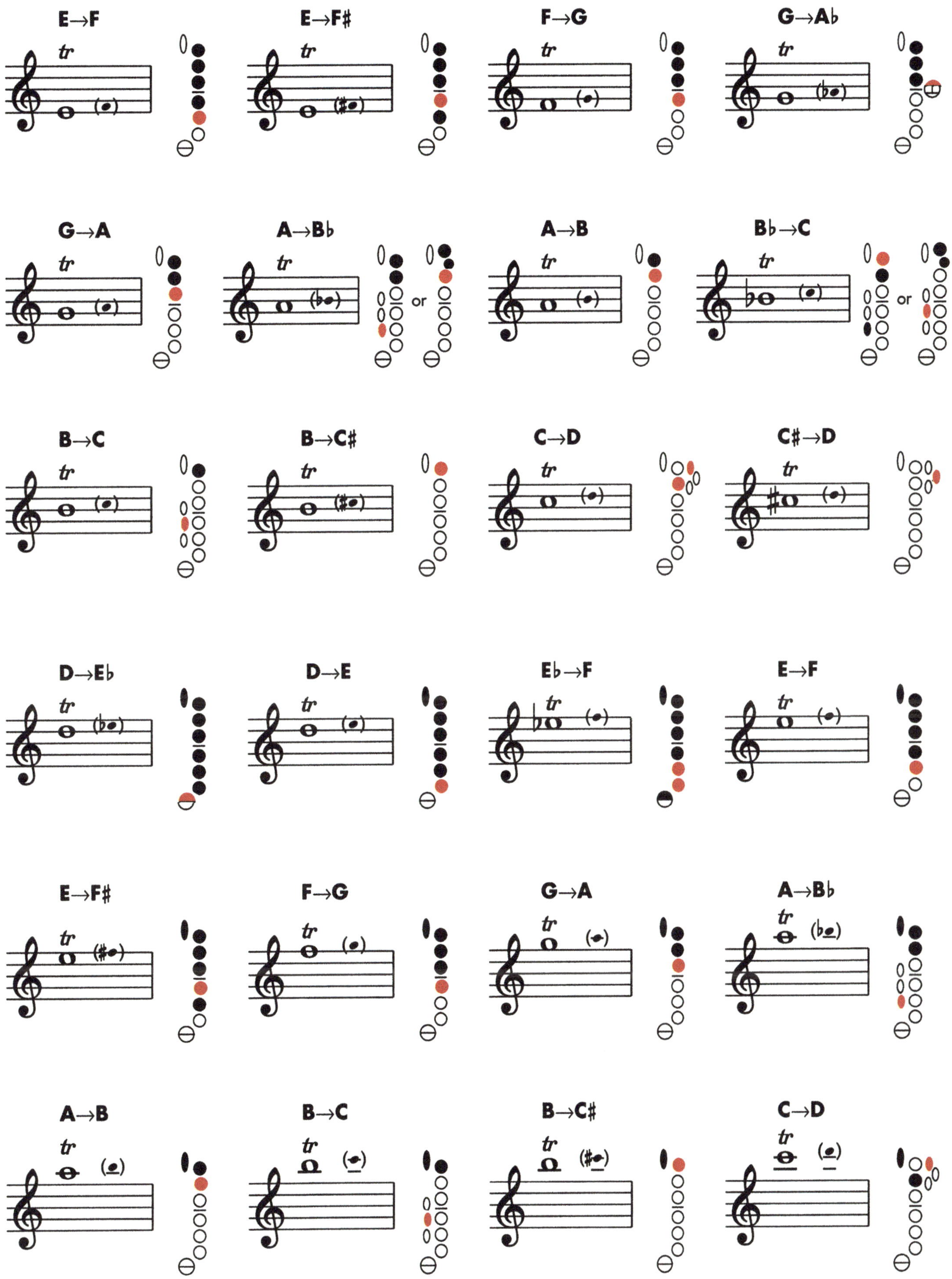

B♭ TRUMPET SPECIAL EXERCISES

LIP SLUR STUDY NO. 1

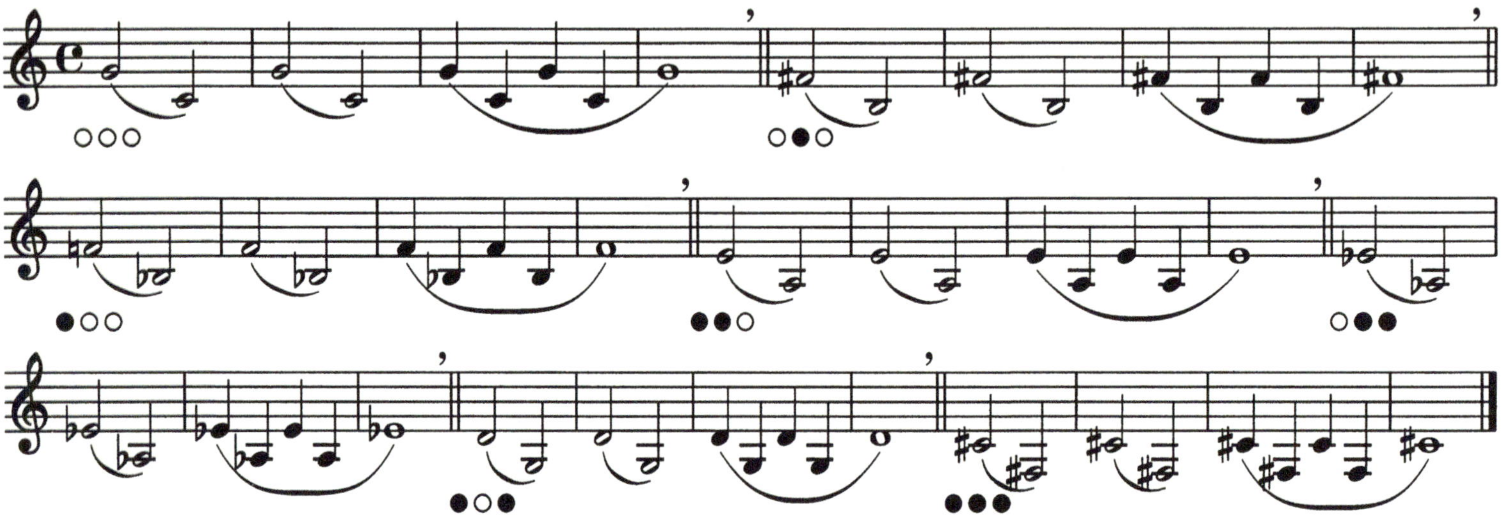

LIP SLUR STUDY NO. 2

FLEXIBILITY FUN

HORN SPECIAL EXERCISES

LIP SLUR STUDY NO. 1

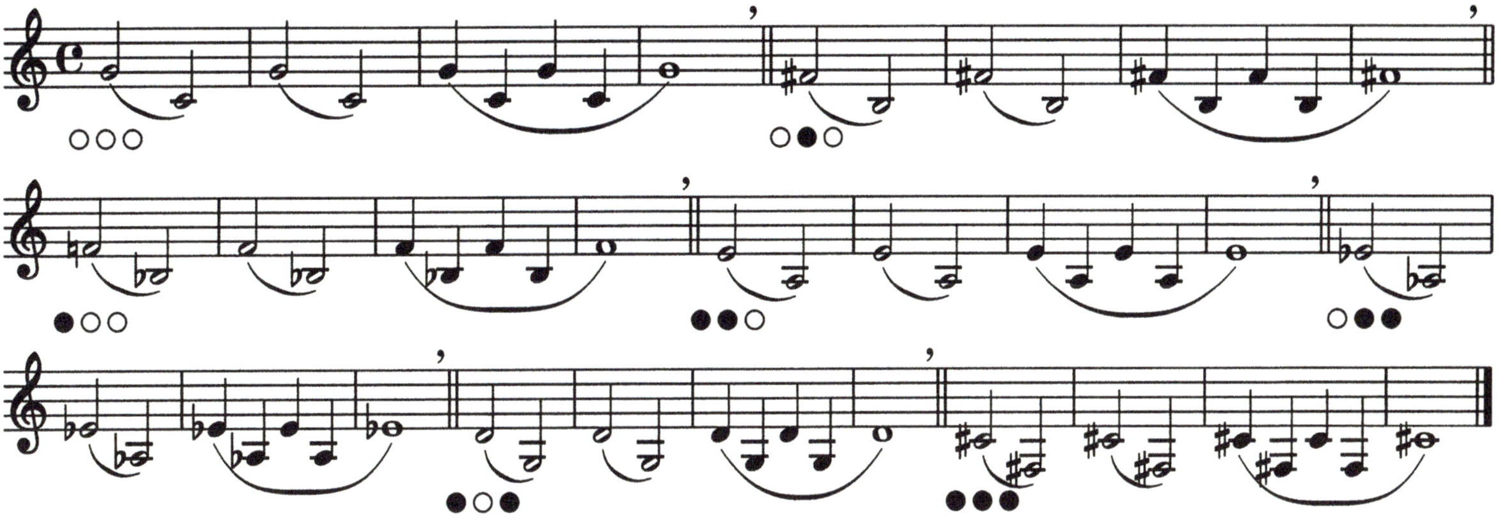

LIP SLUR STUDY NO. 2

FLEXIBILITY FUN

TROMBONE SPECIAL EXERCISES

LIP SLUR STUDY NO. 1

LIP SLUR STUDY NO. 2

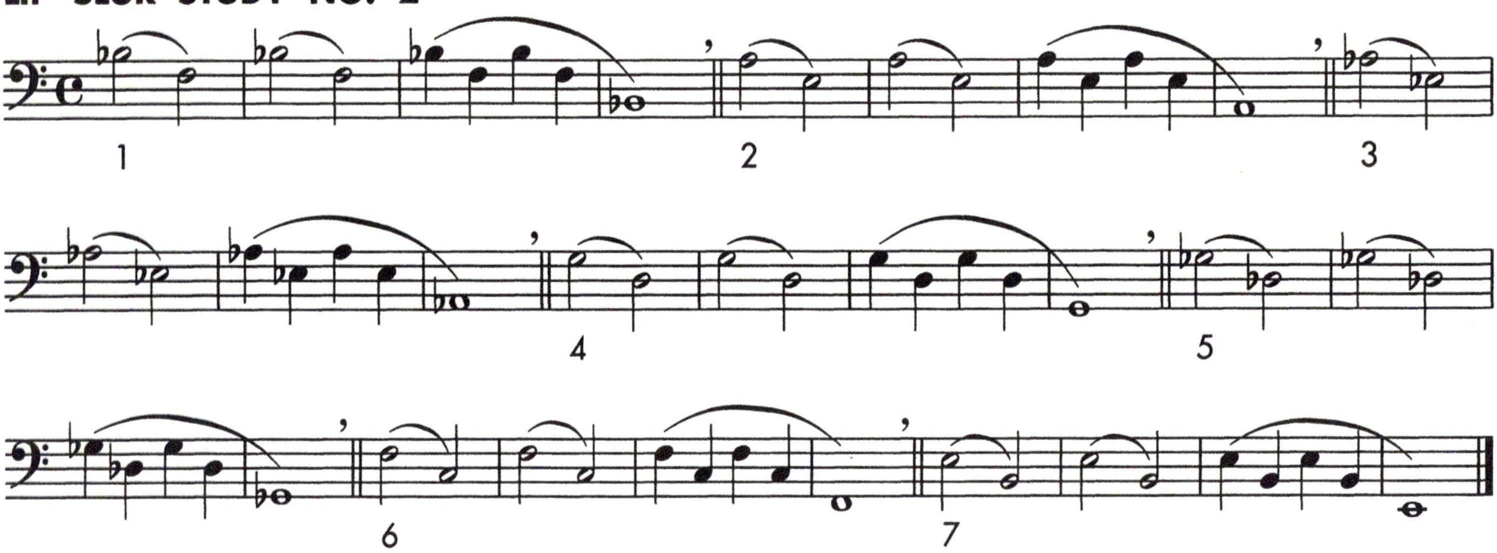

FLEXIBILITY FUN

BARITONE B.C. SPECIAL EXERCISES

LIP SLUR STUDY NO. 1

LIP SLUR STUDY NO. 2

FLEXIBILITY FUN

BARITONE T.C. SPECIAL EXERCISES

LIP SLUR STUDY NO. 1

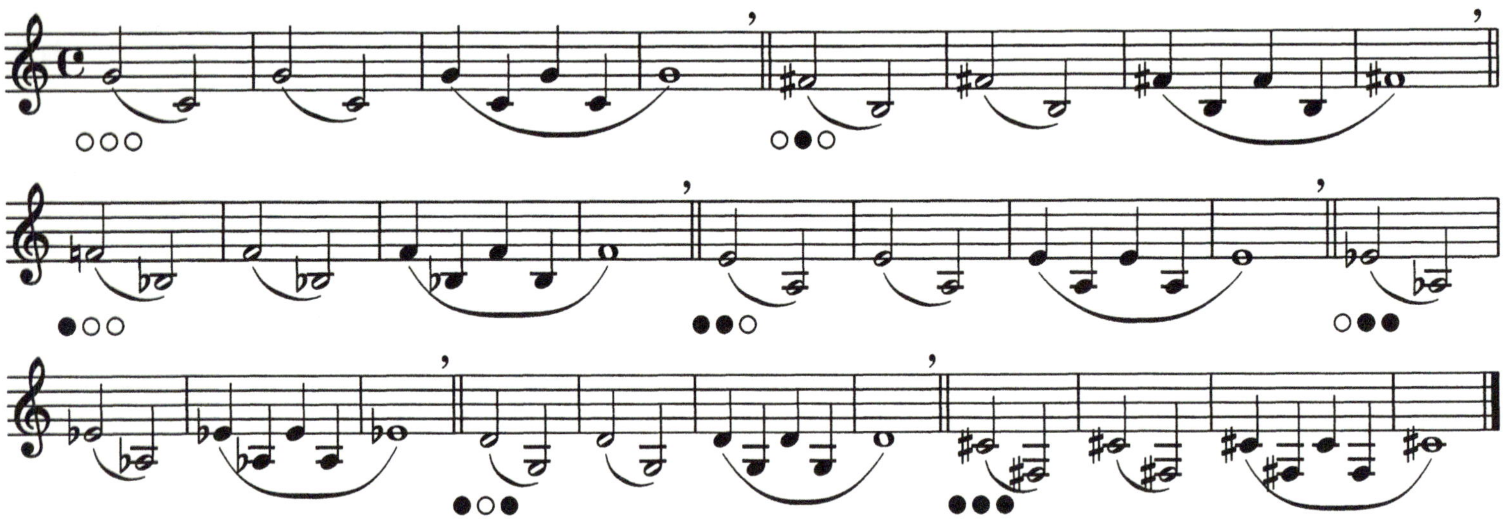

LIP SLUR STUDY NO. 2

FLEXIBILITY FUN

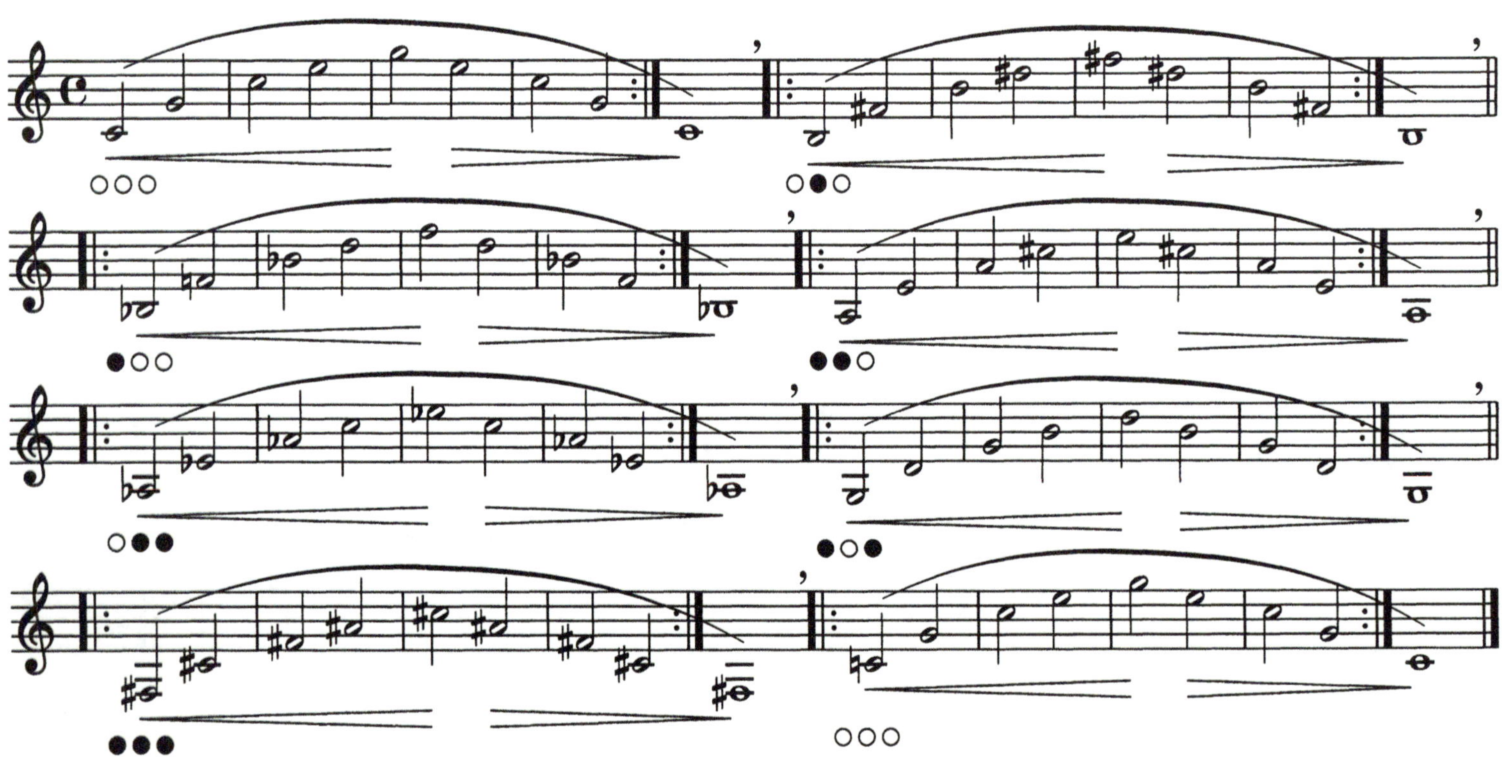

TUBA SPECIAL EXERCISES

LIP SLUR STUDY NO. 1

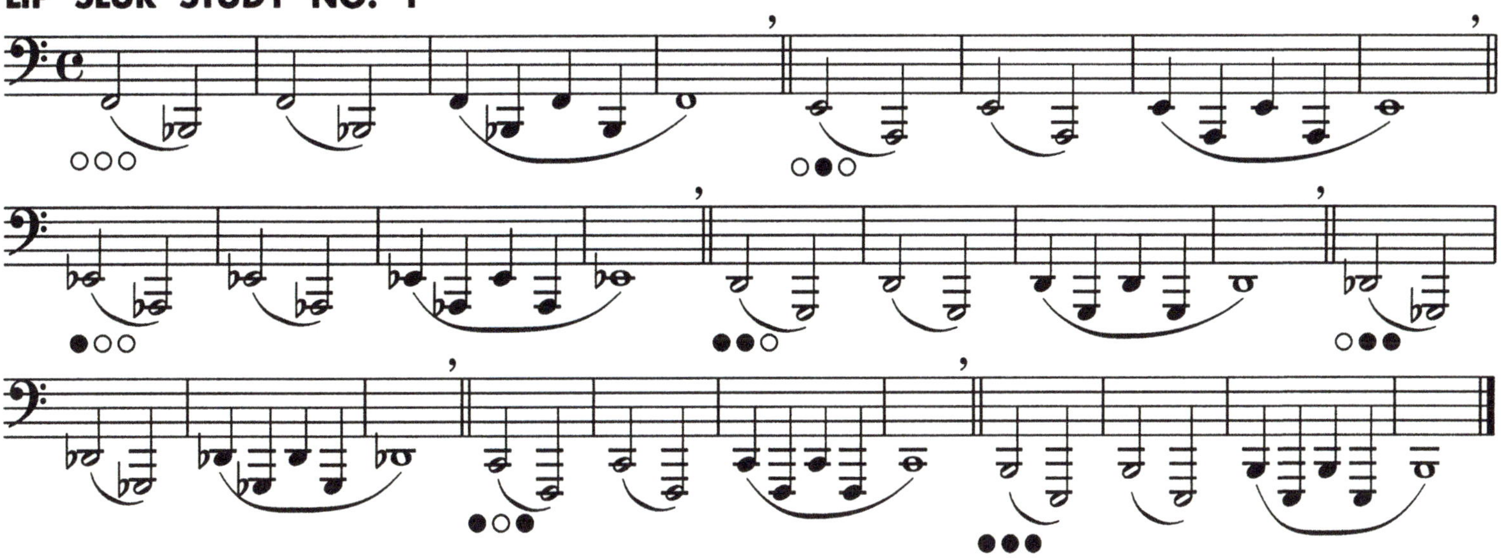

LIP SLUR STUDY NO. 2

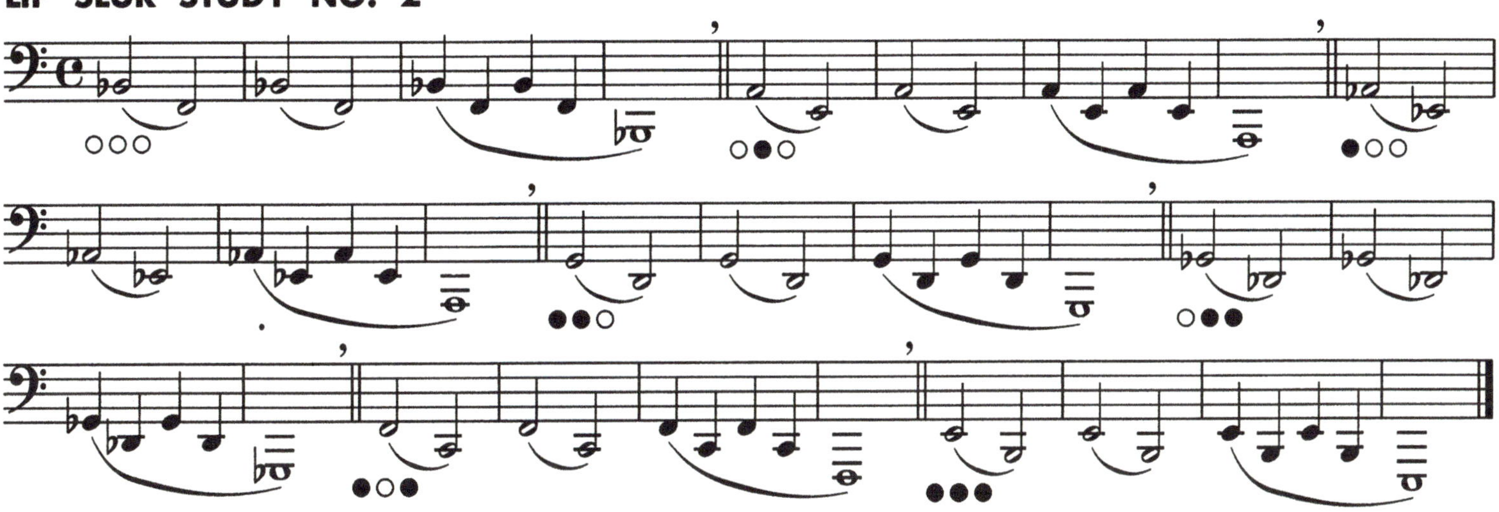

FLEXIBILITY FUN

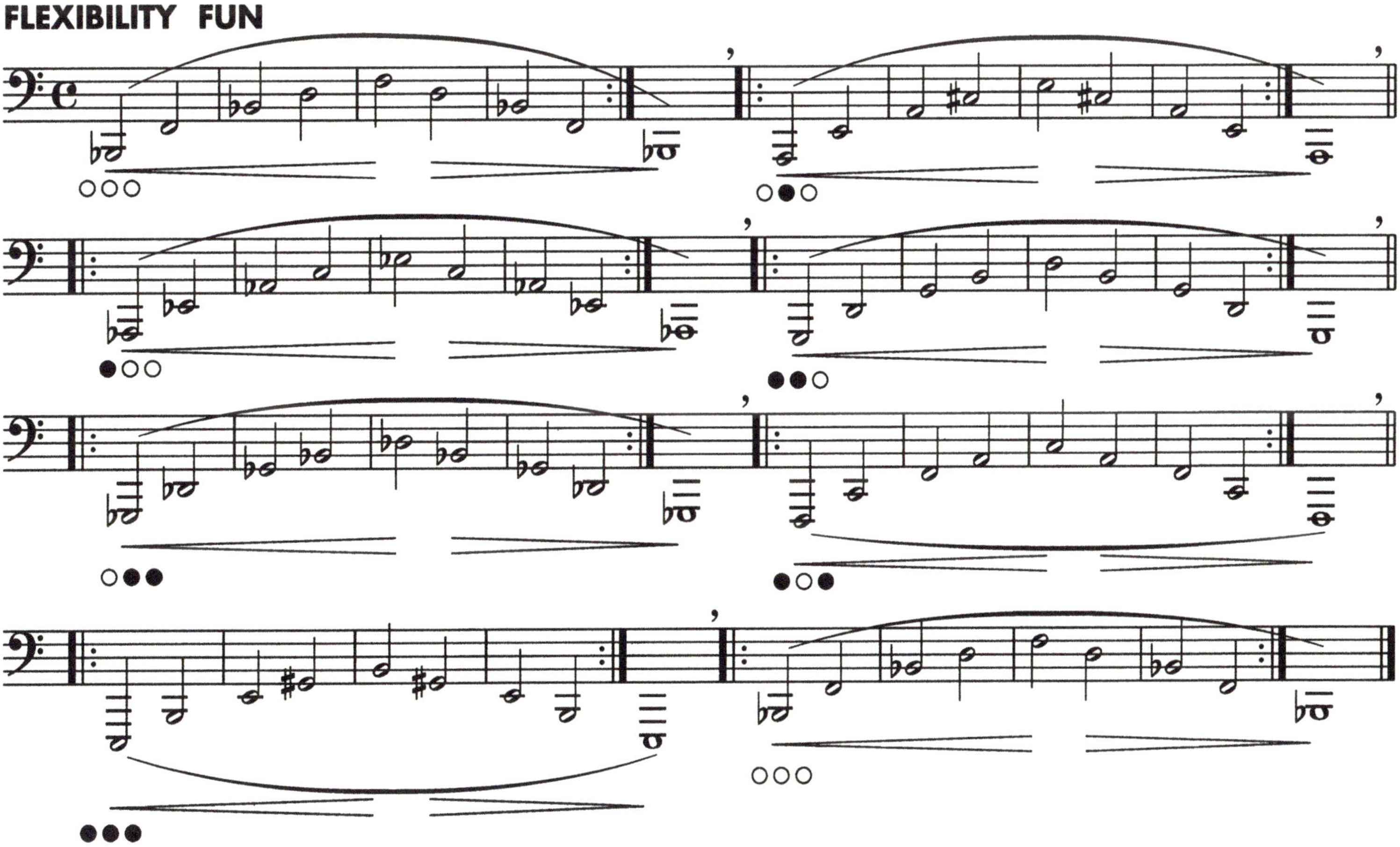

SPECIAL KEYBOARD PERCUSSION EXERCISES

A. INTERVALS

B. OCTAVES

C. ARPEGGIO ENCOUNTER #1

D. ARPEGGIO ENCOUNTER #2

FINGERING CHARTS

(Student Books Pages 46-47)

FLUTE FINGERING CHART

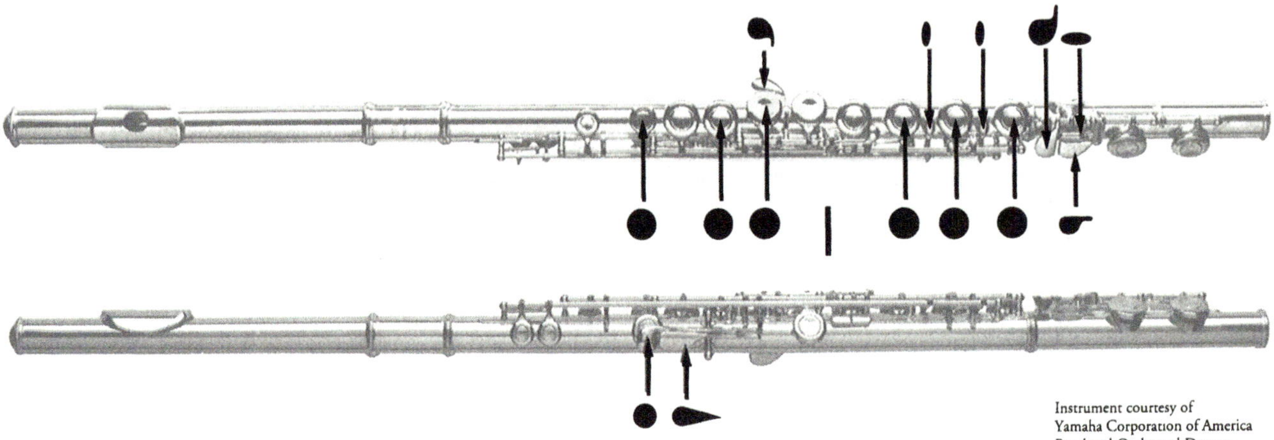

Instrument courtesy of
Yamaha Corporation of America
Band and Orchestral Division

○ = OPEN

● = PRESSED DOWN

The most common fingering appears on top when two fingerings are shown.

Take Special Care

Before putting your instrument back in its case after playing, do the following:

- Carefully shake the water out of the head joint.
- Put a clean soft cloth on the end of your cleaning rod.
- Draw the cleaning cloth and rod through the middle and foot joints.
- Carefully wipe the outside of each section to keep the finish clean.

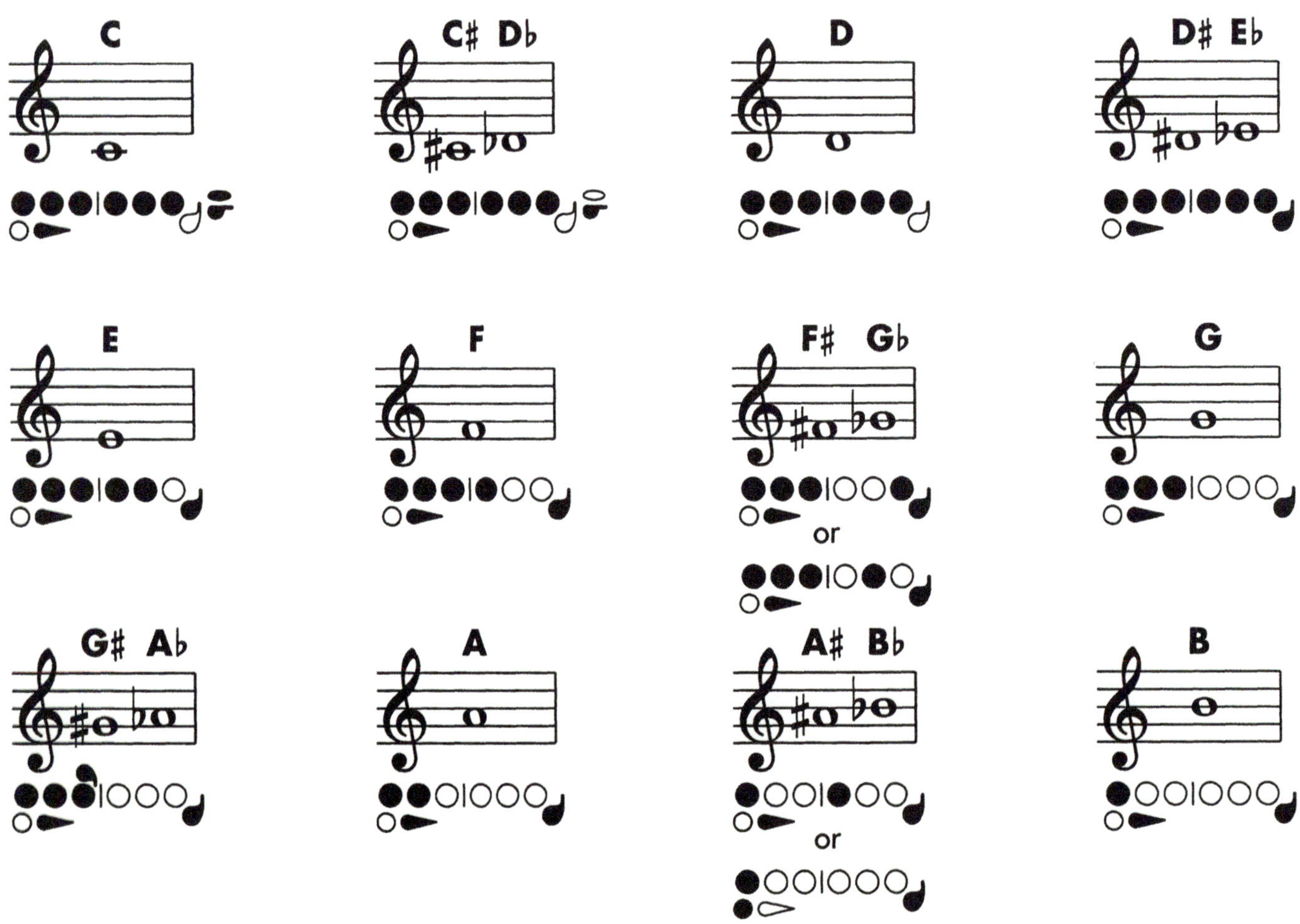

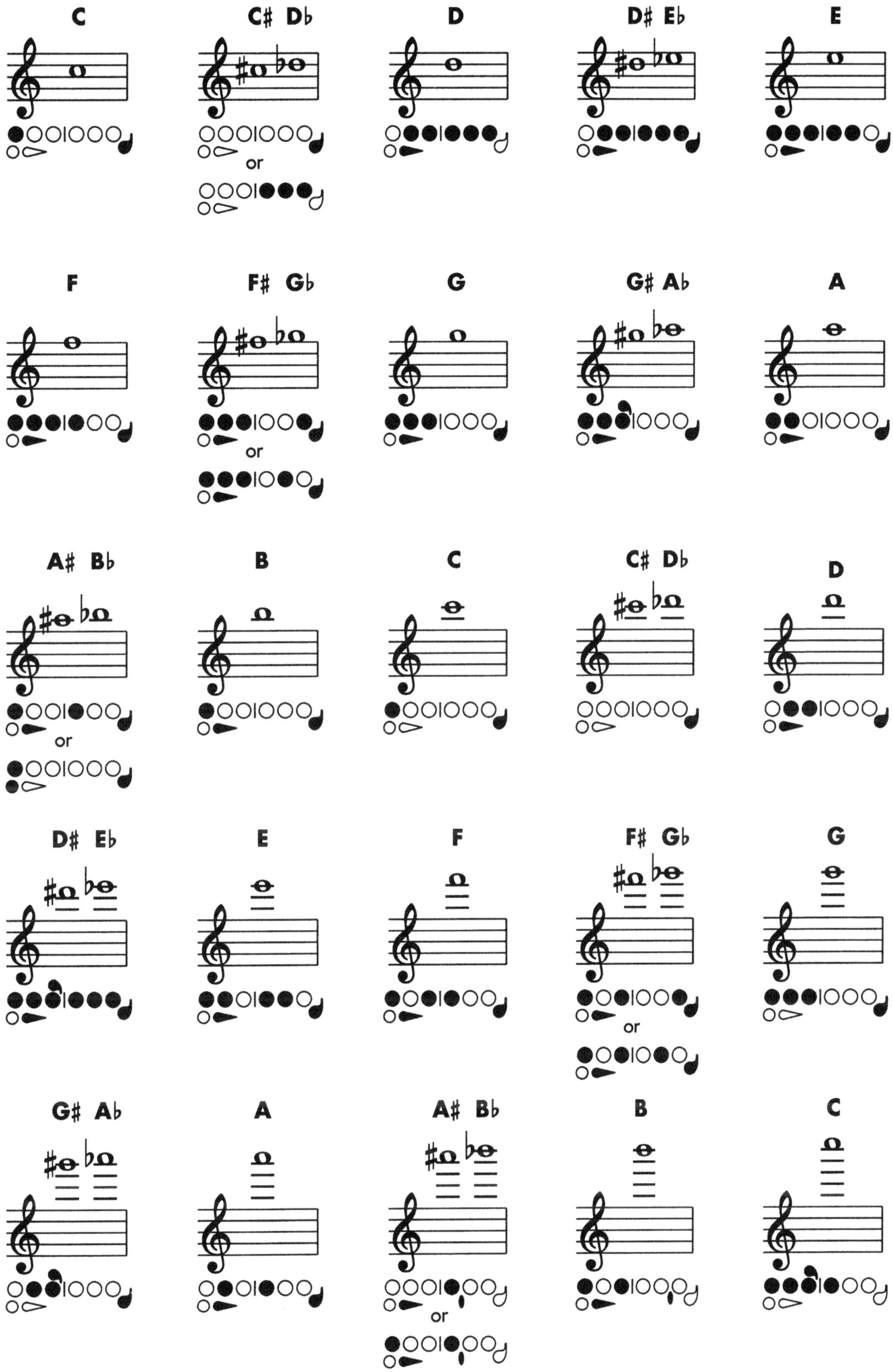
C
C♯ D♭
D
D♯ E♭
E
or
F
F♯ G♭
G
G♯ A♭
A
or
A♯ B♭
B
C
C♯ D♭
D
or
D♯ E♭
E
F
F♯ G♭
G
or
G♯ A♭
A
A♯ B♭
B
C
or

OBOE FINGERING CHART

Take Special Care

Before putting your instrument back in its case after playing, do the following:

- Carefully remove the reed and blow air through it. Return to reed case.
- Take the instrument apart in the reverse order of assembly. Swab out each section with a cloth or feather swab. If the cloth swab has a weight on one end, drop the weight through each section and pull through. Return each section to the correct spot in the case.

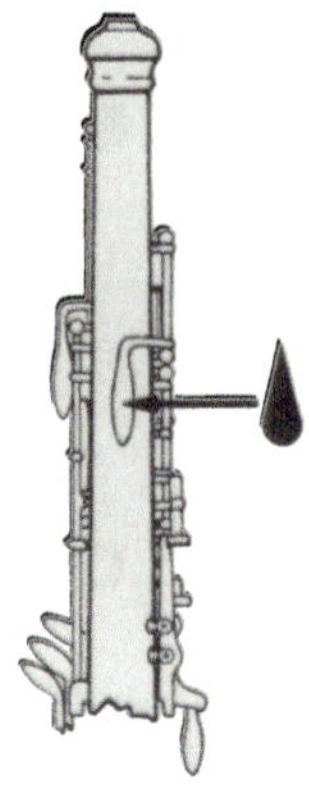

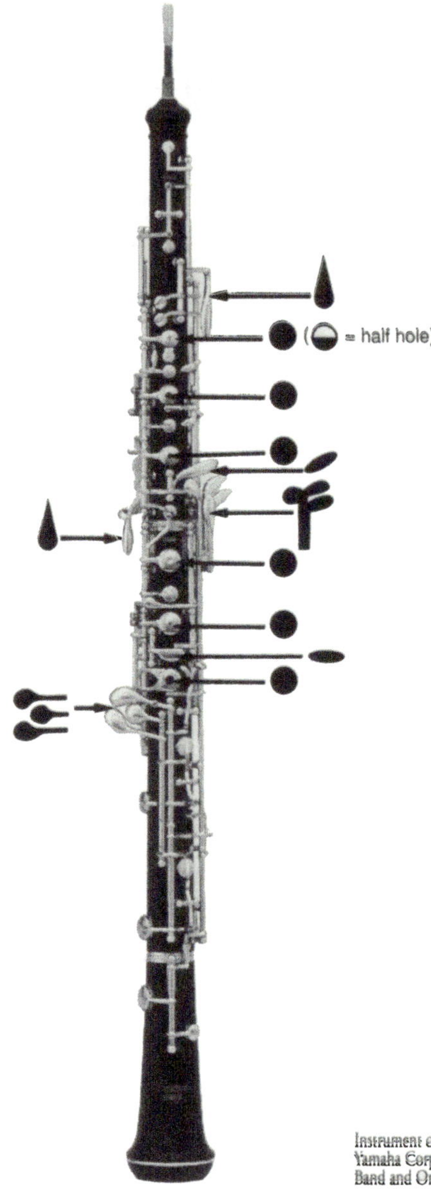

Instrument courtesy of Yamaha Corporation of America Band and Orchestral Division.

○ = OPEN

● = PRESSED DOWN

◒ = HALF HOLE COVERED

The most common fingering appears first when two fingerings are shown.

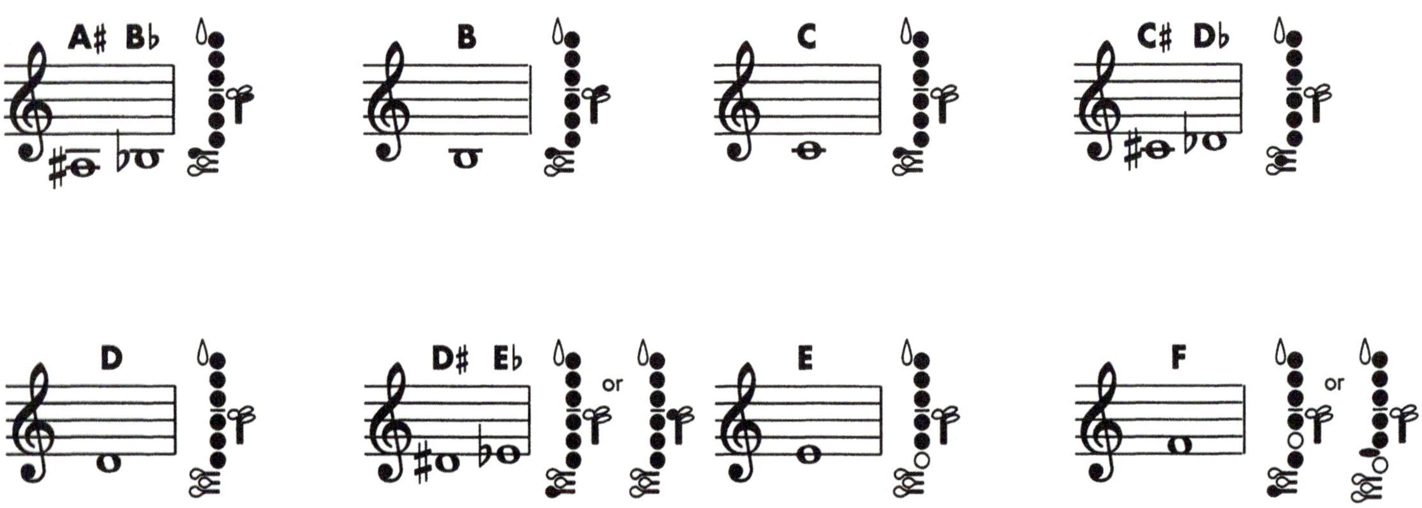

F♯ G♭
G
G♯ A♭
or
A
A♯ B♭
B
C
C♯ D♭
D
D♯ E♭
or
E
F
or
F♯ G♭
G
G♯ A♭
or
A
A♯ B♭
B
C
C♯ D♭
D
D♯ E♭
or
E
F

BASSOON FINGERING CHART

Take Special Care

Before putting your instrument back in its case after playing, do the following:

- Carefully remove the reed and blow air through it. Return to reed case.
- Remove the bocal and blow air through one end to remove excess moisture.
- Take the instrument apart in the reverse order of assembly. Swab out each section with a cloth swab or cleaning rod. Drop the weight of the swab through each section and pull it through. Return each section to the correct spot in the case.

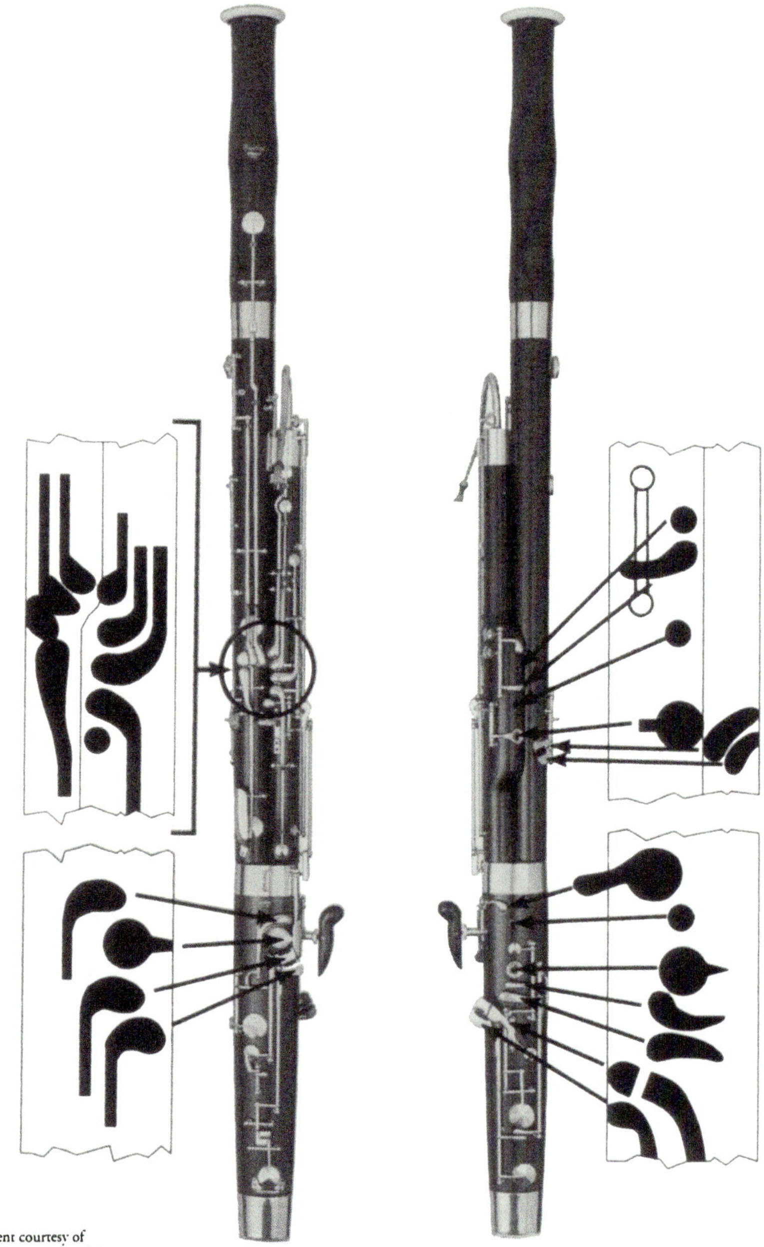

Instrument courtesy of Yamaha Corporation of America Band and Orchestral Division.

○ = OPEN

● = PRESSED DOWN

◒ = HALF HOLE COVERED

The most common fingering appears first when two fingerings are shown.

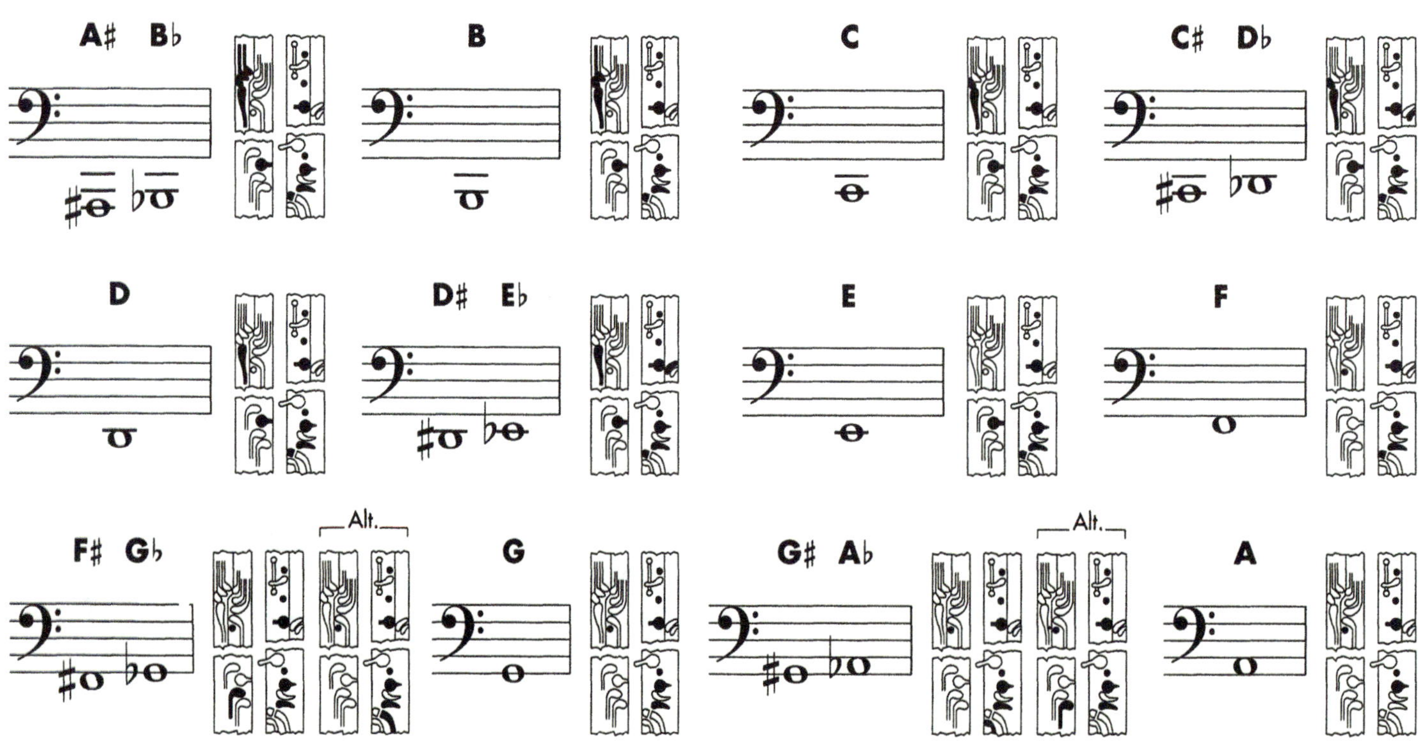

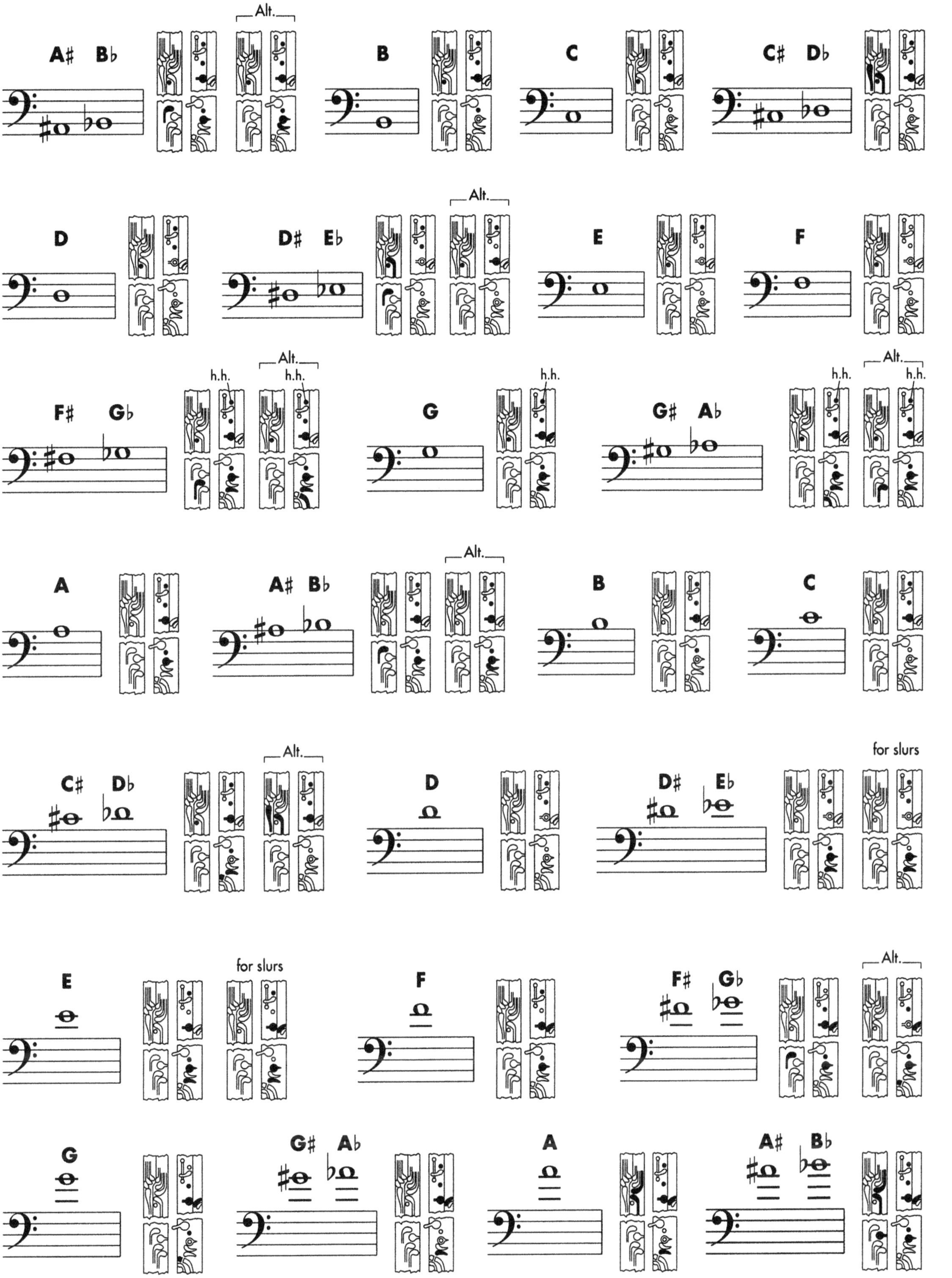
A♯ B♭
Alt.
B
C
C♯ D♭
D
D♯ E♭
Alt.
E
F
F♯ G♭
h.h.
Alt.
h.h.
G
h.h.
G♯ A♭
h.h.
Alt.
h.h.
A
A♯ B♭
Alt.
B
C
C♯ D♭
Alt.
D
D♯ E♭
for slurs
E
for slurs
F
F♯ G♭
Alt.
G
G♯ A♭
A
A♯ B♭

B♭ CLARINET FINGERING CHART

Take Special Care

Before putting your instrument back in its case after playing, do the following:

- Remove the reed and wipe off excess moisture. Return to reed case.
- Remove mouthpiece and wipe the inside with a clean cloth. Wash your mouthpiece once per week with warm tap water. Dry thoroughly.
- Hold the upper section with your left hand and the lower section with your right hand. Gently twist the sections apart. Shake out excess moisture.
- Drop the weight of the chamois or cotton swab and pull through each section. Carefully twist barrel and bell from each section, and place in the instrument case.

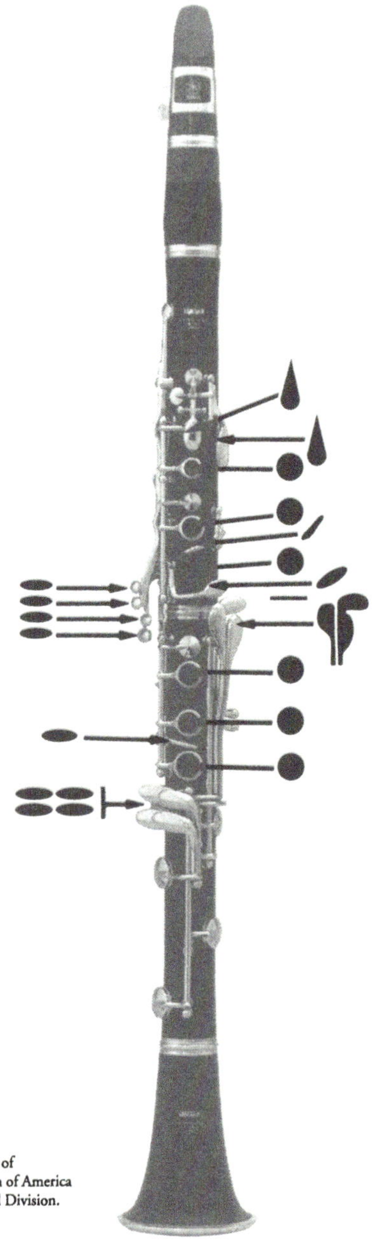

Instrument courtesy of Yamaha Corporation of America Band and Orchestral Division.

○ = OPEN

● = PRESSED DOWN

The most common fingering appears first when two fingerings are shown.

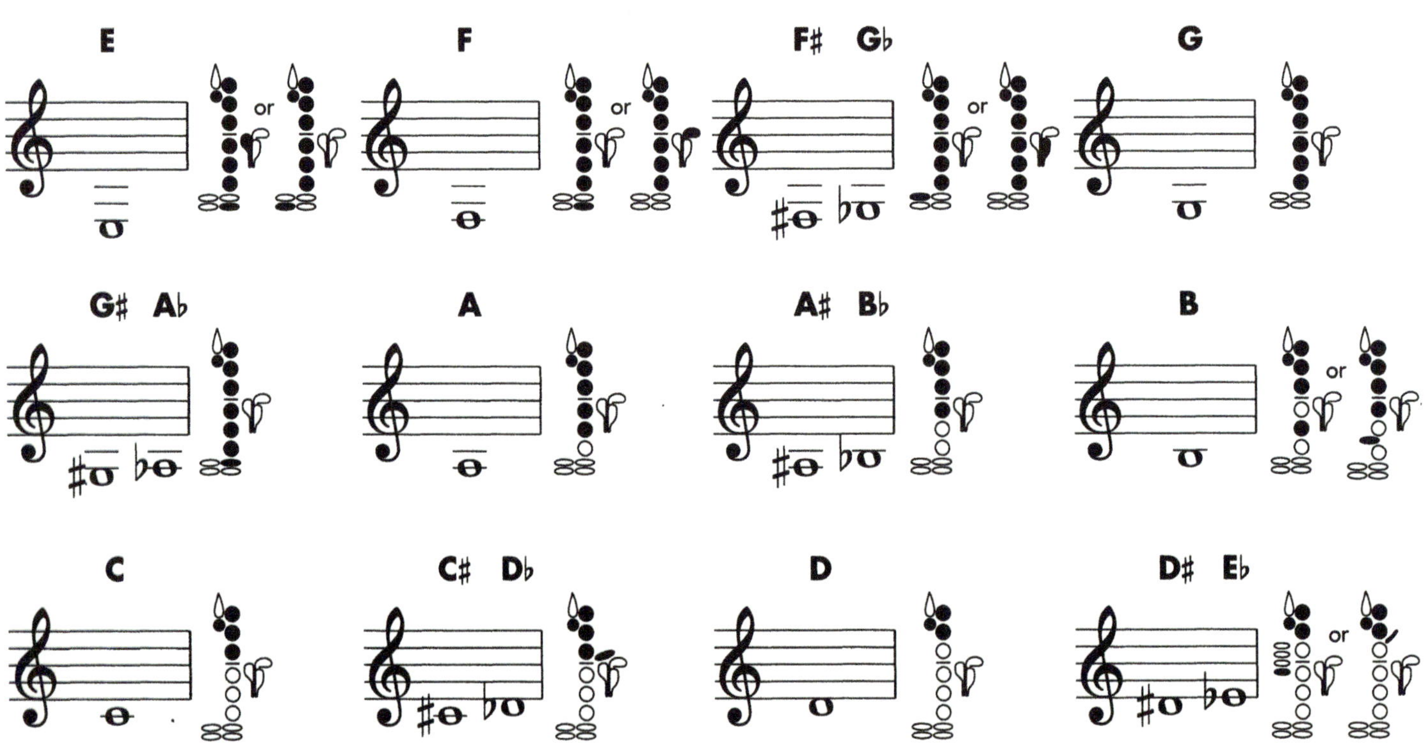

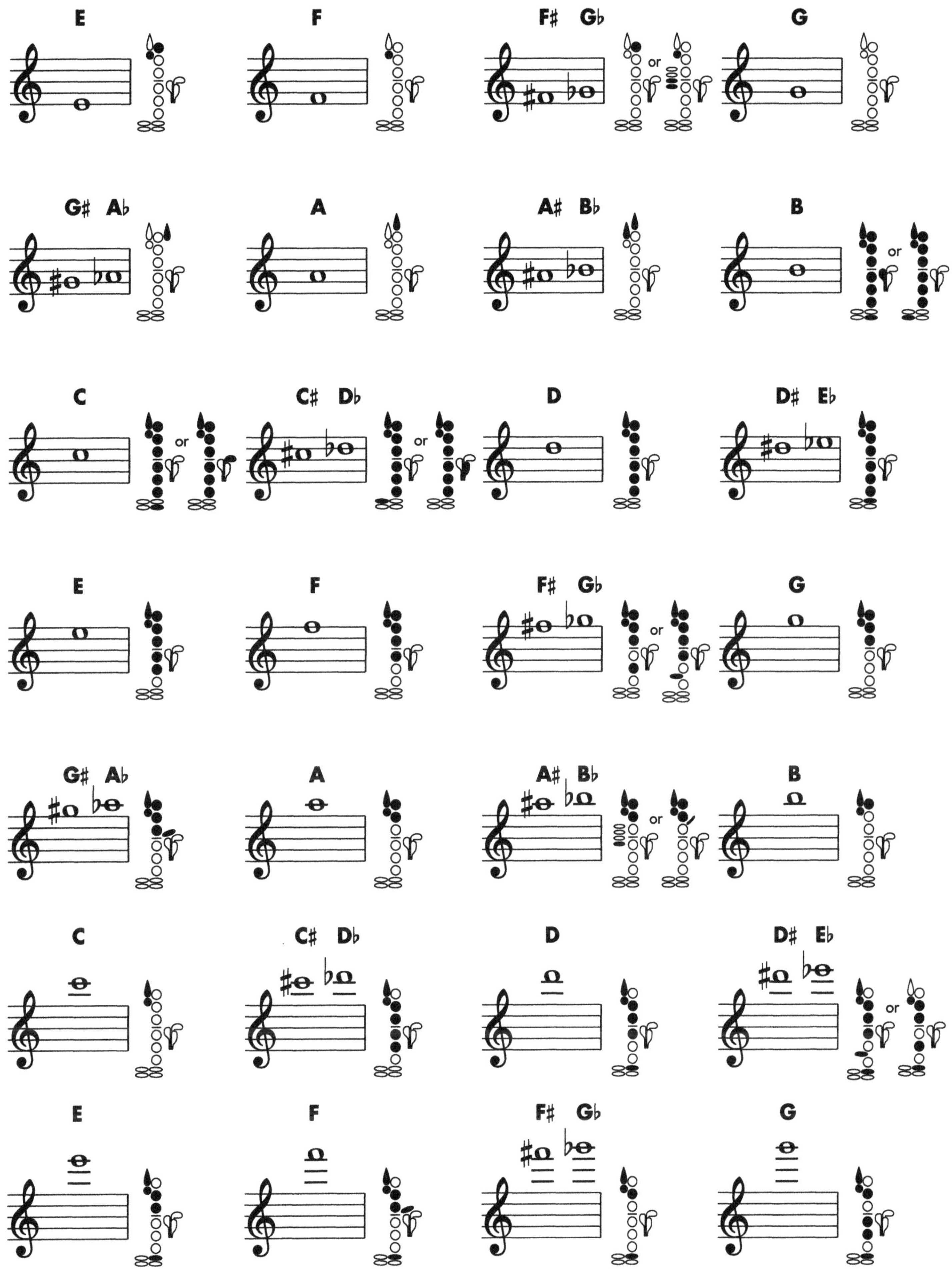
E
F
F♯ G♭
or
G
G♯ A♭
A
A♯ B♭
B
or
C
or
C♯ D♭
or
D
D♯ E♭
E
F
F♯ G♭
or
G
G♯ A♭
A
A♯ B♭
or
B
C
C♯ D♭
D
D♯ E♭
or
E
F
F♯ G♭
G

E♭ ALTO CLARINET FINGERING CHART

Take Special Care

Before putting your instrument back in its case after playing, do the following:

- Remove the reed and wipe off excess moisture. Return to reed case.
- Remove mouthpiece and wipe the inside with a clean cloth. Wash your mouthpiece once per week with warm tap water. Dry thoroughly.
- Remove the neck and bell, and shake out excess moisture. Hold the upper section with your left hand and the lower section with your right hand. Gently twist the sections apart. Shake out excess moisture.
- Drop the weight of the chamois cotton swab and pull through each section. Return the instrument to its case.

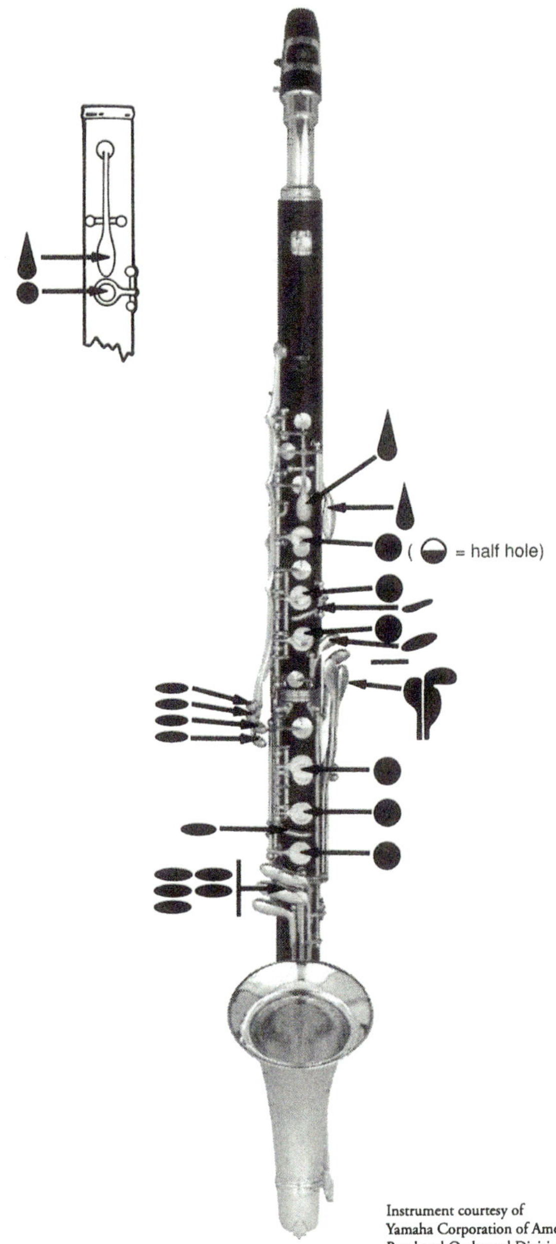

Instrument courtesy of Yamaha Corporation of America Band and Orchestral Division.

○ = OPEN

● = PRESSED DOWN

The most common fingering appears first when two fingerings are shown.

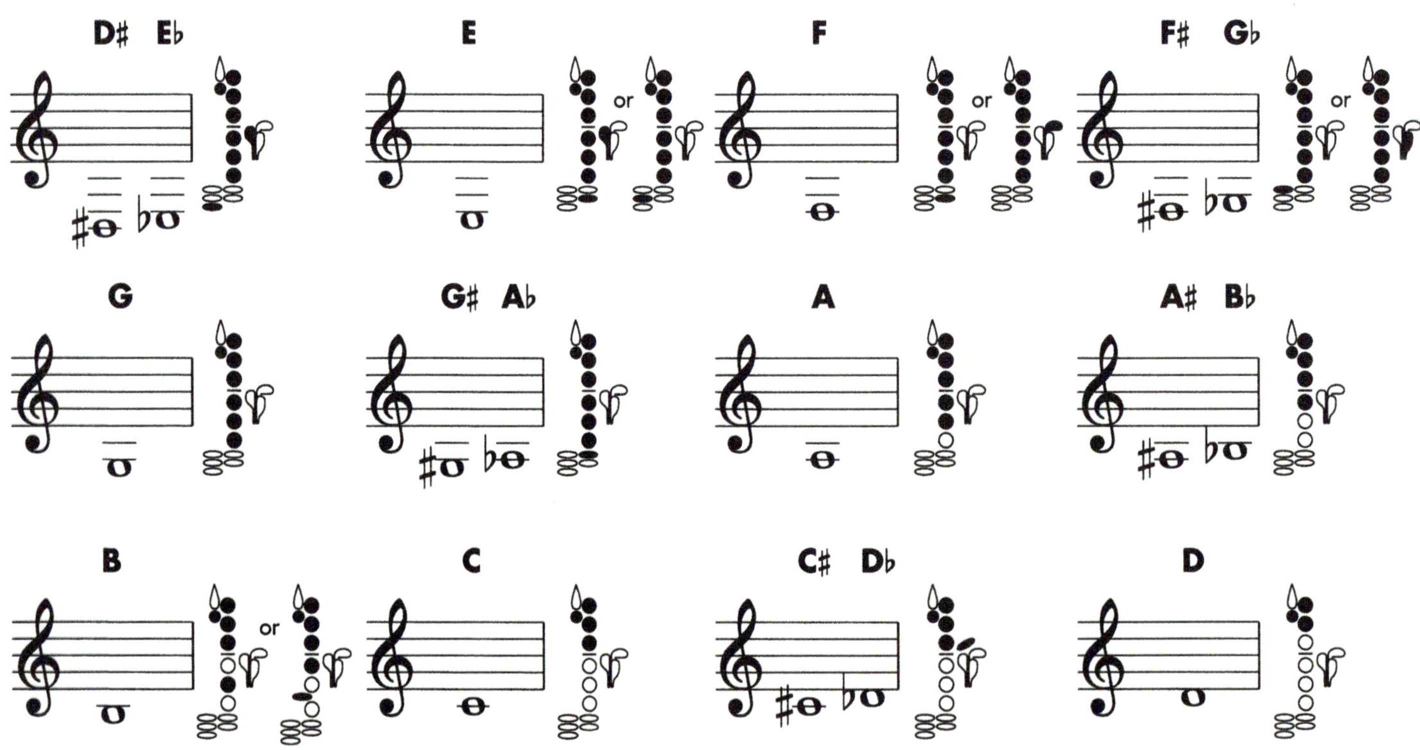

D♯ E♭
or
E
F
F♯ G♭
or
G
G♯ A♭
A
A♯ B♭
B
or
C
or
C♯ D♭
or
D
D♯ E♭
E
F
F♯ G♭
or
G
G♯ A♭
A
A♯ B♭
or
B
C
C♯ D♭
D
D♯ E♭
or
E
F
F♯ G♭

B♭ BASS CLARINET FINGERING CHART

Take Special Care

Before putting your instrument back in its case after playing, do the following:

- Remove the reed and wipe off excess moisture. Return to reed case.
- Remove mouthpiece and wipe the inside with a clean cloth. Wash your mouthpiece once per week with warm tap water. Dry thoroughly.
- Remove the neck and bell, and shake out excess moisture. Hold the upper section with your left hand and the lower section with your right hand. Gently twist the sections apart. Shake out excess moisture.
- Drop the weight of the chamois or cotton swab and pull through each section. Return the instrument to its case.

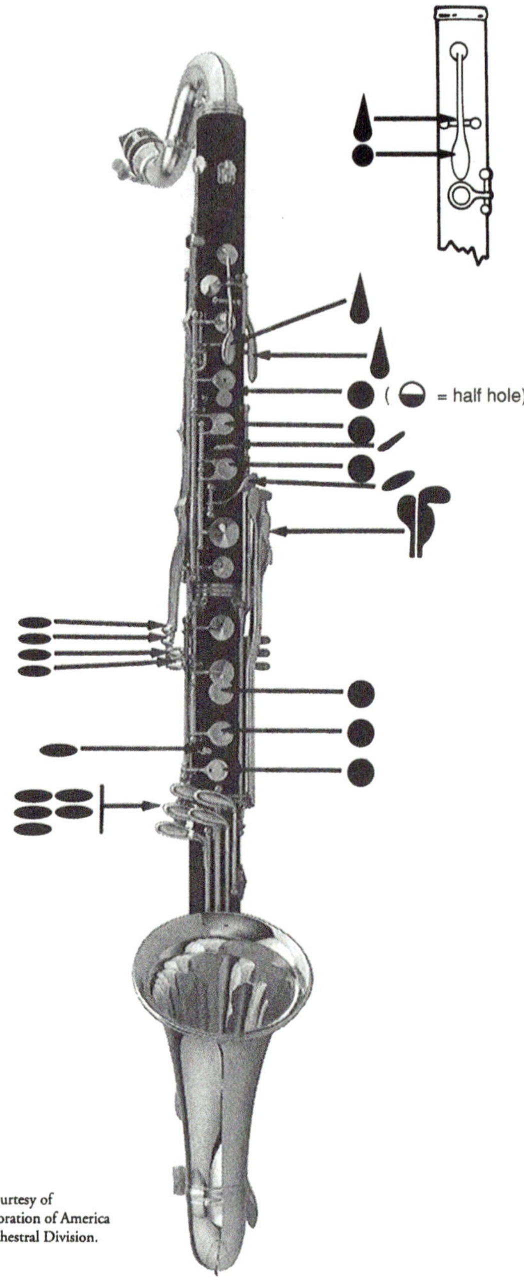

○ = OPEN

● = PRESSED DOWN

The most common fingering appears first when two fingerings are shown.

Instrument courtesy of
Yamaha Corporation of America
Band and Orchestral Division.

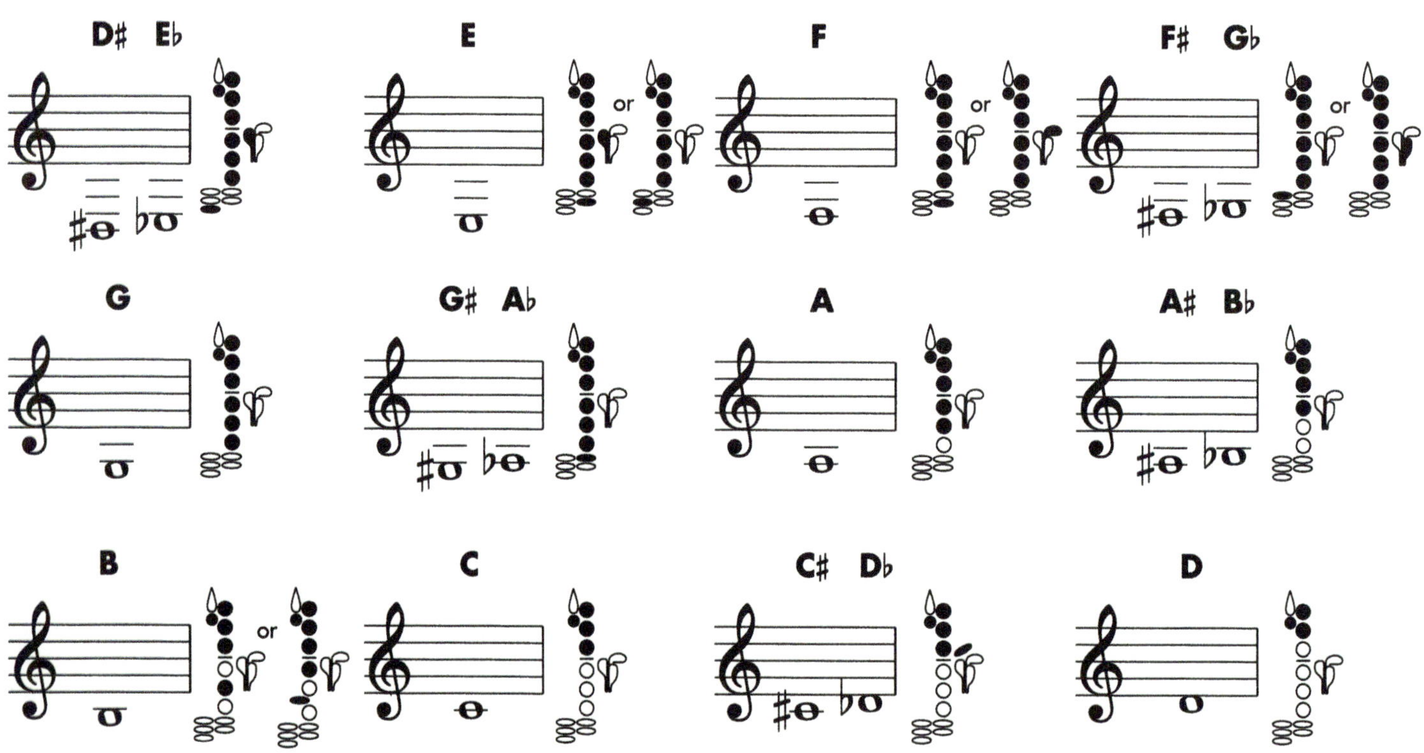

D♯ E♭
or
E
F
F♯ G♭
or
G
G♯ A♭
A
A♯ B♭
B
or
C
or
C♯ D♭
or
D
D♯ E♭
E
F
F♯ G♭
or
G
G♯ A♭
A
A♯ B♭
or
B
C
C♯ D♭
D
D♯ E♭
or
E
F
F♯ G♭

E♭ ALTO SAXOPHONE FINGERING CHART

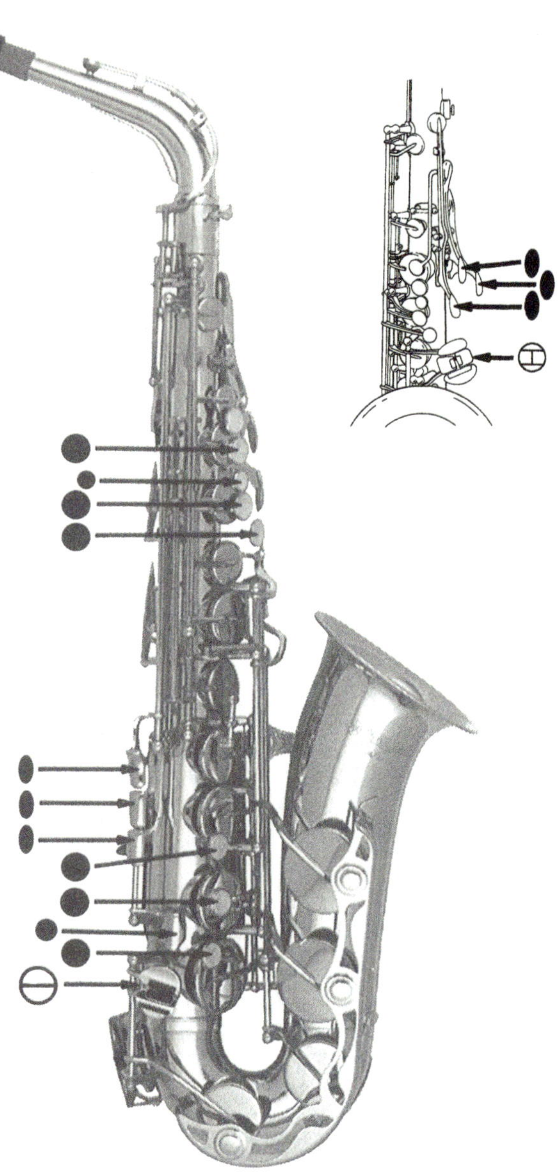

Take Special Care

Before putting your instrument back in its case after playing, do the following:

- Remove the reed and wipe off excess moisture. Return to reed case.
- Remove mouthpiece and wipe the inside with a clean cloth. Wash your mouthpiece once per week with warm tap water. Dry thoroughly.
- Remove the neck and shake out excess moisture. Dry with neck cleaner.
- Drop the weight of the chamois or cotton swab into the bell. Pull the swab through the body several times. Return the instrument to its case.

○ = OPEN

● = PRESSED DOWN

The most common fingering appears first when two fingerings are shown.

Instrument courtesy of Yamaha Corporation of America Band and Orchestral Division.

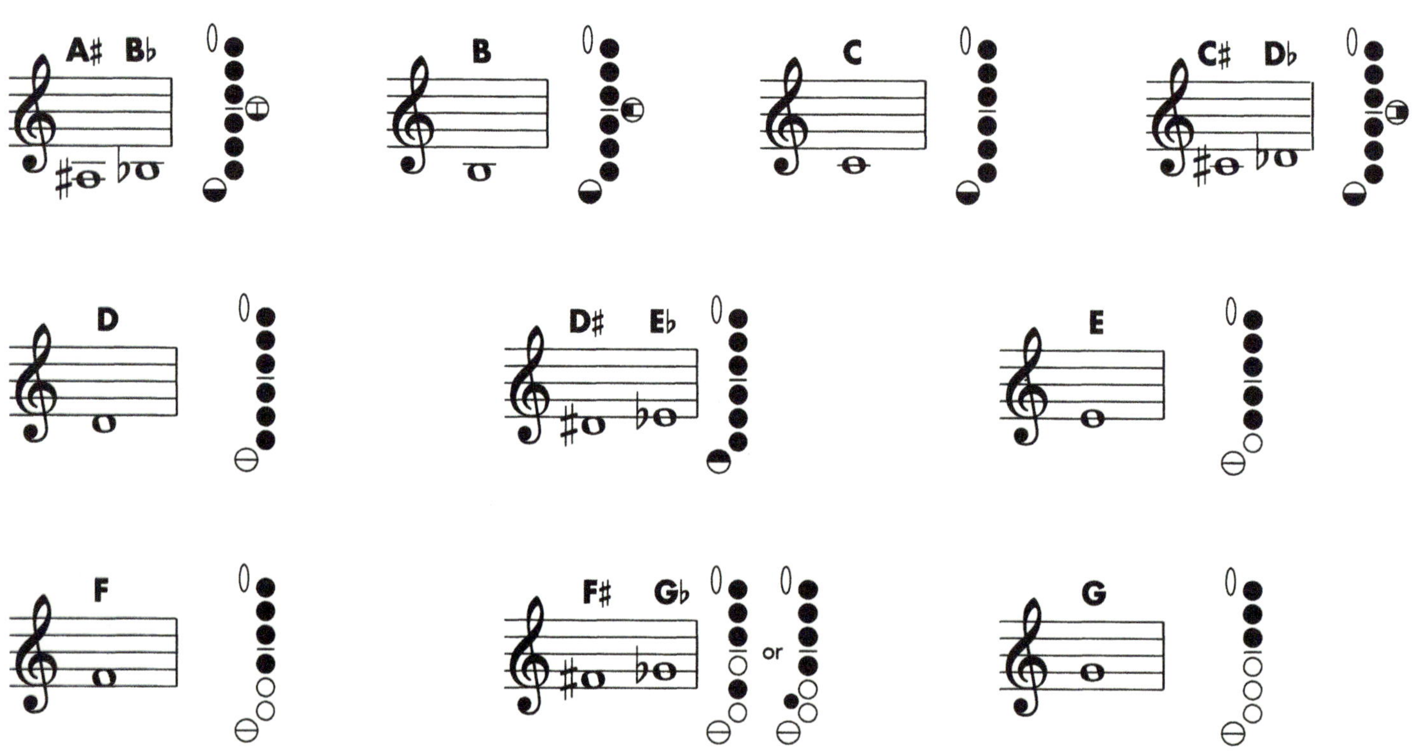

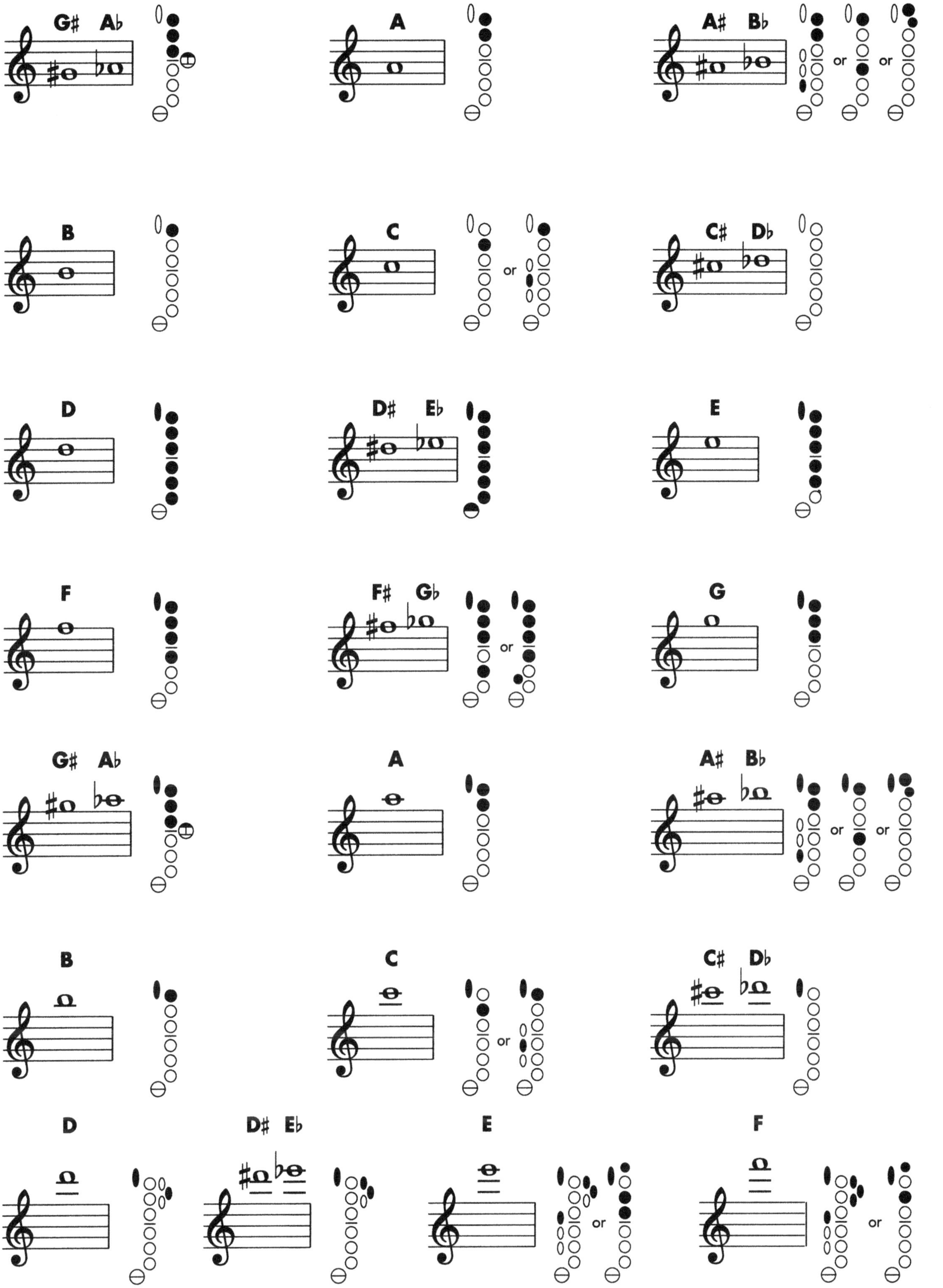
G♯ A♭
A
A♯ B♭
or
or
B
C
or
C♯ D♭
D
D♯ E♭
E
F
F♯ G♭
or
G
G♯ A♭
A
A♯ B♭
or
or
B
C
or
C♯ D♭
D
D♯ E♭
E
or
F
or

B♭ TENOR SAXOPHONE FINGERING CHART

Take Special Care

Before putting your instrument back in its case after playing, do the following:

- Remove the reed and wipe off excess moisture. Return to reed case.
- Remove mouthpiece and wipe the inside with a clean cloth. Wash your mouthpiece once per week with warm tap water. Dry thoroughly.
- Remove the neck and shake out excess moisture. Dry with neck cleaner.
- Drop the weight of the chamois or cotton swab into the bell. Pull the swab through the body several times. Return the instrument to its case.

Instrument courtesy of
Yamaha Corporation of America
Band and Orchestral Division.

○ = OPEN

● = PRESSED DOWN

The most common fingering appears first when two fingerings are shown.

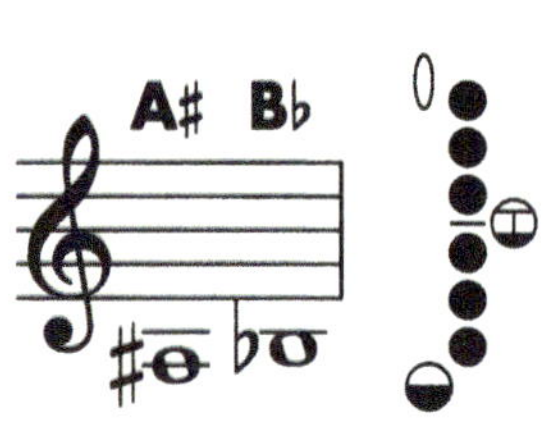

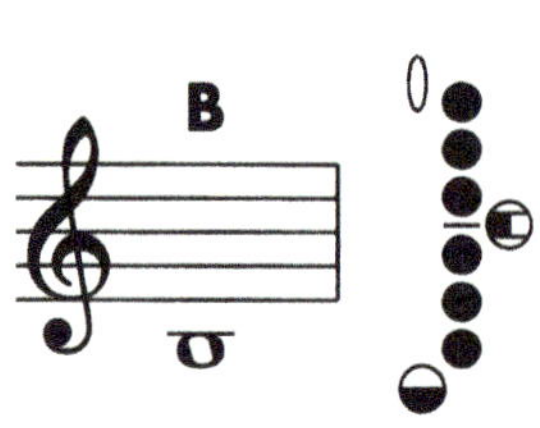

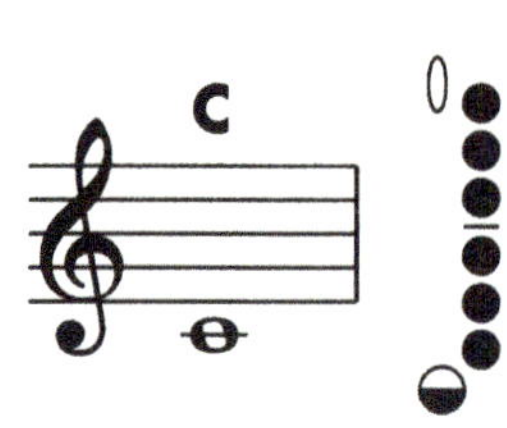

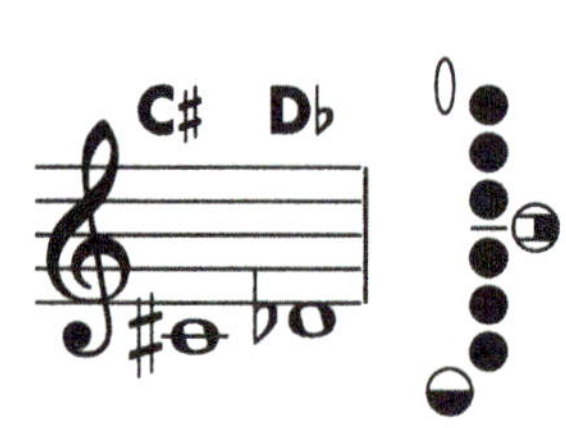

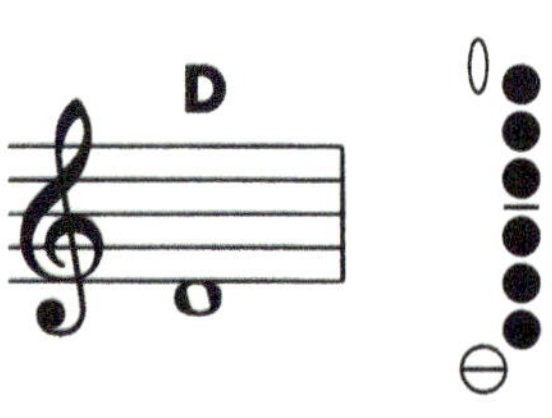

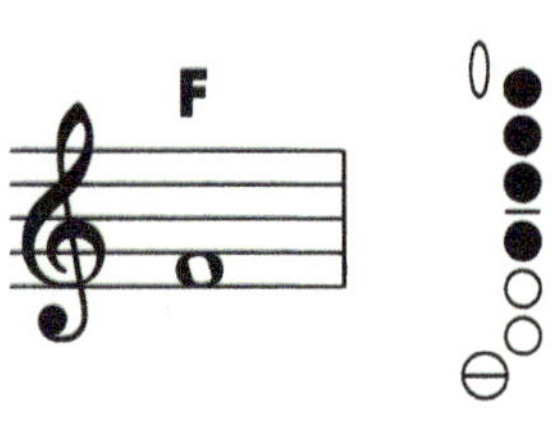

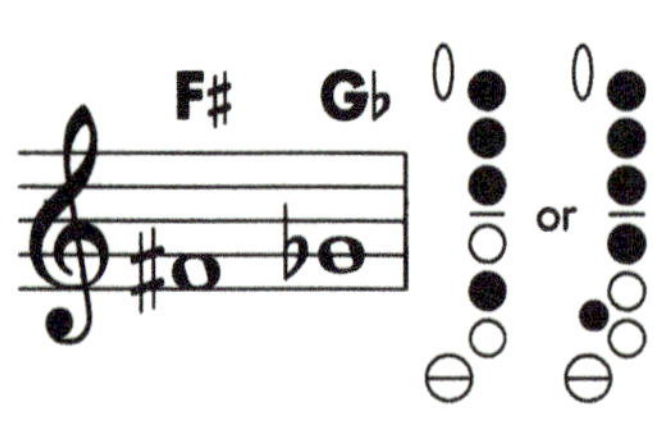

G♯ A♭
A
A♯ B♭
or
or
B
C
or
C♯ D♭
D
D♯ E♭
E
F
F♯ G♭
or
G
G♯ A♭
A
A♯ B♭
or
or
B
C
or
C♯ D♭
D
D♯ E♭
E
or
F
or

E♭ BARITONE SAXOPHONE FINGERING CHART

Take Special Care

Before putting your instrument back in its case after playing, do the following:

- Remove the reed and wipe off excess moisture. Return to reed case.
- Remove mouthpiece and wipe the inside with a clean cloth. Wash your mouthpiece once per week with warm tap water. Dry thoroughly.
- Remove the neck and shake out excess moisture. Dry with neck cleaner.
- Drop the weight of the chamois or cotton swab into the bell. Pull the swab through the body several times. Return the instrument to its case.

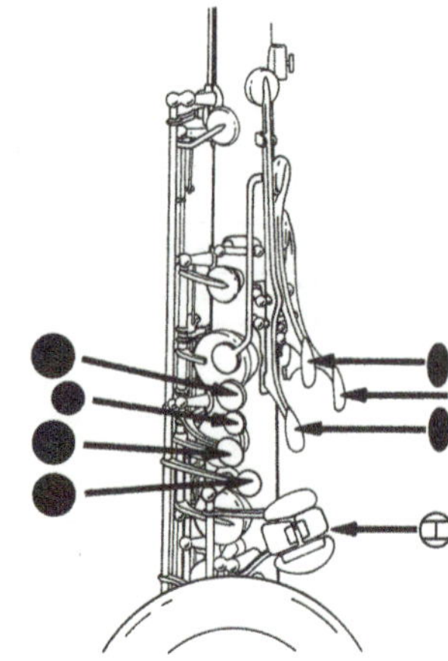

Instrument courtesy of Yamaha Corporation of America Band and Orchestral Division.

 = OPEN

 = PRESSED DOWN

The most common fingering appears first when two fingerings are shown.

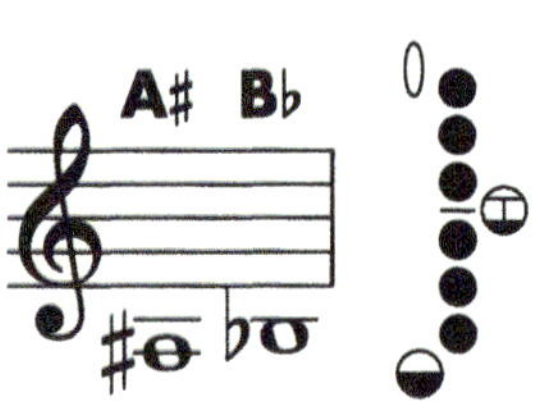

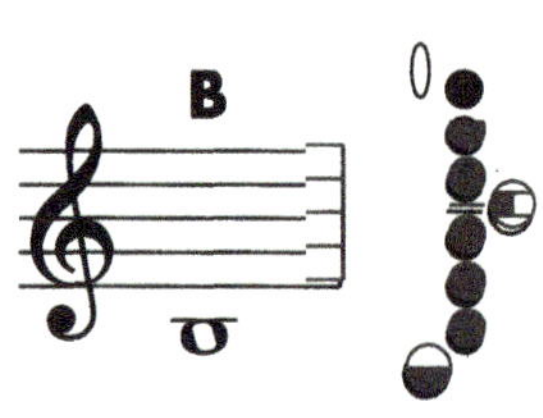

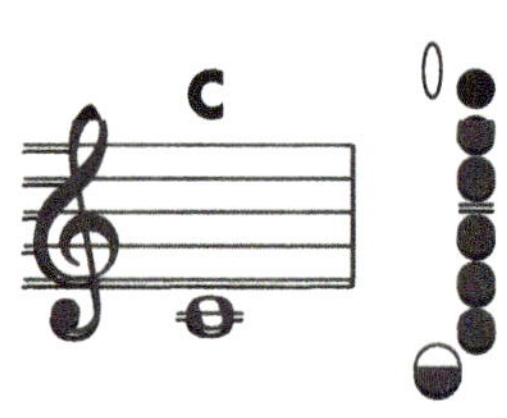

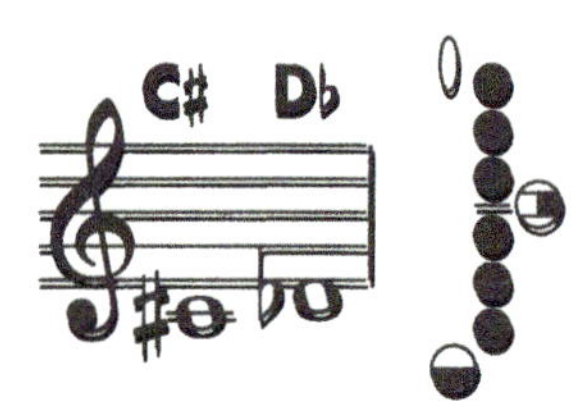

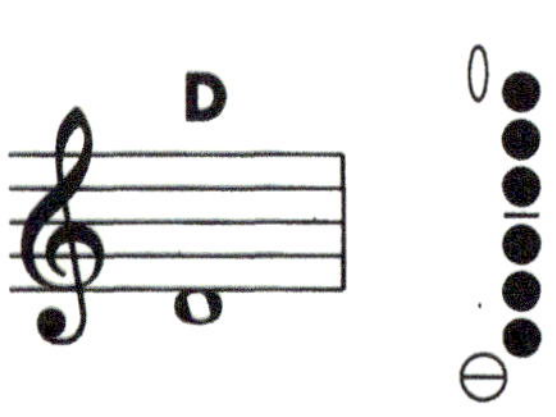

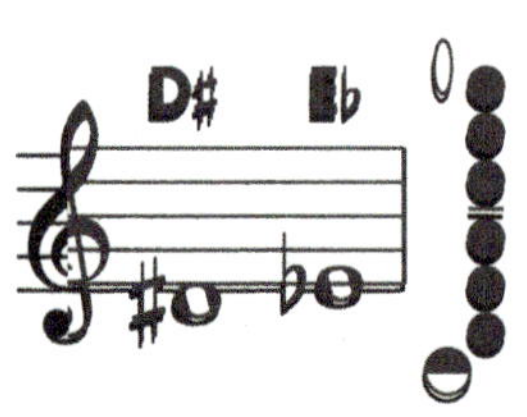

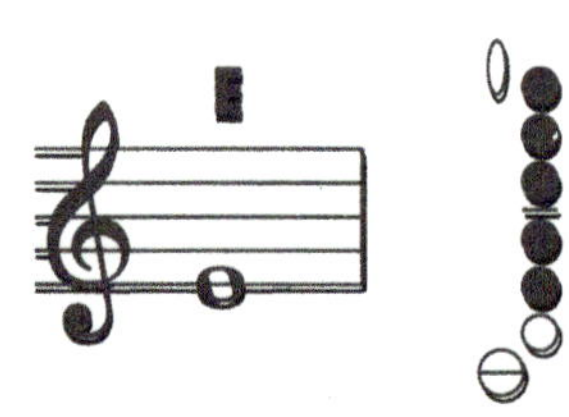

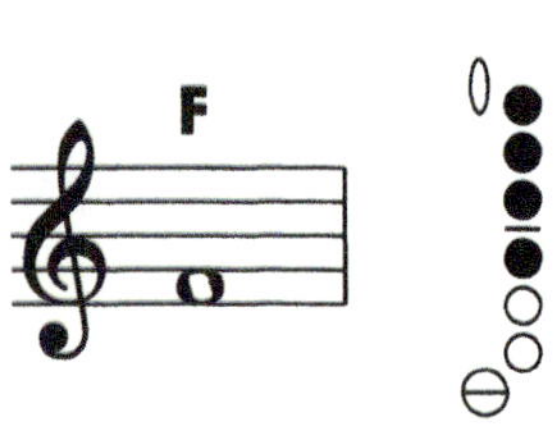

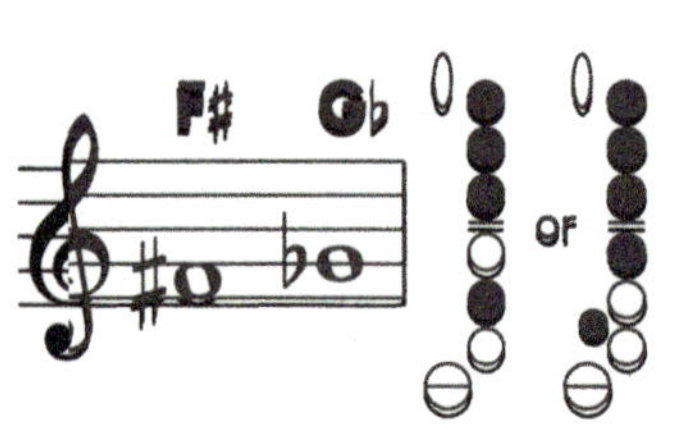

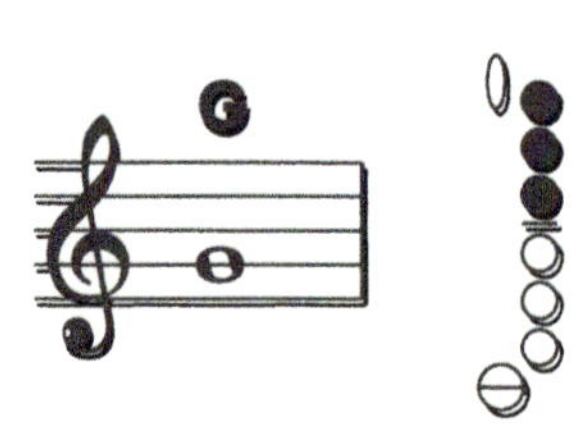

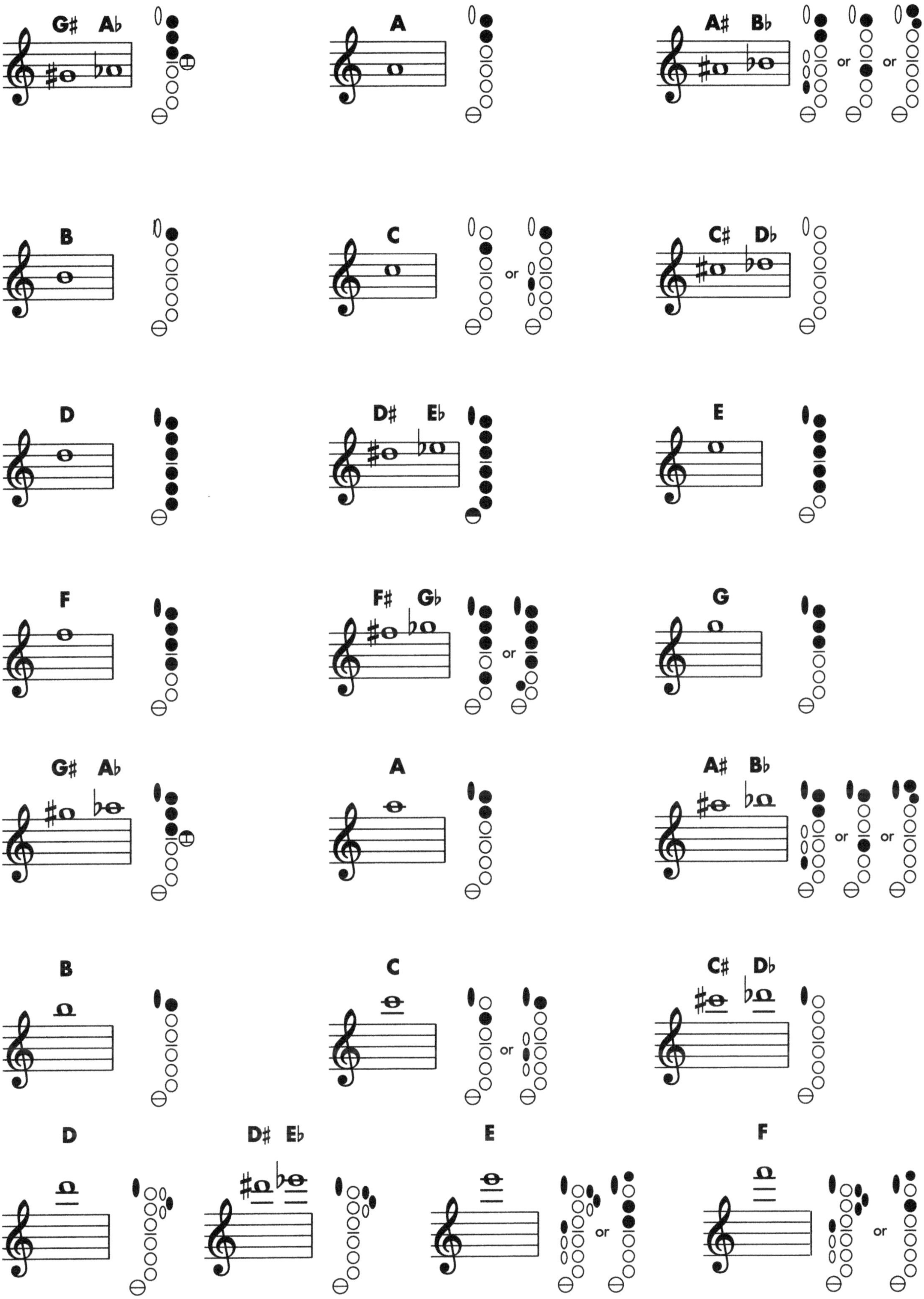
G♯ A♭
A
A♯ B♭
or
or
B
C
or
C♯ D♭
D
D♯ E♭
E
F
F♯ G♭
or
G
G♯ A♭
A
A♯ B♭
or
or
B
C
or
C♯ D♭
D
D♯ E♭
E
or
F
or

B♭ TRUMPET/B♭ CORNET FINGERING CHART

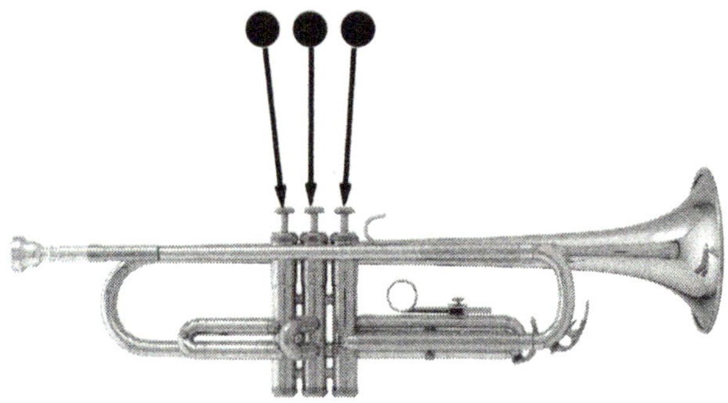

B♭ Trumpet

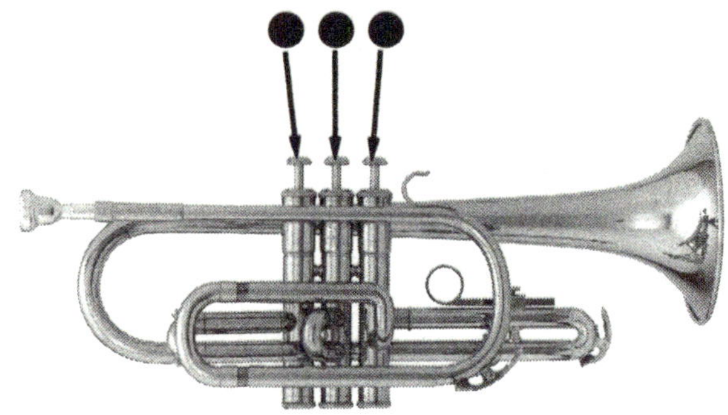

B♭ Cornet

○ = UP ● = PRESSED DOWN

Instruments courtesy of
Yamaha Corporation of America
Band and Orchestral Division.

Take Special Care

Before putting your instrument back in its case after playing, do the following:

- Use the water key to empty water from the instrument. Blow air through it..
- Remove the mouthpiece. Wash your mouthpiece with warm tap water once per week. Dry thoroughly.
- Wipe the instrument off with a clean soft cloth. Return the instrument to its case.

Trumpet valves occasionally need oiling. To oil your trumpet valves, simply:

- Unscrew the valve at the top of the casing.
- Lift the valve half-way out of the casing.
- Apply a few drops of oil to the exposed valve.
- Carefully return the valve to the casing. When properly inserted, the top of the valve should screw back into place.
- Be sure to grease the slides regularly. Your director will recommend valve oil and slide grease, and will help you apply them when necessary.

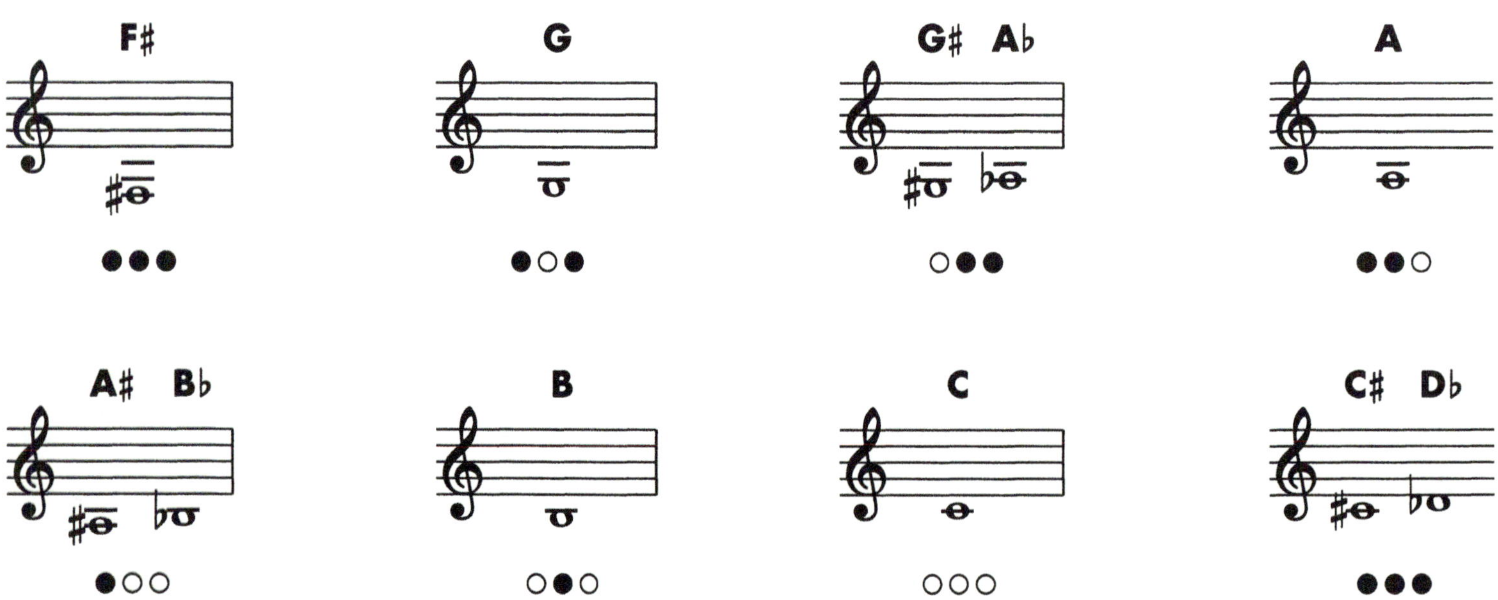

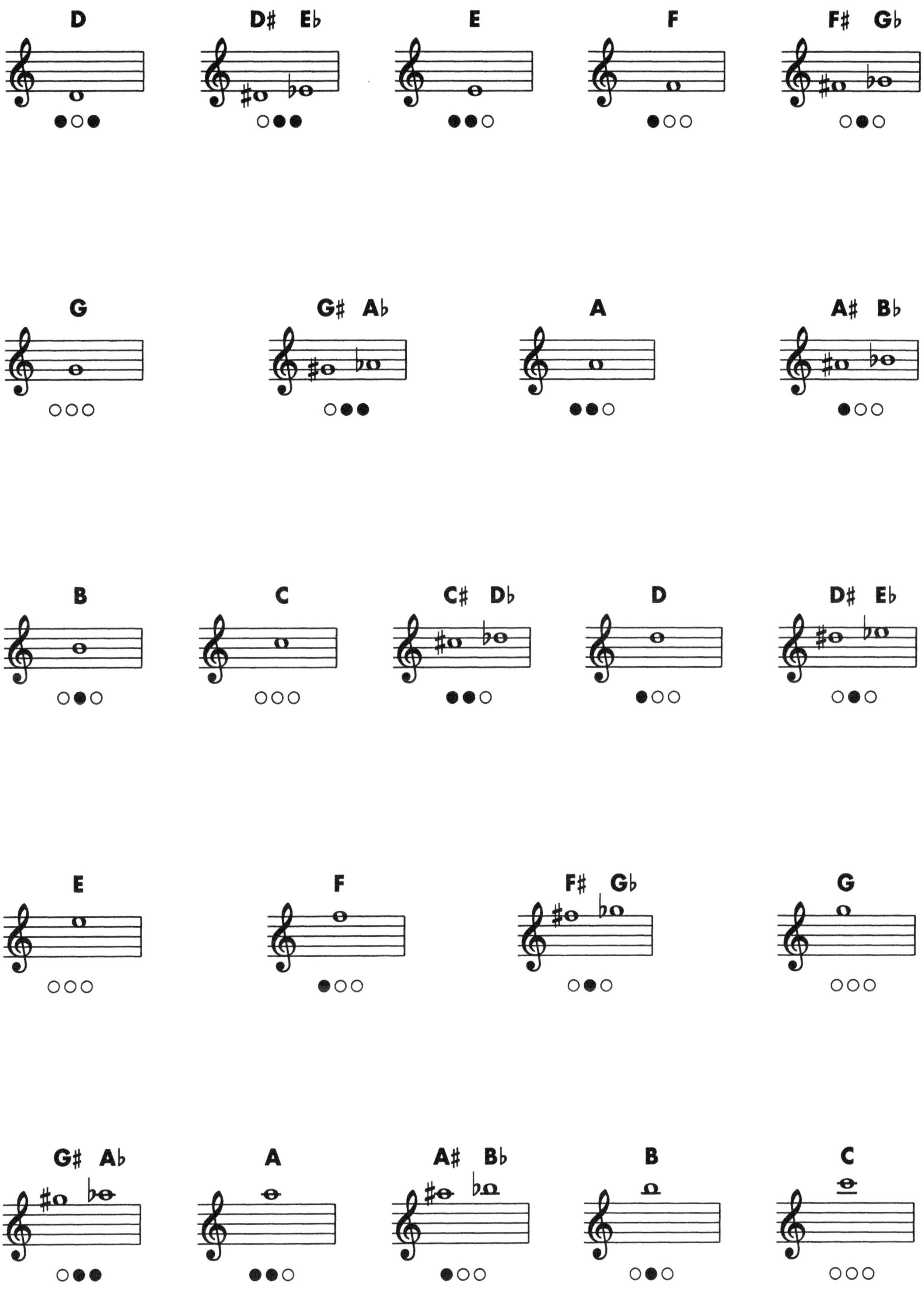
D
D♯ E♭
E
F
F♯ G♭
G
G♯ A♭
A
A♯ B♭
B
C
C♯ D♭
D
D♯ E♭
E
F
F♯ G♭
G
G♯ A♭
A
A♯ B♭
B
C

F HORN FINGERING CHART

○ = UP

● = PRESSED DOWN

Take Special Care

Before putting your instrument back in its case after playing, do the following:

- Use the water key to empty water from the instrument. Blow air through it. If your horn does not have a water key, invert the instrument. You may also remove the main tuning slide, invert the instrument and remove excess water.
- Wipe the instrument off with a clean soft cloth. Return the instrument to its case.
- Remove the mouthpiece. Wash your mouthpiece with warm tap water once per week and dry thoroughly. Horn valves and slides occasionally need lubricating. Your director will recommend valve oil and slide grease, and will help you apply them when necessary.

F Horn players:
- Use the upper fingerings.

Double Horn players:
- Use the lower "T" fingerings when indicated. It is easier to play notes in the upper and extreme lower register of the horn using these fingerings.

B♭ Horn players:
- Use the lower fingerings. The "T" key is only used on double horns.

Instrument courtesy of Yamaha Corporation of America Band and Orchestral Division.

C

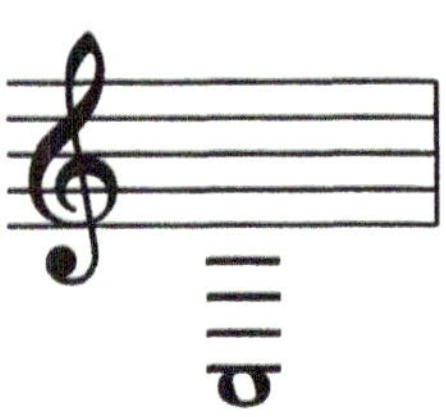

○○○
●○●

C♯ D♭

●●●
T ○●●

D

●○●
T ●●○

D♯ E♭

○●●
T ●○○

E

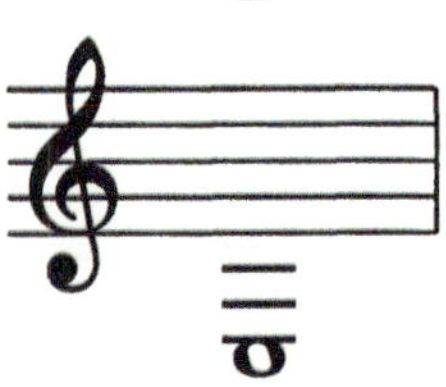

●●○
T ○●○

F

●○○
T ○○○

F♯ G♭

○●○
●●●

G

○○○
●○●

G♯ A♭
A
A♯ B♭
B
C
C♯ D♭
D
D♯ E♭
E
F
F♯ G♭
G
G♯ A♭
A
A♯ B♭
B
C
C♯ D♭
D
D♯ E♭
E
F
F♯ G♭
G
G♯ A♭
A
A♯ B♭
B
C

TROMBONE POSITION CHART

Numbers below the notes = Slide positions

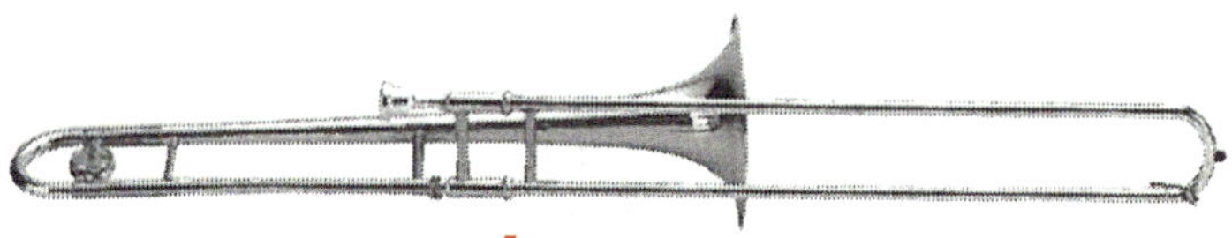

1

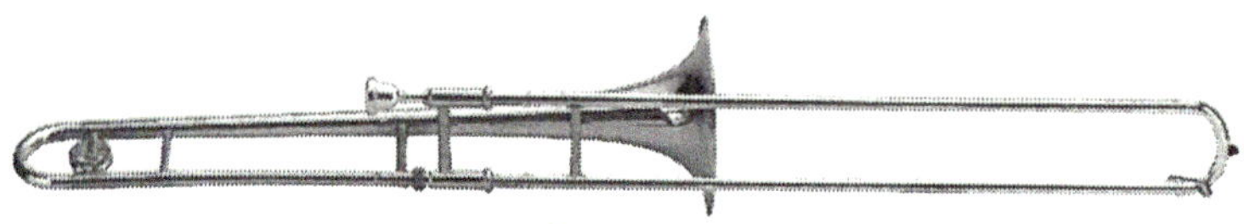

2

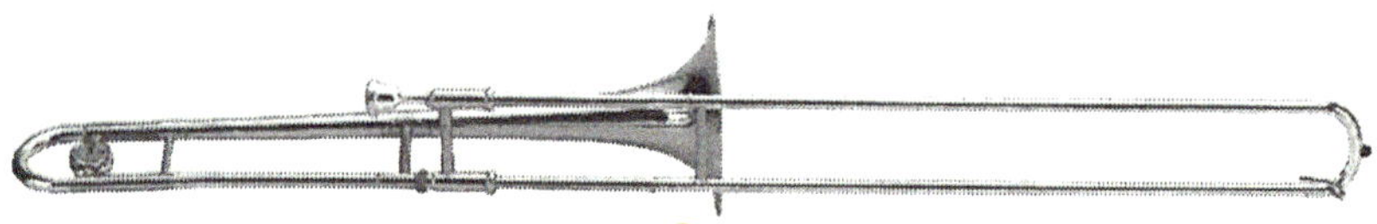

3

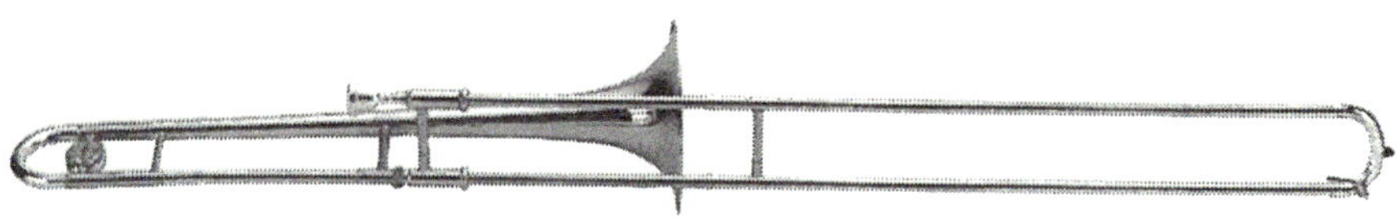

4

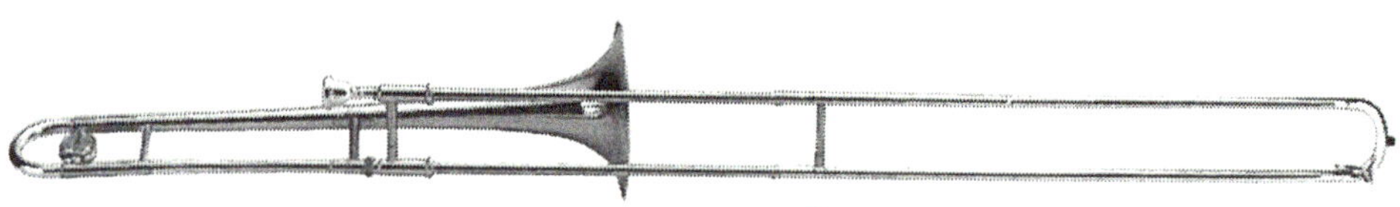

5

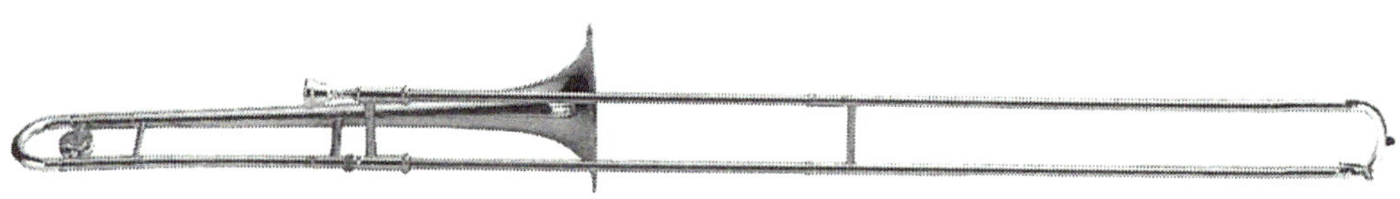

6

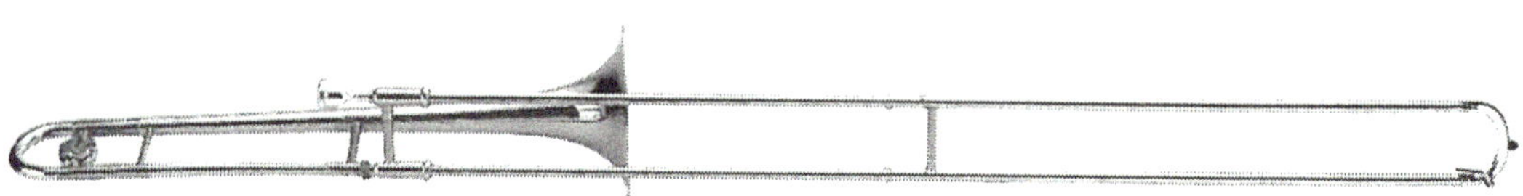

7

Instrument courtesy of
Yamaha Corporation of America
Band and Orchestral Division.

Take Special Care

Before putting your instrument back in its case after playing, do the following:

- Use the water key to empty water from the instrument. Blow air through it.
- Remove the mouthpiece and slide assembly. Do not take the outer slide off of the inner slide piece. Return the instrument to its case.
- Wash your mouthpiece with warm tap water once each week. Dry thoroughly.

Trombone slides occasionally need oiling. To oil your slide, simply:

- Rest the tip of the slide on the floor and unlock the slide.
- Exposing the inner slide, put a few drops of oil on the inner slide.
- Rapidly move the slide back and forth. The oil will then lubricate the slide.
- Be sure to grease the tuning slide regularly. Your director will recommend slide oil and grease, and will help you apply them when necessary.

+ = Make the slide a little longer.
– = Make the slide a little shorter.
T = F Attachment "trigger."

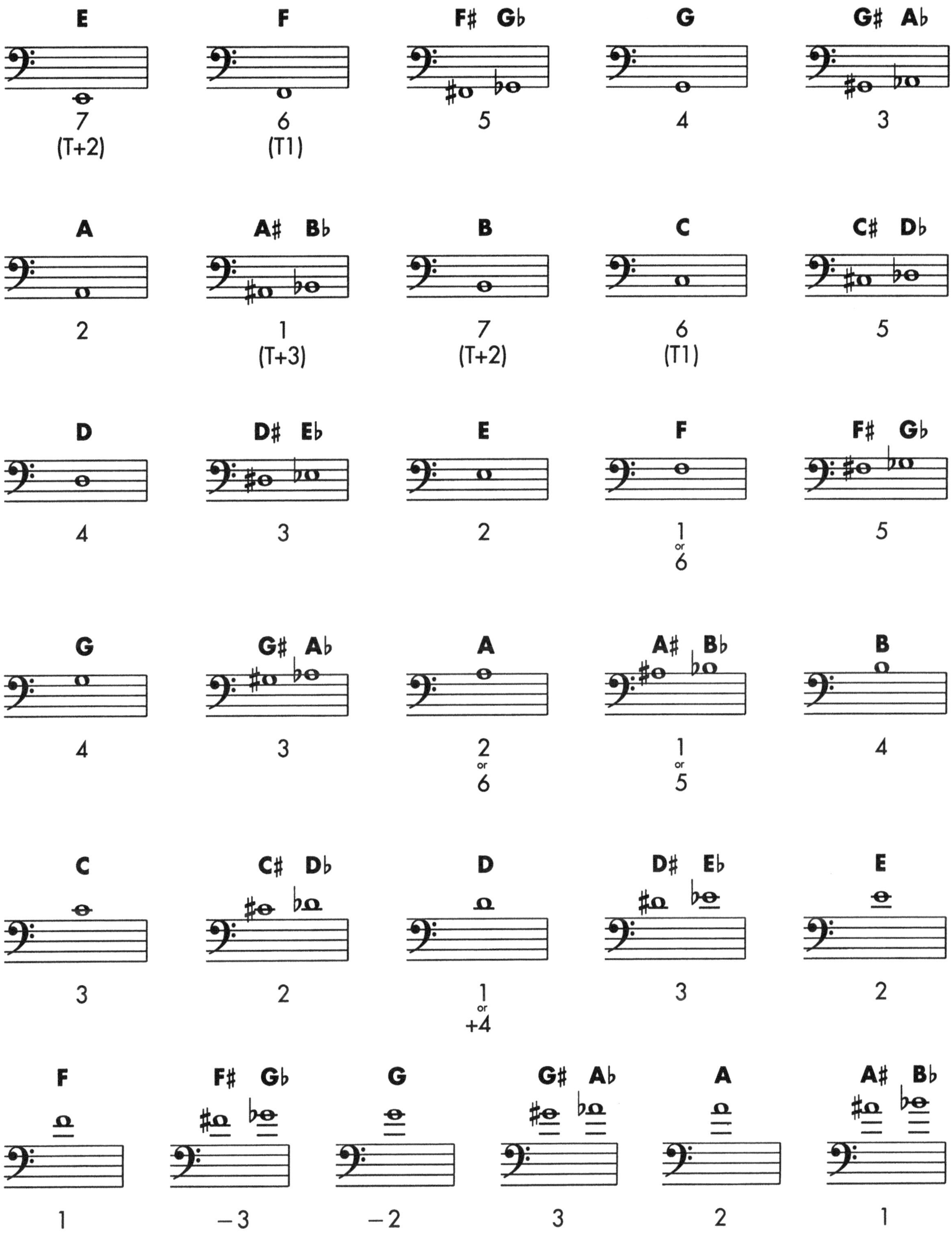

BARITONE B.C. FINGERING CHART

Take Special Care

Before putting your instrument back in its case after playing, do the following:

- Use the water key to empty water from the instrument. Blow air through it.
- Remove the mouthpiece. Wash your mouthpiece with warm tap water once each week and dry thoroughly. Return the instrument to its case.

Baritone valves occasionally need oiling. To oil your valves, simply:

- Unscrew the valve at the top of the casing.
- Lift the valve half-way out of the casing.
- Apply a few drops of oil to the exposed metal valve.
- Carefully return the valve to the casing. When properly inserted, the top of the valve should screw back into place.
- Be sure to grease the slides regularly. Your director will recommend valve oil and slide grease, and will help you apply them when necessary.

○ = UP

● = PRESSED DOWN

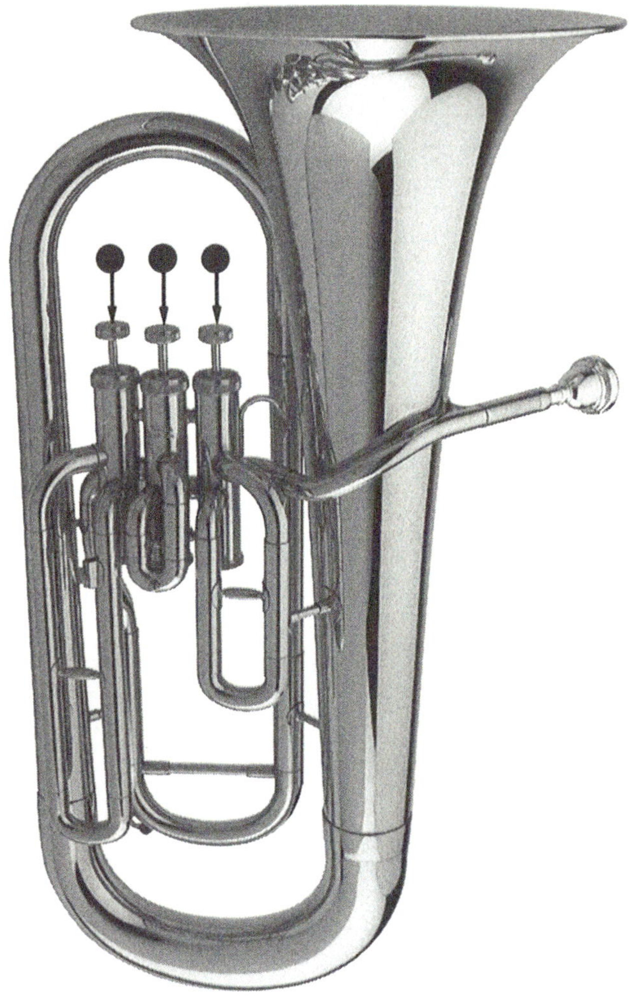

Instrument courtesy of
Yamaha Corporation of America
Band and Orchestral Division.

E

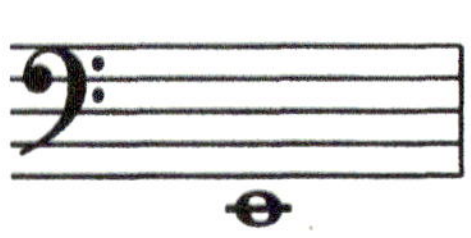

●●●

F

●○●

F♯ G♭

○●●

G

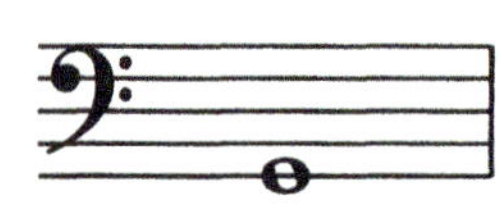

●●○

G♯ A♭

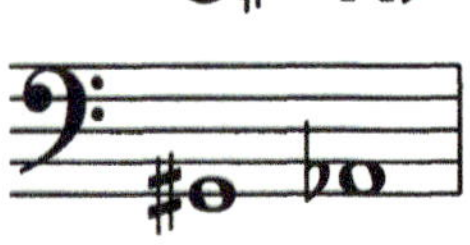

●○○

A

○●○

A♯ B♭

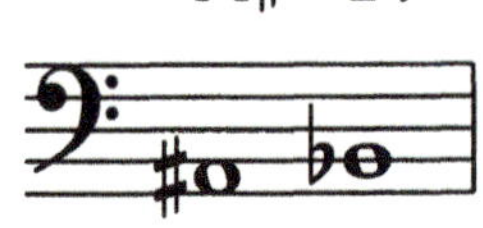

○○○

B

●●●

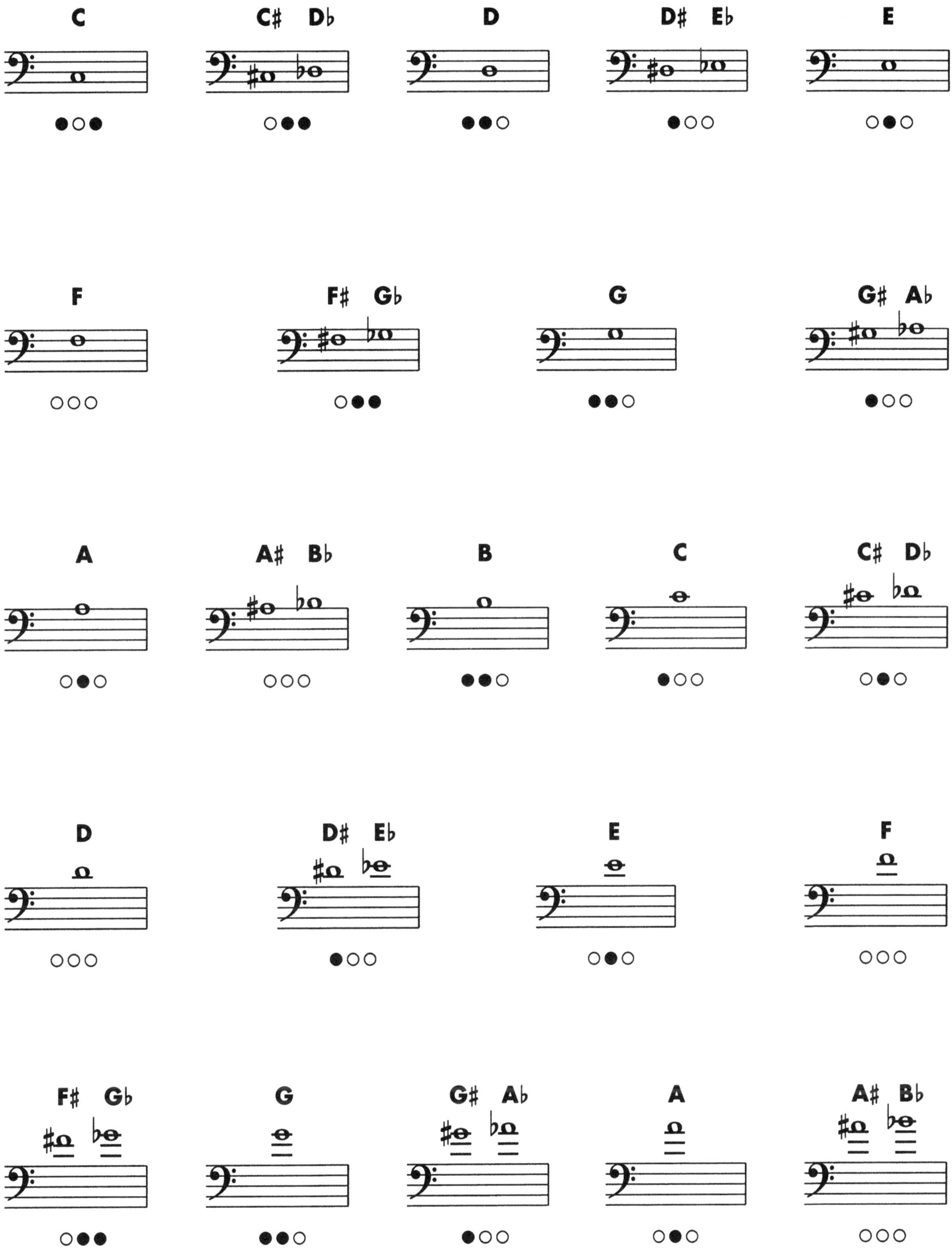
C
C♯ D♭
D
D♯ E♭
E
F
F♯ G♭
G
G♯ A♭
A
A♯ B♭
B
C
C♯ D♭
D
D♯ E♭
E
F
F♯ G♭
G
G♯ A♭
A
A♯ B♭

BARITONE T.C. FINGERING CHART

Take Special Care

Before putting your instrument back in its case after playing, do the following:

- Use the water key to empty water from the instrument. Blow air through it.
- Remove the mouthpiece. Wash your mouthpiece with warm tap water once each week and dry thoroughly. Return the instrument to its case.

Baritone valves occasionally need oiling. To oil your valves, simply:

- Unscrew the valve at the top of the casing.
- Lift the valve half-way out of the casing.
- Apply a few drops of oil to the exposed metal valve.
- Carefully return the valve to the casing. When properly inserted, the top of the valve should screw back into place.
- Be sure to grease the slides regularly. Your director will recommend valve oil and slide grease, and will help you apply them when necessary.

○ = UP

● = PRESSED DOWN

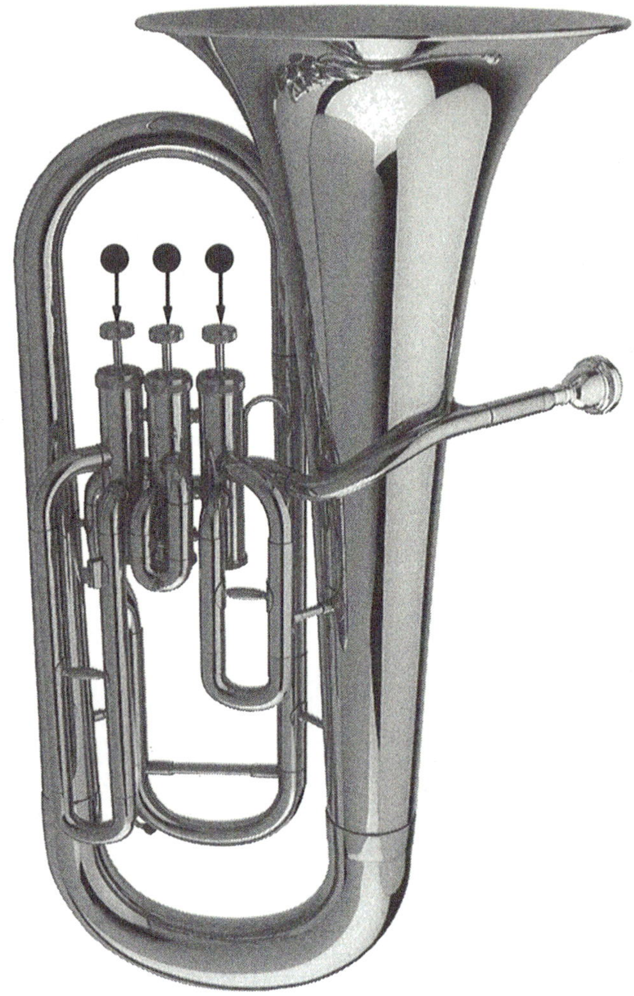

Instrument courtesy of
Yamaha Corporation of America
Band and Orchestral Division.

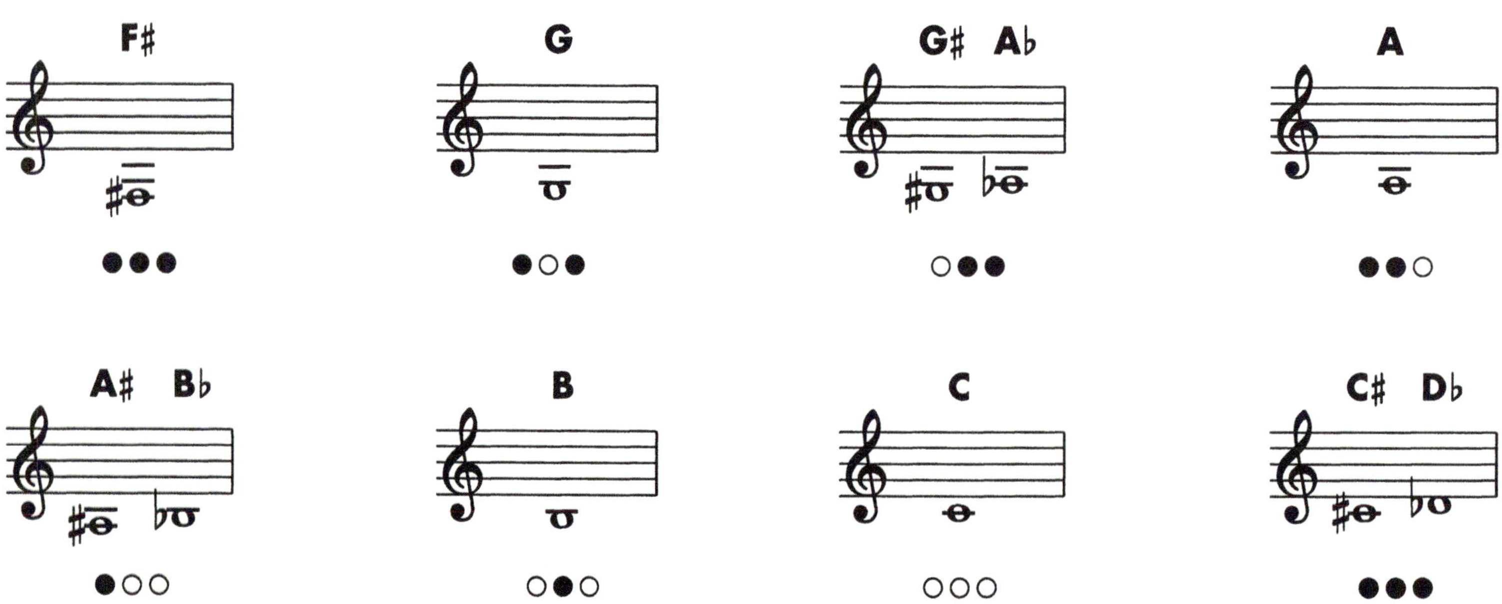

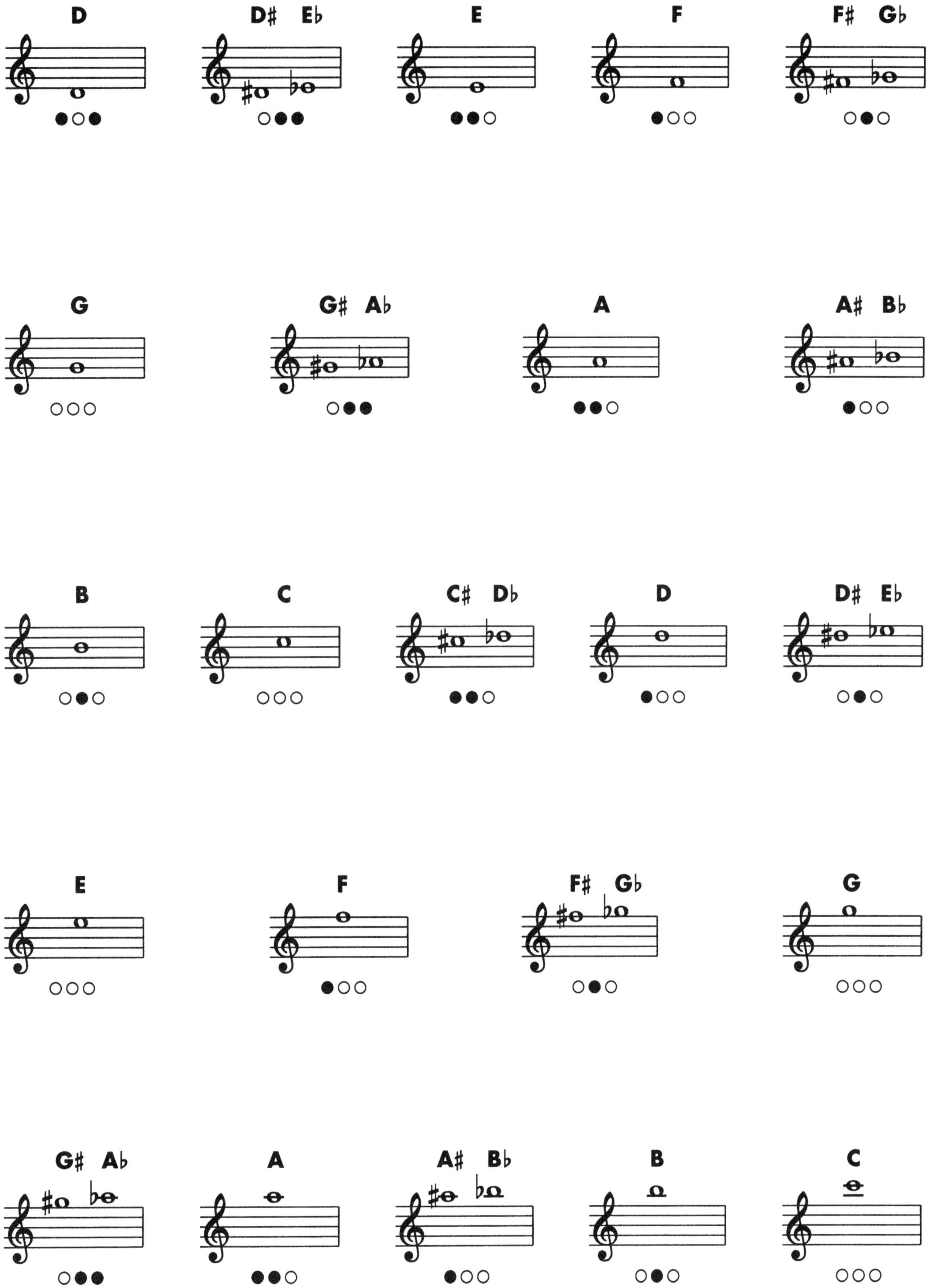
D
D♯ E♭
E
F
F♯ G♭
G
G♯ A♭
A
A♯ B♭
B
C
C♯ D♭
D
D♯ E♭
E
F
F♯ G♭
G
G♯ A♭
A
A♯ B♭
B
C

TUBA FINGERING CHART

Take Special Care

Before putting your instrument back in its case after playing, do the following:

- Use the water key to empty water from the instrument. Blow air through it.
- Remove the mouthpiece. Wash your mouthpiece with warm tap water once each week and dry thoroughly. Return the instrument to its case.

Tuba valves occasionally need oiling. To oil your valves, simply:

- Unscrew the valve at the top of the casing.
- Lift the valve half-way out of the casing.
- Apply a few drops of oil to the exposed metal valve.
- Carefully return the valve to the casing. When properly inserted, the top of the valve should screw back into place.
- Be sure to grease the slides regularly. Your director will recommend valve oil and slide grease, and will help you apply them when necessary.

○ = UP

● = PRESSED DOWN

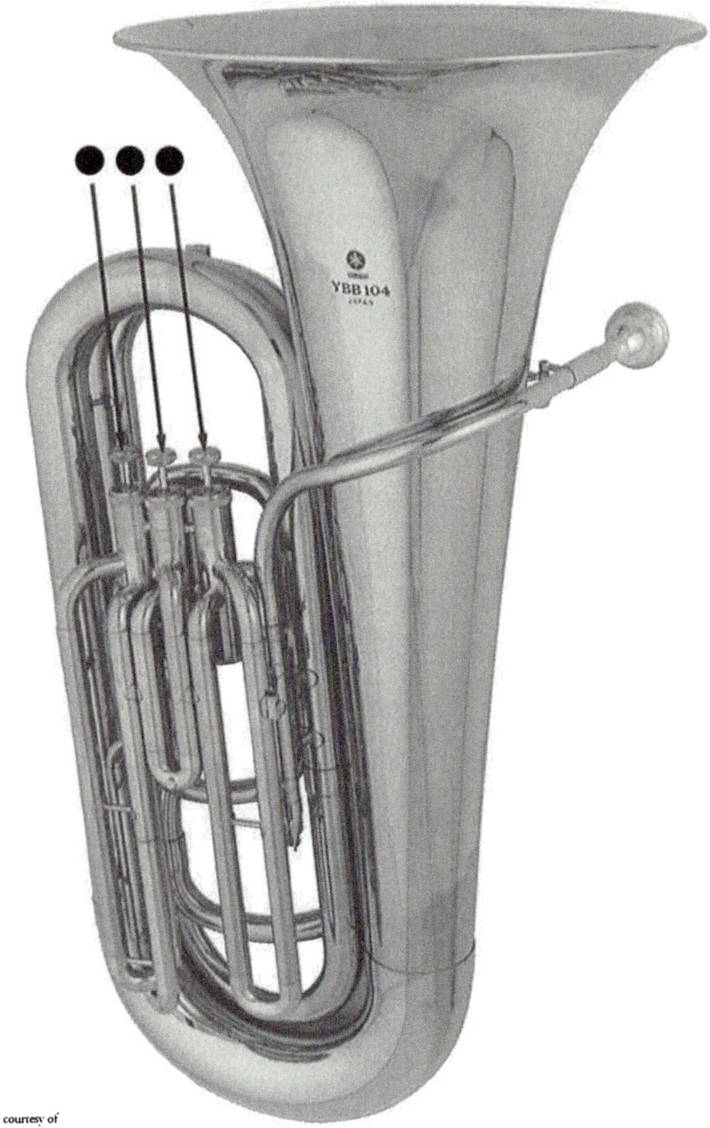

Instrument courtesy of Yamaha Corporation of America Band and Orchestral Division.

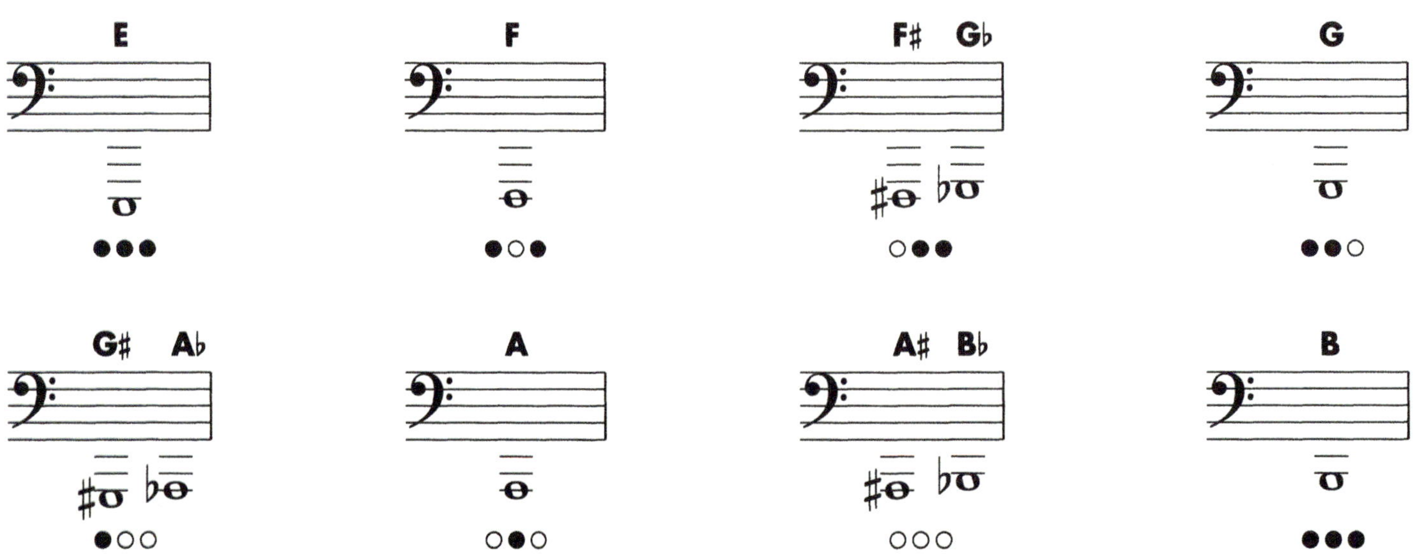

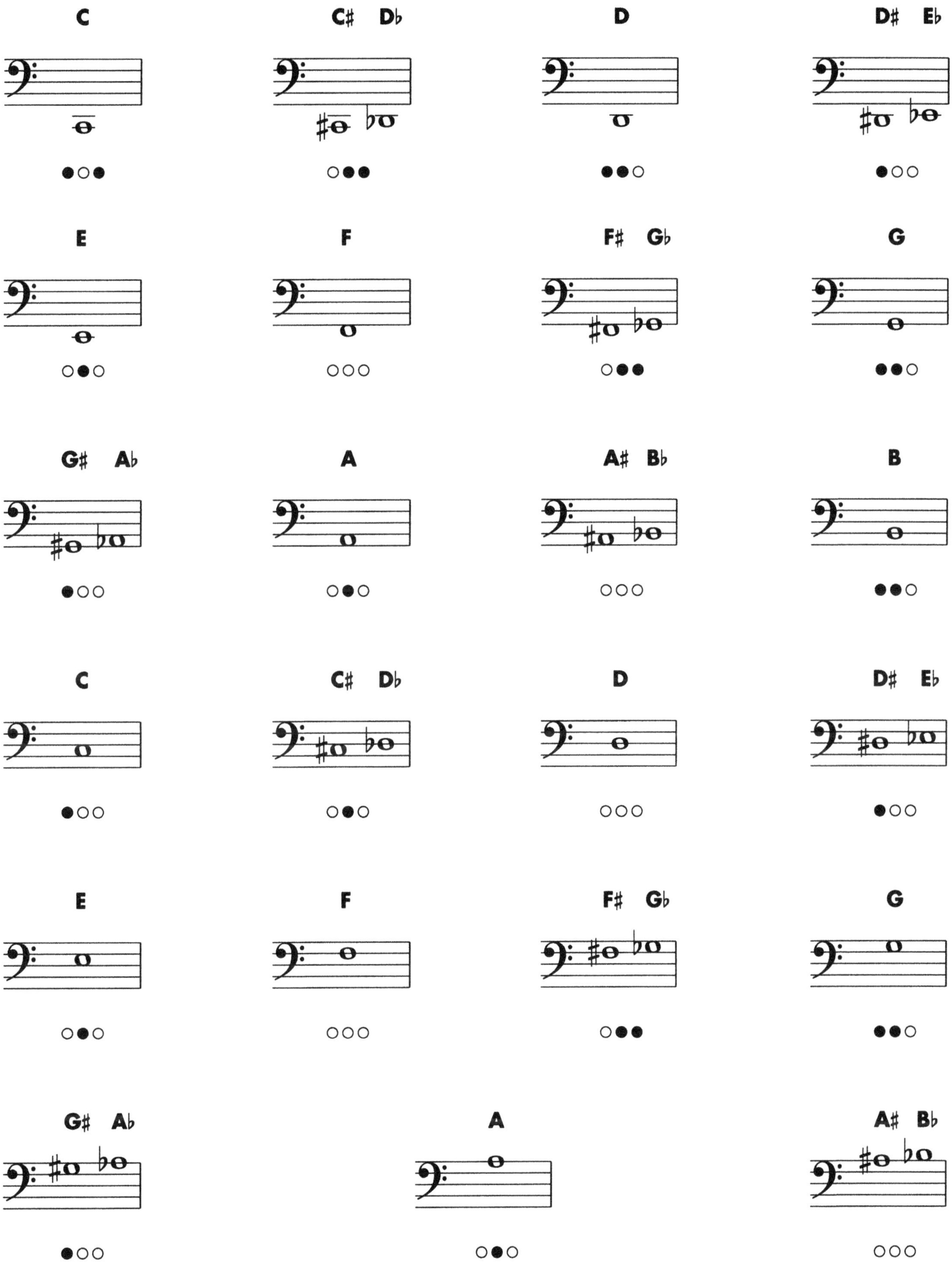
C
C♯ D♭
D
D♯ E♭
E
F
F♯ G♭
G
G♯ A♭
A
A♯ B♭
B
C
C♯ D♭
D
D♯ E♭
E
F
F♯ G♭
G
G♯ A♭
A
A♯ B♭

BASIC PERCUSSION INSTRUMENTS

INSTRUMENT	MALLET/STICK
Concert Snare Drum with stand	5B or 2B sticks
Concert Bass Drum with stand	1 pair medium bass drum mallets
Crash Cymbals (16" to 18")	1 pair medium yarn mallets
Suspended Cymbal and stand (16")	1 pair medium yarn mallets
Triangle with clip	1 pair metal beaters
Wood Block	1 pair medium rubber mallets 1 pair hard rubber mallets
Timpani (26", 29", 23", 32")	1 pair general timpani sticks 1 pair hard timpani sticks
Bells	1 pair very hard lexan mallets 1 pair hard rubber mallets
Xylophone	1 pair hard rubber mallets 1 pair medium rubber mallets
Chimes	2 plastic or 2 rawhide mallets
Marimba	Various yarn and rubber mallets
Vibraphone	Various yarn and rubber mallets

General Accessories:
Tambourines (with and without head),
Cowbell, Bongos, Congas, Timbales,
Maracas, Guiro, Claves, Castenets,
Slapstick, Sleigh Bells, Slide Whistle.

SNARE DRUM INTERNATIONAL DRUM RUDIMENTS

All rudiments should be practiced: open (slow) to close (fast) and/or at an even moderate march tempo.

Take Special Care

Snare drums occasionally need tuning. Ask your teacher to help you tighten each tension rod equally using a drum key.

- Be careful not to over-tighten the head. It will break if the tension is too tight.
- Loosen the snare strainer at the end of each rehearsal.
- Cover all percussion instruments when not in use.
- Put sticks away in a storage area. Keep the percussion section neat!
- Sticks are the only things which should be placed on the snare drum. NEVER put or allow others to put objects on any percussion instrument.

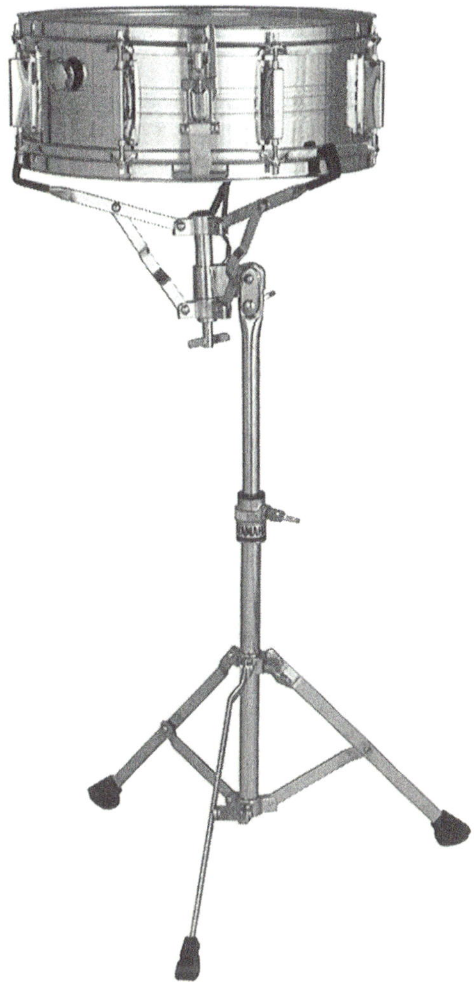

Instrument courtesy of
Yamaha Corporation of America
Band and Orchestral Division

I. ROLL RUDIMENTS

A. SINGLE STROKE ROLL RUDIMENTS

1. Single Stroke Roll

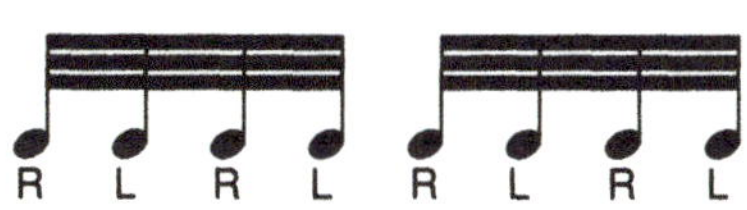

2. Single Stroke Four

3. Single Stroke Seven

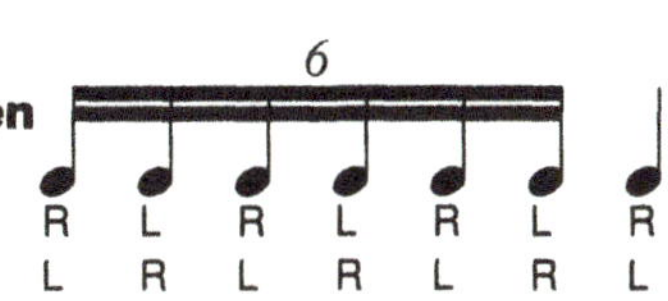

B. MULTIPLE BOUNCE ROLL RUDIMENTS

4. Multiple Bounce Roll

5. Triple Stroke Roll

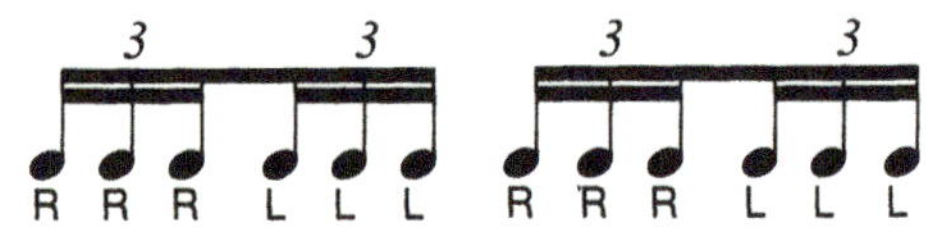

C. DOUBLE STROKE OPEN ROLL RUDIMENTS

6. Double Stroke Open Roll

7. Five Stroke Roll

8. Six Stroke Roll

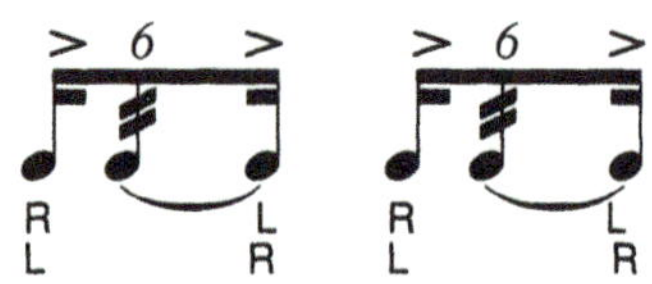

9. Seven Stroke Roll

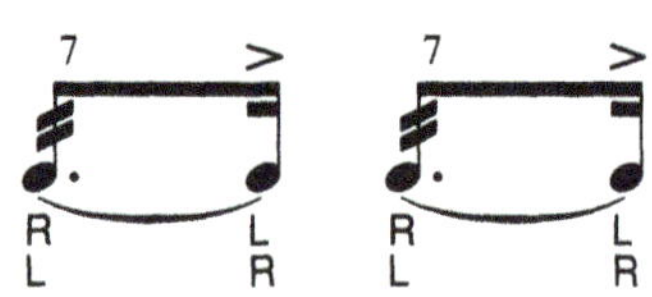

10. Nine Stroke Roll

11. Ten Stroke Roll

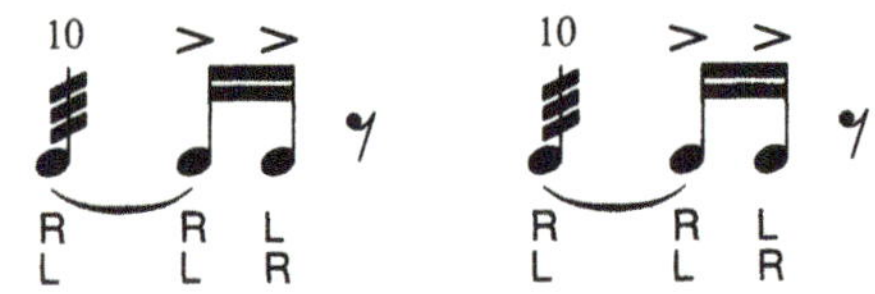

12. Eleven Stroke Roll

13. Thirteen Stroke Roll

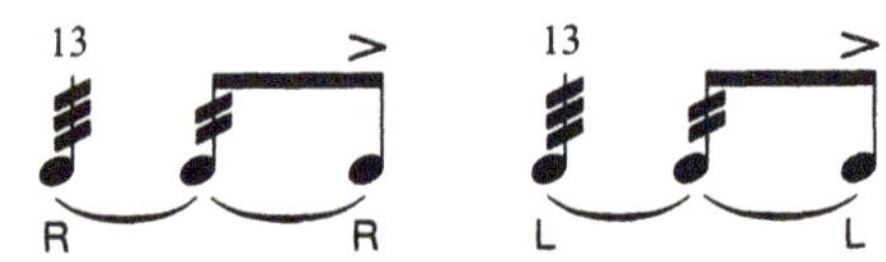

14. Fifteen Stroke Roll

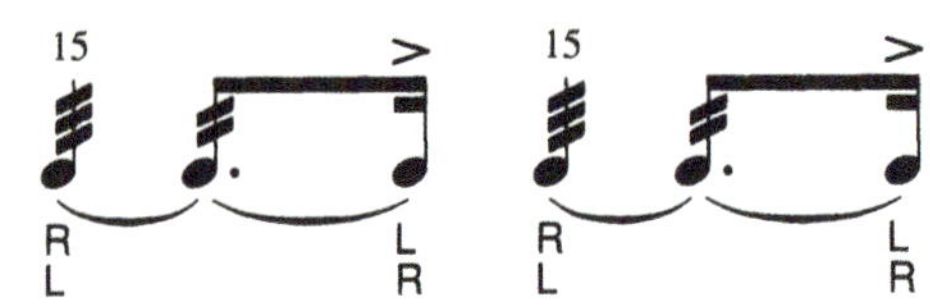

15. Seventeen Stroke Roll

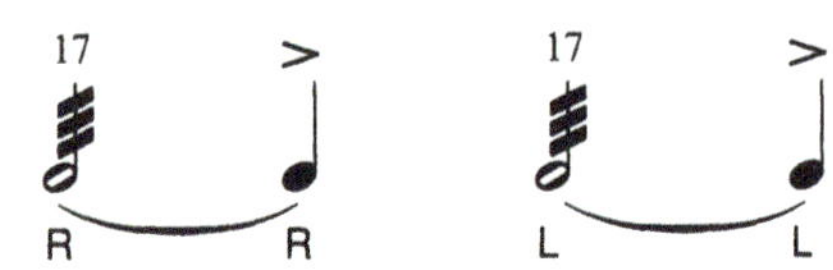

II. DIDDLE RUDIMENTS

16. Single Paradiddle

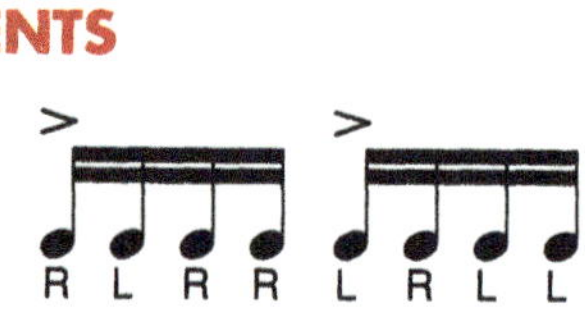

17. Double Paradiddle

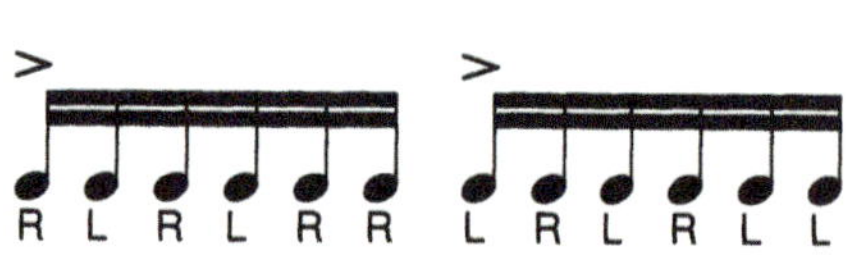

18. Triple Paradiddle

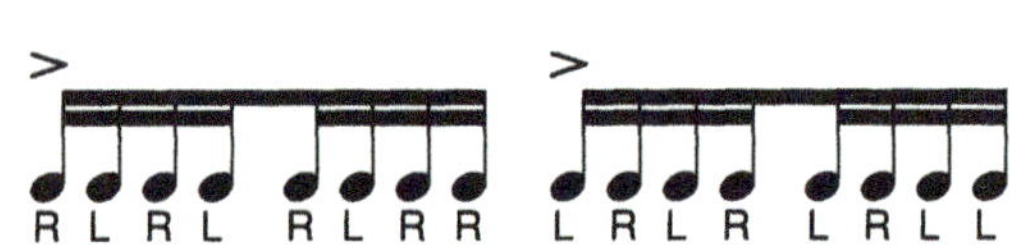

19. Single Paradiddle-Diddle

III. FLAM RUDIMENTS

20. Flam

21. Flam Accent

22. Flam Tap

23. Flamacue

24. Flam Paradiddle

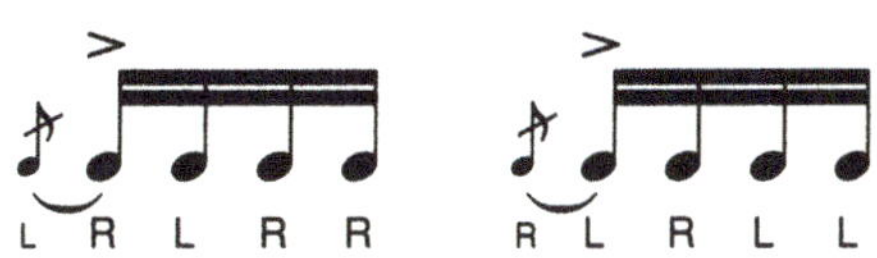

25. Single Flammed Mill

26. Flam Paradiddle-Diddle

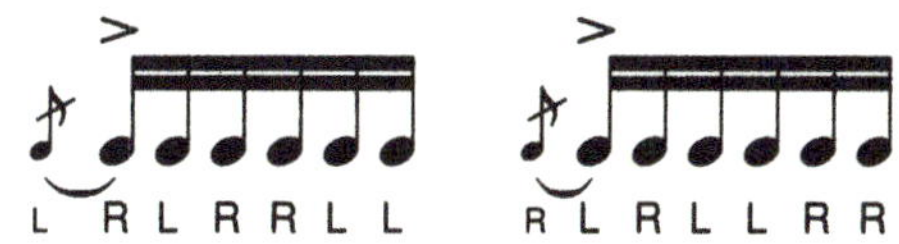

27. Pataflafla

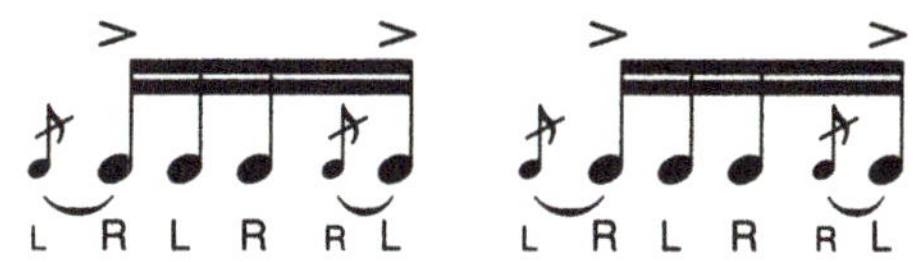

28. Swiss Army Triplet

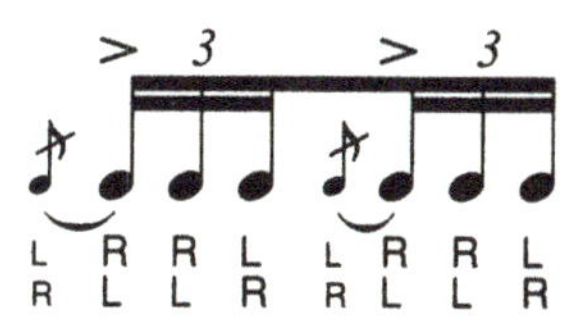

29. Inverted Flam Tap

30. Flam Drag

IV. DRAG RUDIMENTS

31. Drag

32. Single Drag Tap

33. Double Drag Tap

34. Lesson 25

35. Single Dragadiddle

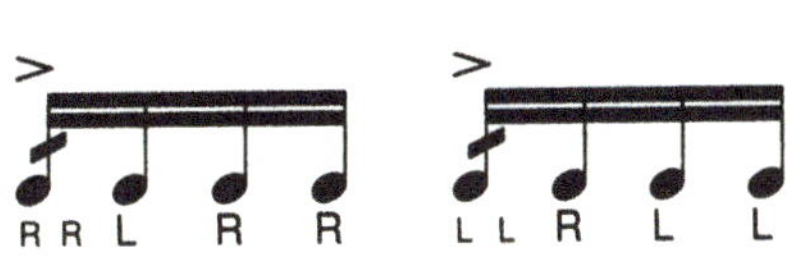

36. Drag Paradiddle #1

37. Drag Paradiddle #2

38. Single Ratamacue

39. Double Ratamacue

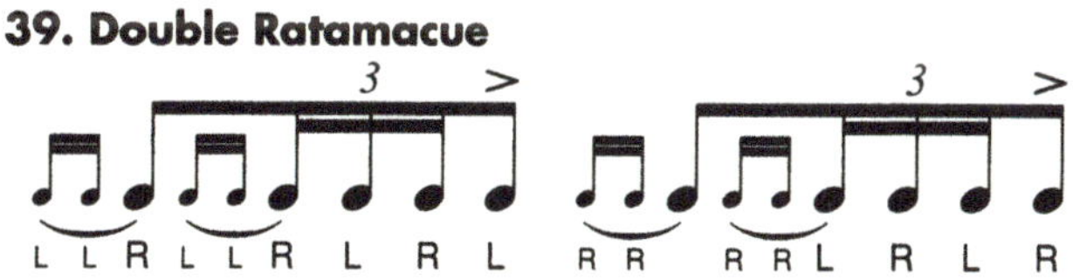

40. Triple Ratamacue

KEYBOARD PERCUSSION INSTRUMENTS

Each keyboard percussion instrument has a unique sound because of the materials used to create the instrument. Ranges may differ with some models of instruments.

Take Special Care

- Cover all percussion instruments when they are not being used.
- Put mallets away in a storage area. Keep the percussion section neat!
- Mallets are the only things which should be placed on your instrument. NEVER put or allow others to put objects on any percussion instrument.

BELLS (Orchestra Bells)

- Bars - metal alloy or steel
- Mallets - lexan (hard plastic), brass or hard rubber
- Range - 2 1/2 octaves
- Sounds 2 octaves higher than written

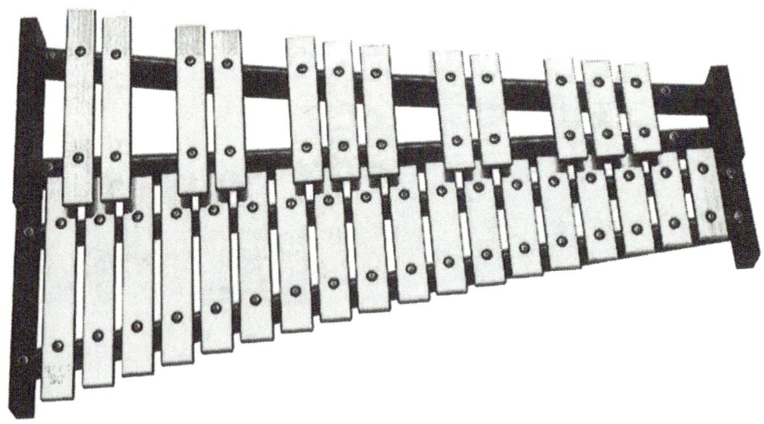

XYLOPHONE

- Bars - wooden or synthetic
- Mallets- hard rubber
- Range - 3 octaves
- Sounds 1 octave higher than written

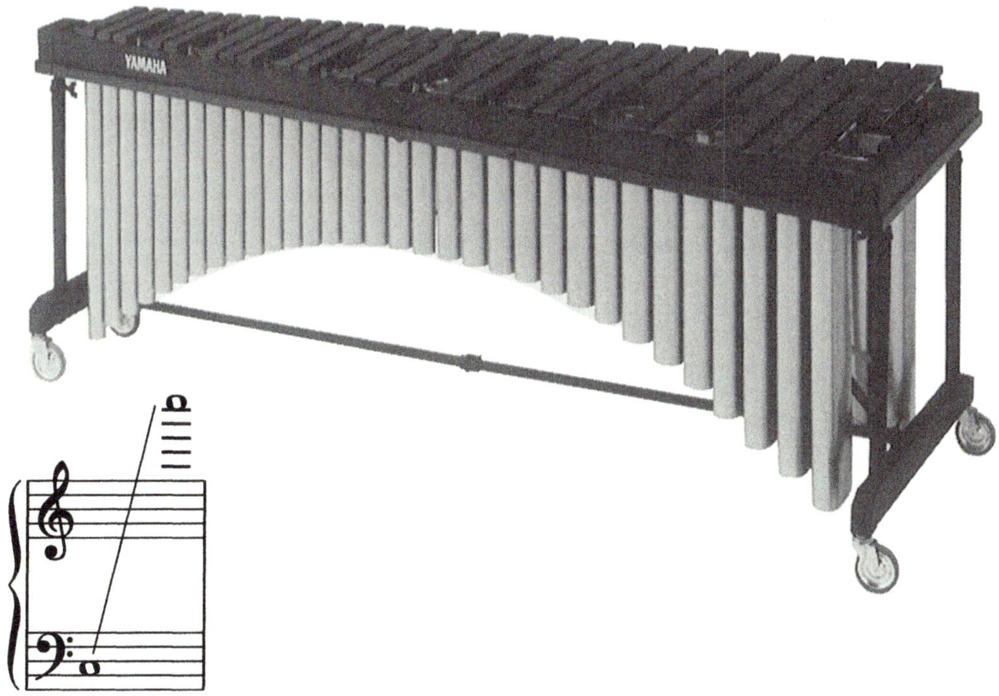

MARIMBA

- Bars - wooden (wider than xylophone bars)
  Resonating tube located below each bar
- Mallets - soft to medium rubber or yarn covered
- Range - 4 1/2 octaves (reads bass and treble clefs)
- Sounding pitch is the same as written pitch

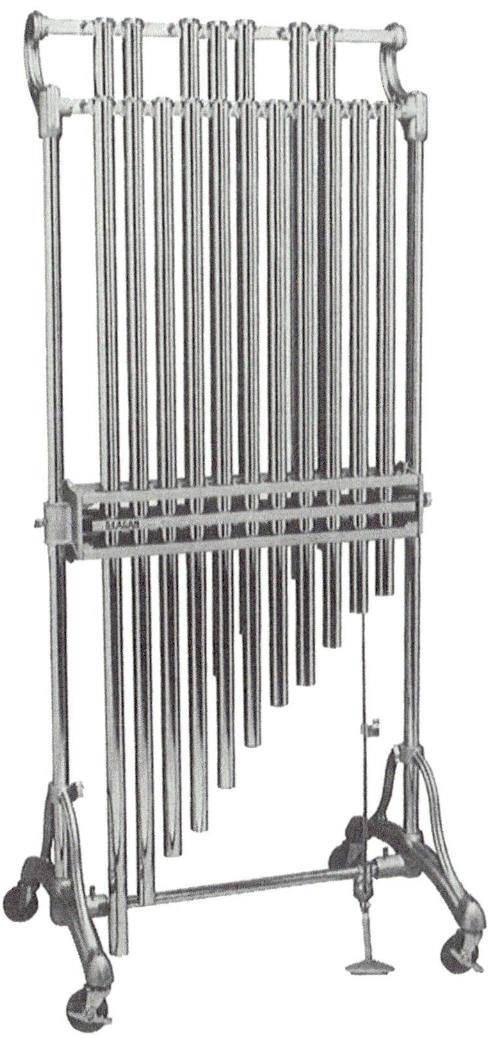

VIBRAPHONE

- Bars - metal alloy or aluminum
  Resonating tubes located below each bar
  Adjustable electric fans in each resonator create "vibrato" effect
- Mallets - yarn covered
- Range - 3 octaves
- Sounding pitch is the same as written pitch

CHIMES

- Bars - metal tubes
- Mallets - plastic, rawhide or wooden
- Range - 1 1/2 octaves
- Sounding pitch is the same as written pitch

Instruments and photos courtesy of
Yamaha Corporation of America
Band and Orchestral Division.

GLOSSARY

Essential Element	Definition
Accelerando *accel.*	Gradually increase the tempo.
Accent	Emphasize the note.
Accidentals	Sharps, flats, and naturals found in the music.
Adagio	Slow tempo, slower than Andante.
Agitato	Agitated.
Allegretto	A lively tempo.
Allegro	Fast, bright tempo.
Andante	Slow walking tempo.
Animato	Animated, lively.
Arpeggio	A sequence of notes from any scale.
Articulation	The way we tongue or slur notes.
Balance	The proper adjustment of volume from all instruments.
Bass Clef	"F" clef used by trombone, baritone, bassoon, and tuba.
Chord	Two or more notes sounding simultaneously.
Chromatic Scale	Sequence of notes in half-steps.
Chromatics	Notes that are altered with sharps, flats and naturals.
Common Time **C**	Another way to write $\frac{4}{4}$.
Crescendo	Gradually increase volume.
Cut Time ¢	Meter in which the half note gets one beat.
D.C. al Fine	*Da Capo al Fine* - Play until *D.C. al Fine.* Go back to the beginning and play until *Fine.*
D.S. al Fine	*Del Segno al Fine* - Play until *D.S. al Fine.* Go back to the sign (𝄋) and play until *Fine.*
Decrescendo	Gradually decrease volume.
Divisi *div.*	Divide the notes between players.
Dixieland	A popular form of early jazz.
Dolce	Sweet, gentle style.
Double Bar	Indicates the end of a piece of music.
Dynamics	The volume of music.
Enharmonics	Notes that are written differently but sound the same.
Espressivo	Expressivly.
Fermata	Hold the note longer, or until your director tells you to release it.
1st and 2nd Endings	Play the first ending the first time through. Then repeat the same music, skip the first ending and play the 2nd.
Flat ♭	Lowers the note and remains in effect the entire measure.
forte ***f***	Play loudly.
fortissimo ***ff***	Play very loudly.
Giocosso	Lightly, happily.
Grace Note	A small note played on or slightly before the beat.
Grazioso	Gracefully.
Half-step	The smallest distance between two notes.
Harmonic Minor Scale	Like the natural minor scale, except the 7th scale step is raised one half-step.
Interval	The numerical distance between two notes.
Jazz	American form of music combining African and European styles.
Key Signature	Flats or sharps next to the clef that apply to the entire piece.
Legato	Play in a smooth and connected style.
Leggiero	Lightly.
Lento	Very slow tempo.
Maestoso	Play in a majestic, stately manner.
Major Scale	Series of 8 notes with a definite pattern of whole steps and half steps.
Marcato Accent	A loud accented note of short duration.
Marziale	March-like style.
Measure Repeat	Repeat the previous measure.
Melodic Minor Scale	Like the natural minor, except the 6th and 7th scale steps are raised by one half-step when the scale is ascending. Same as natural minor when descending.
mezzo forte ***mf***	Play moderately loud.
mezzo piano ***mp***	Play moderately soft.
Minor Chord	Made up of the 1st, 3rd, and 5th scale steps of a minor scale.
Minor Scale	Series of 8 notes with a definite pattern of whole steps and half-steps.
Moderato	Moderate tempo.
Mysterioso	Mysteriously.
Natural Minor Scale	Minor scale with half-steps between scale steps 2-3 and 5-6.
Natural Sign ♮	Cancels a flat ♭ or sharp ♯ in the measure.
Pentatonic Scale	Five note scale.
pianissimo ***pp***	Play very softly.
piano ***p***	Play softly.
Pick-up Notes	Notes that come before the first full measure.
Rallentando *rall.*	Gradually slow the tempo.
Repeat Sign	Go back to the beginning and play again. Repeat the section of music enclosed by the repeat signs.
Ritardando *rit.*	Gradually slow the tempo.
Sharp ♯	Raises the note and remains in effect the entire measure.
Sightreading	Playing a musical selection for the first time.
Simile *sim.*	Continue in the same style.
Staccato	Play the notes with separation.
Stagger breathing	Players breathe at different times so the phrase is not broken.
Style Mark	Indicates the manner or style in which music is to be played.
Swing	A style of music in which eighth notes are played as if they were written:
Tempo di valse	Waltz tempo.
Tempo	The speed of music.
Tenuto	Play notes for their full value.
Time Signature (Meter)	Tells how many beats are in each measure and what kind of note gets one beat.
Treble Clef	"G" clef used by flute, oboe, clarinet, sax, trumpet, and horn.
Trill	Rapid alternation between two adjacent notes.
Triplet	Group of three notes.
Unison *unis.*	Tells performers to play the same note.
Waltz	Dance in moderate $\frac{3}{4}$ meter.

BIBLIOGRAPHY

Baker, Theodore. *The Concise Baker's Biographical Dictionary Of Musicians.* Edited by Nicholas Slonimsky. New York: Schimer Books, 1988.

Barlow, Harold and Sam Morgenstern, comps. *A Dictionary Of Musical Themes.* rev. ed. New York: Crown Publishers, 1975.

Cadman, Charles Wakefield. *Music Of The American Indian.* New York: Edwin H. Morris & Company, Inc., 1976.

Corp, Ronald, ed. *Folksongs From The British Isles.* London: Faber Music Ltd., 1991.

Corp, Ronald, ed. *Folksongs Of The Sea.* London: Faber Music Ltd., 1991.

The Classical Fake Book. Milwaukee: Hal Leonard Publishing Corporation, 1992.

Fake Book Of The World's Favorite Songs. Milwaukee: Hal Leonard Publishing Corporation, 1990.

Floyd, Malcolm, ed. *Folksongs From Africa.* London: Faber Music Ltd., 1991.

Gilmore, Jeanne and Robert, ed. *Chantez Encore: Folksongs Of French Louisiana.* Gretna, Louisiana: Pelican Publishing Company, 1977.

Gritton, Peter, ed. *Folksongs From The Far East.* London: Faber Music Ltd., 1991.

Grout, Donald J. *A History Of Western Music.* rev. ed. New York: W.W. Norton & Company, 1988.

Hattori, Ryutaro, ed. *Japanese Folk Songs.* Tokyo: Japan Times Ltd., 1950.

Rhodes, Tom C., Donald Bierschenk, Tim Lautzenheiser, John Higgins. Linda Petersen, ed. *Essential Elements Comprehensive Band Method.* Books 1 and 2. Milwaukee: Hal Leonard Publishing Corporation, 1991.

Sadie, Stanley, ed. T*he New Grove Dictionary Of Music And Musicians.* 20 vols. London: Macmillan Publishers, 1980.

Sadie, Stanley and Alison Latham, eds. *The Norton/Grove Concise Encyclopedia Of Music.* London: Macmillan Publishers, 1988.

Westphal, Frederick W. *Guide To Teaching Woodwinds.* 5th ed. Dubuque, Iowa: William C. Brown Publishers, 1990.